New Readings of *The Merchant of Venice*

New Readings of *The Merchant of Venice*

Edited by

Horacio Sierra

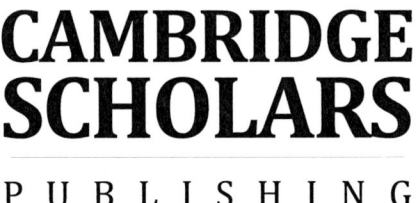

CAMBRIDGE
SCHOLARS

P U B L I S H I N G

New Readings of *The Merchant of Venice*,
Edited by Horacio Sierra

This book first published 2013

Cambridge Scholars Publishing

12 Back Chapman Street, Newcastle upon Tyne, NE6 2XX, UK

British Library Cataloguing in Publication Data
A catalogue record for this book is available from the British Library

ISBN (10): 1-4438-4176-5, ISBN (13): 978-1-4438-4176-4

TABLE OF CONTENTS

ACKNOWLEDGMENTS

Horacio Sierra thanks his parents, Maria and Horacio Sierra, for their unconditional love and support; Wess Brooker for his encouragement; Sidney Homan and Mihoko Suzuki for their mentoring; as well as the University of Saint Joseph, the Folger Shakespeare Library, the University of Florida, the University of Miami, Miami Coral Park Senior High School, Cambridge Scholars Publishing, and Bowie State University for their invaluable resources and education.

Audrey Birkett thanks the students of the English 3000 at the University of Colorado-Colorado Springs class for helping me work through the theoretical issues of *The Merchant of Venice*.

Rebecca Olson thanks Horacio Sierra and Allison Hobgood for their helpful questions and suggestions for this essay.

Paul Dingman thanks Professor Richard W. Kaeuper at the University of Rochester for his guidance, belief, and support.

James Newlin thanks Richard Burt, Kristin Denslow, Peter Gitto, and R. Allen Shoaf for offering their invaluable assistance with earlier drafts of this chapter.

Russell McConnell thanks his family for their love and support, in particular his wife, Dr. Emma Annette Wilson.

WHY NEW READINGS?

HORACIO SIERRA

The first two decades of the twenty-first century have witnessed a spate of high-profile presentations of *The Merchant of Venice*: the 2004 Michael Radford film, 2010's New York City "Shakespeare in the Park" production, as well as the play's Tony Award-nominated 2010-11 Broadway run. Likewise, new scholarly works such as Kenneth Gross's *Shylock is Shakespeare* (2006) and Janet Adelman's *Blood Relations: Christian and Jew in The Merchant of Venice* (2008) have offered poignant insights into this drama. Why has this play garnered so much attention of late? What else can we learn from this contentious comedy? How else can we read the drama's characters? Where do studies of *The Merchant of Venice* go from here?

When asked why Shakespeare's dramas are as popular today as they were hundreds of years ago, those in academia and the performing arts often cite the universal nature of the emotions, philosophies, and themes explored in his plays. Star-crossed lovers, humorous disguises, and bawdy jokes are some of the more enjoyable timeless elements of Shakespeare's comedies and tragedies. Incompetent rulers, religious prejudices, and racist taunts, however, are just as, if not more, relevant to contemporary audiences who seek a connection to the sometimes confusing early modern English of Shakespeare's plays. While an enchanted forest and shipwrecked twins seem the stuff of myth and slapstick comedy, respectively, the plight of ostracized minorities and state-sanctioned discrimination are all too real, which promises an uncanny verisimilitude for twenty-first century audiences. Though the magical charms of *A Midsummer Night's Dream* and the political turmoil of *Hamlet* continue to intrigue readers and theatergoers from grammar school to adulthood, we must wonder why there is still so much fascination with a play such as *The Merchant of Venice*.

The play cannot escape its anti-Semitic elements. Yet its more inoffensive thematic elements, such as the dichotomy between justice and mercy and conflations of love and money, save the play from being racist propaganda. After all, as many would attest, Shakespeare knew better than that. To say the least, the character of the usurious Jew Shylock is problematic, complex, and unforgettable. Audiences despise him at the same time that, increasingly, they sympathize with him or understand where he is coming from. Educated by post-Nazi Holocaust humanist studies and forced to confront our previous prejudices and complicity in the oppression of others, we realize, perhaps better than previous generations, that Shakespeare's portrayal of Shylock, the stereotypical Renaissance-era Jewish usurer, is so much more than we see at first glance. He is not a hero. In fact, he is the antagonist and yet we still feel for him. It need not be said that the play would be another creature without Shylock – this is obvious. However, without him and the religious conflict that emerges because of his presence, this play runs the risk of being another run-of-the-mill comedy, an early modern *Mamma Mia!* wherein three men are potential caretakers for a beautiful young woman and the curtain closes on felicitous unions.

Although not as popular among the secondary school set as feel-good comedies such as *Twelfth Night* or classic romantic tragedies such as *Romeo and Juliet*, *The Merchant of Venice* is experiencing a revival in high school productions thanks to the heightened attention the issue of bullying has received of late. Directors of high school productions of the drama are sure to keep the cruel verbal barbs that are thrown at Shylock in their scripts so as to present teachable moments about discrimination and prejudice.

This collection of essay thrives on teachable moments that are influenced by watershed critical twentieth-century scholarly works such as Paulo Freire's *Pedagogy of the Oppressed*, Eve Kosofsky Sedgwick's *Epistemology of the Closet*, and James Shapiro's *Shakespeare and the Jews*, and contextualized within new ways of approaching both the primary text and these critical texts with an eye towards the horizons of twenty-first-century intellectual inquiry. *New Readings of The Merchant of Venice* showcases a sampling of ways this culturally arresting play can be read and interpreted. The strength of this monograph lies in the disparate approaches we offer – from a feminist view of Portia and Nerissa's friendship inspired by a viral YouTube clip to psychoanalytic readings of allegories between the play and Shakespeare's *Pericles* to a visual and textual analysis of a Manga version of *The Merchant of Venice*. Each essay is supported by a strong basis in traditional close reading practices. Our collection of scholars then buttresses such work with the theoretical or pedagogical frameworks that reflect their area of expertise.

Although professors and graduate students can appreciate and employ the scholarship of this collection, we write with our primary audience in mind: undergraduate students and professors who work with them. We've all had the experience of checking out a book and then finding it was a waste of time because the author spends three hundred pages discussing a perspective of which we have no interest. We hope that in this collection you will not only see how multi-faceted interpretations of the play can be but also find essays that appeal to your own research interests.

"What news on the Rialto?": *The Merchant of Venice* Then and Now

Spanning Venice's Grand Canal, the Rialto Bridge connects the Venetian *sestierie* (districts) of San Polo and San Marco. Construction on this permanent stone bridge, which replaced less reliable pontoon and wooden bridges, began in 1591 and was completed a few years before William Shakespeare penned *The Merchant of Venice* sometime between 1596 and 1598. Yet the fame of this bustling bridge, teeming with pedestrians, merchants, and investors, was established centuries before Shakespeare would set the Rialto as the spatial nexus for Shylock's interactions with the Christian community in *The Merchant of Venice*. San Polo, known for its main commercial market area, is named after the Church of San Polo, a Roman Catholic church dedicated to Saint Paul the Apostle. Saint Paul differentiates between a physical and spiritual circumcision in the New Testament: "But he is a Jew, that is one inwardly; and the circumcision is that of the heart, in the spirit, not in the letter; whose praise is not of men, but of God" (Romans 2:29). The San Marco district is named after Venice's patron, Saint Mark, and includes the heart of the city's religious identity with Saint Mark's Basilica, and its political character with the Doge's Palace. The fact that the Rialto links Venice's commercial identity with Christianity's most influential early proselytizer prods us to think about connections, tensions, and conflations: between church and state, mercy and justice, love and money, Jews and Christians, and men and women. Mostly, though, as we examine and appreciate the scholarly work that has been done in the twentieth century, we try to read *The Merchant of Venice* with twenty-first-century eyes informed by new and alternative modes of analyses that are refreshing in their indebtedness to and departure from older forms of study.

Keeping in mind undergraduate students who want a basic rundown of how and when *The Merchant of Venice* first came to be, this section will provide undergraduates with a rudimentary understanding of *The Merchant of Venice*'s early history. Because the issue of usury and the character of Shylock are the play's most commonly studied elements, I will offer a brief contextualized history of the play's publication as it relates to usury and anti-Semitic discourse before previewing the topics covered by this collection's set of essays.

The Merchant of Venice and the 1590s

On 22 July 1598 the play was entered into the London Stationers' Register by James Roberts as "the Marchaunt of Venyce or otherwise called the Jewe of Venice." Roberts was a printer who entered the play into the Register in order to control the license to print its script. On 28 October 1600 Roberts transferred the rights to publish the drama to Thomas Heyes. This collaboration resulted in the first printed edition of the play, the 1600 First Quarto. The title for this printed copy reads "The most excellent History of the Merchant of Venice" with a subtitle of "With the extreame crueltie of Shylocke the Jew towards the sayd Merchant . . ." The 1623 Folio edition simplifies the title to *The Merchant of Venice*.

Shakespeare wrote *The Merchant of Venice* sometime between 1596 and 1598. Many scholars believe the play was first performed as *The Jew of Venice* to capitalize on the popularity of Christopher Marlowe's *The Jew of Malta*, which was written sometime between 1588 and 1592. Marlowe's play was an early modern equivalent of a hit when it was performed at least thirty six times by the Admiral's Men acting company between February 1592 and June 1596. Although much credit for the tragedy's popularity must go to Marlowe's "mighty line" and his unparalleled craftsmanship, the 1594 execution of Rodrigo Lopez must also be cited as a reason for its commercial success.

Highly regarded and trusted by the English court, Lopez was Queen Elizabeth I's physician for thirteen years and had practiced medicine in the homes of Sir Francis Walsingham, Robert Dudley, and Sir Robert Cecil among other members of the royal court's upper echelon. In fact, Marlowe satirized Lopez for the high fees he charged for his services as early as 1588 in *Doctor Faustus*.

Lopez was born in Portugal and is now seen by many as a closeted Jew who clandestinely practiced his religion in the hostile environs of the anti-Semitic Iberian Peninsula, which was obsessed with *limpieza de sangre* (purity of blood) distinctions and rooting out heretics under the authority of the Spanish Inquisition. Publicly, of course, Lopez lived as a Jew who had converted to the dominant and legally sanctioned Christian religion of the day. Nonetheless, known as a *converso*, New Christian, or, more pejoratively in Spain, a *marrano*, Lopez, like other Jews-cum-Christians would always be doubted as to the genuineness of his newly found faith.

When he was caught up in a treasonous plot to poison Queen Elizabeth, Lopez's links to Catholic Spain and his Jewish roots marked him as a man set for failure by the Christian majority – much like Shylock. Just as Shylock's property and money is forfeited by the end of Act 4, Lopez's home had been confiscated by the law and his goods were seized by the Customs House. Lopez was hanged, drawn, and quartered at Tyburn on 1594 after being convicted of plotting to poison the queen.

Shakespeare was no doubt influenced by Lopez in his portrayal of Shylock – how much so is debatable. Scholars such as Charles Edelman and Christopher Spencer suggest that Shylock's origins might not necessarily lie in Lopez. It is certain that Shakespeare knew how popular an earlier stage Jew was: Barabas from Marlowe's *The Jew Of Malta.* Many scholars suggest that the now standard title of *The Merchant of Venice* was eventually created to avoid confusion with Marlowe's tragedy. After all, Marlowe's play, which can be seen as nothing short of virulently anti-Semitic, was a blockbuster even before Lopez was executed in June 1594. All the same, the notoriety of Lopez's trial and execution, as well as *The Jew of Malta's* popularity, surely was not missing on Shakespeare. The web of conspiracy, rumors, secret dealings, and, bloodshed that swirled around Lopez's death must have played some role in the darkness that pervades *The Merchant of Venice*, which is ostensibly meant to be viewed as a comedy.

The 1623 First Folio edition of the play places *The Merchant of Venice* under the category of comedies right between *A Midsummer Night's Dream* and *As You Like It.* The listing seems innocuous enough, but if we remember the older titles under which the play was printed and published, or even the subtitle of the 1598 licensing of the play, "Otherwise Called *The Jew of Venice*," we can easily problematize readings of the play as a straightforward comedy. When we consider *The Merchant of Venice* alongside Shakespeare's other comedies, we note the lack of a catchy title imbued with a fanciful or substantive theme stemming from a popular proverb or phrase (think *All's Well That End's Well* or *Much Ado About Nothing*). Although the title is absent a proper noun like those we see in his tragedies, the play's anomalous title hints that more than a run-of-the-mill comedy is in the works. The seventeenth-century categorization of *The Merchant of Venice* as a comedy, even if it was later classified as one of Shakespeare's problem plays in the 1930s and 1940s by W. W. Lawrence and E. M. W. Tillyard, belies the virulent anti-Semitism, high-wire tension, and threat of death that permeates this play.

In a post-WWII era, rare is the reader or viewer of *The Merchant of Venice* that is ignorant to the atrocities the Nazis perpetrated on Europe's

Jewish population. Nudged to be more inclusive and humanist with the help of cultural products such as Anne Frank's *Diary of a Young Girl* (1947), Elie Wiesel's *The Night* (1958), and the Hollywood film *Schindler's List* (1993), Western society has become increasingly sensitive to negative stereotypes about Jews in culture, politics, and quotidian life. So how does the patently anti-Semitic nature of *The Merchant of Venice* survive in the classroom, on the stage, and, to a lesser extent, on film? The cultural capital we have invested in all things Shakespeare plays an important role in the continued fascination with *The Merchant of Venice* as much as it does in the continued interest in the unsettling misogyny of *Taming of the Shrew* and the caustic racism of *Othello*. However, as this collection argues, Shakespeare the genius, legend, and enduring English icon, is not the only factor fueling *The Merchant of Venice*'s longevity.

Shylock, the play's Jewish villain, appears in only five scenes in the play but dominates the Venetian community's psyche not only as a religious Other but also as a catalyst for the early modern world's anxiety about capitalism, usury, inter-faith friendships and relationships, homosocial bonds, and the inability to decipher the signified from the signifier. Shylock exists in surprising ways as the indelible focal point of the comedy. However, as many are keen on pointing out, he is not the title character of the play.

How important of an issue was usury in Elizabethan England? By some accounts, the necessity of interest (and even usury) was a foregone conclusion.

Although the Jewish community in England served the kingdom as money-lenders before their banishment in 1290, by the late sixteenth century, many a Christian venture capitalist could be found lending money at interest. Nonetheless, anti-Semitic legends, myths, and folklore contributed to a history of Jewish prejudice, especially in respect to the alleged greediness of Jews. The essentials regarding usury and Jews, as it relates to *The Merchant of Venice*, are as follows.

The first legislation to sanction the charging of interest in England was the Act of 1545, which allowed the practice as long as it did not exceed 10%. The Act was repealed in 1552 with possible punishments including a fine, imprisonment, and the forfeiture of interest and principal. It was not until 1571 that the charging of interest was once again legally sanctioned in England. Interest, as opposed to usury, was once more set at a maximum of 10%. With a numerical limit placed on legal interest, individuals could argue that usury was interest above the allowable ten percent.

Of course, human flesh is unquantifiable save in terms of weights and measurements, making the flesh bond plot of *The Merchant of Venice* all the more horrific and engrossing. Shylock's thirst for Christian flesh (and, as Portia argues, blood) allows him to live up to the stereotype and caricature of the evil and devilish Jew that was rumored to use the blood of Christian children in religious rituals. From Martin Luther's sermons against Jews, most notably 1543's *On the Jews and Their Lies*, to Marlowe's Barabas and Medieval portrayals of Judas as a usurer, Jews had few, if any, positive portrayals in the popular discourse on which to count.

Yet Shylock endures because he is different. He challenges the stereotype. In fact, Shylock is the only character in the drama to employ any form of the term "usury" when he says that Antonio "was wont to call me usurer" (3.1.47). Although he is quoting Antonio, Shylock's reference to this name-calling demonstrates his offense at the term. Other characters, however, are more likely to call him "Jew" (sixty one times) rather than his given name (fifteen times). If we consider the dramatic form of the text, Shylock is referred to as "Jew" in the stage direction and speech prefixes of the First Quarto thirty times while his proper name is given fifty seven times in the directions and prefixes. Can we assign some sympathy to Shakespeare's more respectful usage of the Shylock's name in the stage directions? After all, whereas Barabas is more of a well-rounded misanthrope scorning Christians, Turks, and even other Jews, Shylock speaks of his "sacred nation." He is cognizant of his community and asks us to consider as much in his pathos-rich "If you prick us do we not bleed?" speech.

New Readings of *The Merchant of Venice*

Despite the vexing character of Shylock, this play, as much as it is indebted to the controversy over usury for its infamy, is so much more than a play about Shylock, money, and religious rivalry. As this collection stands testament to, just as with all of Shakespeare's works, readers and viewers of *The Merchant of Venice* can choose sundry topics to analyze, reflect on, and be inspired by.[1]

---

[1] *The Merchant of Venice* has long been a rich field to mine in academia with respect to literary studies, history, and the performing arts. It has also increasingly become a key text in studies of Judaism and Jewish culture. In fact, three authors in this collection (Horacio Sierra, James Newlin, and Sidney Homan) have ties and are indebted to the University of Florida and its Jewish Studies Center, which hosted a symposium in 2010 entitled "Convergences and Conversions: The Merchant of Venice into the 21st Century" under the direction of Judith Page. The

Regardless of how much scholarship is done on early modern life, culture, and theater-going customs, we can never know how the original audience of *The Merchant of Venice* interpreted the play. Likewise, even in our own era, we can never take an accurate survey of how even a single production of *The Merchant of Venice* is received by audience members. Imagine yourself in the theater and seeing Shylock, Portia, and Antonio on stage. Consider how you might feel during the first two acts, during intermission, a few minutes after the performance, and a few days later when you discuss it with a friend. Our feelings and interpretations are likely to change based on what we saw, what our friends and spouses tell us they felt, what popular press reviews focus on, etc. In a nod to the infinite variety of such interpretations, this collection presents different readings of *The Merchant of Venice* that are indebted to twentieth-century scholarship and invigorated by twenty-first century appreciations, contexts, and theoretical frameworks. This collection does not purport to be the bedrock on which future scholarship is founded. Rather, it is one piece of an ever-changing stream of academic studies dedicated to enjoying and making sense of *The Merchant of Venice*.

Just as there are myriad ways to interpret Shylock as a redeemable or incorrigible villain, there are a variety of ways to read, understand, perform, and appropriate *The Merchant of Venice* within a twenty-first century context. This collection of essays offers new and sometimes alternative systems of analyses for comprehending the complex masterpiece that is *The Merchant of Venice*. The authors in this collection are a little looser with their language – not so much for the fun of using slang as for reflecting colloquial vocabulary that would not sound strange in the contemporary undergraduate classroom. Such vocabulary, phrases, idioms, and pop culture allusions make a discussion of this work relatable without being condescending. Just as Shakespeare made hay (and gold) with the language of his day, so must we continue to respect, challenge, and utilize our vernacular to the best of our ability so that we can communicate as inclusively as possible in the spirit of the humanities without obfuscating jargon or esoteric language.

This collection's first essay, Audrey Birkett's "Theoretical Investigations and Critical Answers in *The Merchant of Venice*" offers undergraduates a brief set of primers on critical theory that are then applied to *The Merchant of Venice*. An added bonus to such an introduction is Birkett's ability to

---

symposium's focus on considering *The Merchant of Venice* within the context of the twenty-first century complements the heart of this collection's goals as we seek to read, decipher, and experience *The Merchant of Venice* as a cultural product and literary artifact that responds to, reflects, and informs our everyday lives.

articulate the "real world" applications of employing theoretical lenses to interpret literature. This chapter explores how different theoretical readings of *The Merchant of Venice* provide disparate answers to the array of social, political, gender, religious, and racial questions posed in the text. By guiding students to understand the ideas, structures, and divides in *The Merchant of Venice*, Birkett arrives at a sustained, focused reading of the play that elucidates the nuances of theory in a fashion palatable to undergraduate vocabulary. Birkett focuses on four of the more popular schools of critical theory: queer theory, feminism, post-colonialism, and Marxism. This chapter gives us a better idea of what the play can do, what we can learn about it, and how we can apply theory to understand and solve difficult literary problems, such as those posed in *The Merchant of Venice*. This chapter examines the slipperiness of genre as Birkett argues that, more than any other Shakespeare text, *The Merchant of Venice*'s fluidity mirrors our current state of theoretical play as we study literature and drama in a "post"-theoretical moment.

Working with the theoretical apparatuses Birkett deconstructs in her chapter, the collection's subsequent three essays employ various styles of feminism, queer theory, and gender studies to examine the characters of Antonio, Bassanio, Portia, and Nerissa.

Paul Dingman starts off this thread with "'Why then you are in love': Close Male Friendship and Ethical Identity in Early Modern Drama," which explores Antonio and Bassanio's amity as a manifestation of Renaissance-era male-male friendships as influenced by notions of chivalric friendship in the Middle Ages. Fierce loyalty or even love between knights on campaign or adventures helped define good chivalric character in medieval times as indicated by the wildly popular romances and epic poems of the period. Although the ideological dominance of chivalry began to fade—ever so slowly—in the Early Modern era, some of its central tenets critical to elite male identity did not. Strong, emotional friendships between men, for example, transferred easily across time and topography from the battlefield to the marketplace. In *The Merchant of Venice*, Bassanio and Antonio are beloved yet beleaguered friend-heroes in the knightly tradition even though they never enter a joust or seek a religious artifact. By examining chronicle sources and older, influential tales such as the anonymous *Amis and Amiloun*, the *Gesta Romanorum*, and Malory's *Le Morte D'arthur*, this chapter highlights enduring ideas of male friendship and chivalric virtue in Shakespeare's dark comedy while revealing the medieval context of the play in a mode similar to the recent scholarship of Curtis Perry, James Simpson, Brian Walsh, and others. Understanding the link between bonds of emotional male friendship and accompanying ethics/esteem may help illuminate the perennial fascination with this complex drama.

Rebecca Olson's study of female friendship complements Dingman's chapter and offers a closer look at Shakespeare's comedic heroines who typically have "BFFs" (sisters or close female friends of comparable social standing) in contrast to the heroines in the tragedies and romances who tend to confide in sympathetic servants or lack female camaraderie altogether. "The Genre of Female Friendship in *The Merchant of Venice*" launches this investigation with a nod to Brian Gallivan's YouTube viral video series "Sassy Gay Friend" and by employing a recent Oregon Shakespeare Festival production of *Merchant* that problematized the allegedly easy relationship between Portia and Nerissa by highlighting one of the heiress's uglier moments, when she dismisses her suitor the Prince of Morocco with "Let all of his complexion choose me so." This chapter attends to the "girlfriend problem" in *The Merchant of Venice* to argue that Portia's social isolation may set the stage for the play's less traditional comedic conclusion.

The following essay in the collection, Horacio Sierra's "'Thrift is blessing, if men steal it not': Usury and Cuckoldry in *The Merchant of Venice*," appropriates the tenets of gender studies and queer theory to offer a new way of understanding Shylock. This chapter proposes one more motivation for Shylock's cruelty: his anxieties about having been cuckolded. The scholarly silence on cuckoldry in *The Merchant of Venice* belies the numerous references to it in the play. There is no literal reading of Shylock-as-cuckold. Rather, Shylock is cuckolded through verbal innuendo, rumor, imagery, double entendre, and subtext. Because Renaissance conceptions about usury originate in classical prohibitions of the practice because of its unnaturalness, this chapter argues that Shylock sublimates his paternal unease by substituting financial regeneration for biological reproduction. As such, Sierra asserts that Shylock's bond is a hyperbolic, psychosexual manifestation of anti-usury polemics. Antonio is a foil to Shylock in this proposition since he neither charges interest nor fears about his nonexistent offspring. Antonio's queer acceptance of his childlessness contrasts with Shylock's doubts about being Jessica's father. This chapter showcases how the text questions Shylock's paternity and reflects concern about conflations of love and money while interrogating early modern angst over capitalism's reliance on usury. This chapter also models for undergraduates how even the most radical interpretations of literature can be credibly supported with careful close readings of the text and the employment of critical resources, historical contextualization, and theoretical structures.

Just as Sierra's unconventional reading of Shylock's back story shifts the reader's perspective of the villainized Jew, James Newlin takes on the very notion of reading *The Merchant of Venice* as a conduit for understanding intertextual allegorical residue between two Shakespearean works in "How Every Fool Can Play Upon The Word!': Allegories of Reading in *The Merchant of Venice* and *Pericles*." Unlike Sigmund Freud, who links the choice of three caskets in *The Merchant of Venice* with the love test in *King Lear*, Newlin compares the riddles of the caskets—and the suitors' accompanying answers—with Antiochus's riddle at the beginning of *Pericles*. As this chapter's subtitle's allusion to Paul de Man indicates, Newlin's study employs a method inspired by deconstruction to read the two plays and their riddles. With a particular focus on the characters' accounts of the various contracts and bonds in *The Merchant of Venice*, these two plays are read as allegories of their own reading, or as Lorenzo puts it, how we "can play upon the word!" But rather than simply mapping de Man's famous notion of the impossibility of reading unto the plays, such "play" will illuminate many of the specific riddles that have plagued the critical history of these works, such as *The Merchant of Venice*'s treatment of anti-Semitism and the textual difficulties of *Pericles*.

Jeffrey Wilson's work in "Hath Not a Jew a Nose? Or, the Danger of Deformity in Comedy" dovetails with this introductory essay's engagement with the most vexing element of the play, Shylock as the embodiment of early modern anti-Semitic stereotypes, in respect to theoretical and practical stage considerations. In more than the obvious way, an obnoxiously large nose has been attached to Shakespeare's Shylock. This prosthetic comes neither from the text of *The Merchant of Venice* nor from a Shakespearean theatrical tradition, but from "the artificiall Iewe of Maltas nose," as William Rowley's *A Search for Money* (1609) remembers the costume of Edward Alleyn's Barabas in Marlowe's play. The play influencing Shakespeare's invention of Shylock uses an artificial nose to signal a Jewish villainy, and so do at least two plays influenced by Shakespeare's Shylock: George Chapman's *The Blinde Begger of Alexandria* (1598) and John Marston's *Jack Drum's Entertainment* (1601). Some historicists reason an artificial nose onto Shylock due to early English theatrical and cultural conventions, but other strict textualists cannot credit this unsubstantiated suggestion, and the issue of Shylock's artificial nose is so tricky that analysts such as James Shapiro and Joan Holmer have thrown up their hands in uncertainty. Did Shakespeare's Shylock actually wear an artificial Jew's nose on the Elizabethan stage? This chapter responds to this question, not by scouring the historical record of Elizabethan performances, which yields no answer, but by extrapolating from Shakespeare's other thematic considerations and compositional decisions in *The Merchant of Venice*.

In our increasingly visual culture, Shakespeare's plays have been appearing more frequently in the popular form of comic books and graphic novels. *The Merchant of Venice* is no exception. To understand how these texts are adapting and interpreting Shakespeare for a new generation requires an interpretive approach that can engage both with Shakespeare's poetry and with the medium of sequential art. Russell McDonnell's chapter "Reading Law and Ethnicity in the Manga Shakespeare *Merchant of Venice*" examines Faye Yong's *Manga Shakespeare* edition of the play by combining a traditionally formalist close reading with detailed attention to Yong's use of the comics medium, using a method derived from the pioneering work of visual theorist Scott McCloud, who provides a basic descriptive grammar of the comics form. Yong's adaptation carefully deploys Shakespeare's words in combination with sequential images to present a version of the play in which Shylock exposes how the order and prosperity of Venice rests upon a self-contradictory system of law, dependent upon the racially-other "strangers" that it marginalizes and excludes. This chapter not only provides insight into a fresh new way of interpreting *The Merchant of Venice*, but it also models an interpretation of Shakespeare in graphic novels, thus opening up a new field of inquiry for the further study of Shakespeare and visual culture.

As I often remind my students, Shakespeare's plays were meant to be seen on stage. One of the most prolific and astute scholars on Shakespeare and acting, Sidney Homan, concludes our collection with a masterful chapter that is more of a vision than an essay. Given his knack for bringing Shakespeare to life as a professor of undergraduates and graduates at the University of Florida for more than thirty years, Homan employs his skills as a community theater director and his expertise as a scholar to bring to life the ideas that this collection's authors explore. Amalgamating his trademark academic astuteness with his passion for the performing arts, Homan offers a zestfully imagined vision of how a production of *The Merchant of Venice* would work using the new readings proffered in this collection. Intellectually curious and artistically open-minded, Homan focuses on eight distinct scenes that can offer rich rewards for actors and offers a plan along with a slew of questions to inspire further inquiry. This final chapter, "With These Essays in Hand: Re-Stagings of *The Merchant of Venice*," embodies the potential that new scholarship and alterative analysis offers students, professors, directors, actors, and viewers. Homan's coda, if you will, reminds us to pay attention to every new opinion on *The Merchant of Venice*, for without a reading/viewing and response to the play, it would be dead.

The Merchant of Venice has long been a rich field to mine in academia with respect to literary studies, history, and the performing arts. It has also increasingly become a key text in studies of Judaism and Jewish culture. In fact, three authors in this collection (Sierra, Newlin, and Homan) have ties and are indebted to the University of Florida and its Jewish Studies Center, which hosted a symposium in 2010 entitled "Convergences and Conversions: The Merchant of Venice into the 21st Century." The symposium's focus on considering *The Merchant of Venice* within the context of the twenty-first century complements the heart of this collection's goals as we seek to read, decipher, and experience *The Merchant of Venice* as a cultural product and literary artifact that responds to, reflects, and informs our everyday lives.

Bibliography

Adelman, Janet. *Blood Relations: Christian and Jew in The Merchant of Venice*. Chicago: University of Chicago Press, 2008. Print.

Barnet, Sylvan. Ed. *Twentieth Century Interpretations of The Merchant of Venice*. Englewood Cliuffs, NJ: Prentice-Hall, Inc., 1970.

Casillas, Martín. *Apuntes sobre El mercader de Venecia*. Mexico City: Ultradigital Press, 2005.

Danson, Lawrence. *The Harmonies of the Merchant of Venice*. New Haven, CT: Yale University Press, 1978.

Edelman, Charles. *Shakespeare in Production: The Merchant of Venice*. Cambridge: Cambridge University Press, 2003. Print.

Gellert, James. "Shylock, Huckleberry, and Jim: Do They Have a Place in Today's High Schools?" *Children's Literature Association Quarterly*. 12.1 (Spring 1987): 40-43.

Green, Dominic. *Spies, Shakespeare, and the Plot to Poison Elizabeth I: The Double Life of Doctor Lopez*. London: Century Press, 2003.

Gross, Kenneth. *Shylock is Shakespeare*. Chicago: University of Chicago Press, 2006.

Janik, Vicki K. *The Merchant of Venice: A Guide to the Play*. Westport, CT: Greenwood Press, 2003.

Kitch, Aaron. "Shylock's Sacred Nation." *Shakespeare Quarterly*. 59.2 (Summer 2008): 131-55.

Lawrence, W. W. *Shakespeare Problem Comedies*. New York: 1931.

Leimberg, Inge. *"What may words say . . . ?" A Reading of The Merchant of Venice*. Lanham, MD: Fairleigh Dickinson University Press, 2011.

O'Rourke, James L. "Racism and Homophobia in *The Merchant of Venice*." *ELH* 70.2 (Summer 2003): 375-97.

Penuel, Suzanne. "Castrating the Creditor in *The Merchant of Venice*." *Studies in English Literature: 1500-1900*. 44.2 (Spring 2004): 255-75.

Shatzmiller, Joseph. *Shylock Reconsidered: Jews, Moneylending, and Medieval Society*. Berkeley: University of California Press, 1990.

Spenser, Christopher. *The Genesis of Shakespeare's Merchant of Venice*. Lampeter, Wales: Edwin Mellen Press, 1988.

Tillyard, E. M. W. *Shakespeare's Problem Plays*. Toronto: 1949.

Wright, Celeste Turner. "Some Conventions Regarding the Usurer in Elizabethan Literature." *Studies in Philology* 35 (1938): 178-94.

THEORETICAL QUESTIONS AND CRITICAL ANSWERS IN *THE MERCHANT OF VENICE*

AUDREY BIRKETT

At the end of his article, "The Merchant of Venice and the Possibilities of Historical Criticism," Walter Cohen suggests that "if we attempt to use *The Merchant of Venice* . . . to interrogate literary theory, rather than the other way around, it will be evident, the need to account for both its familiarity and its otherness" (784). I will do just that in this chapter: show the familiarity and the otherness of the play in respect to how it is reflected in contemporary society. An examination of four specific literary theories – queer theory, feminism, postcolonialism, and Marxism – when used to explain different interpretations of *Merchant* provides a series of insights into twenty-first-century society. The issues at the play's core, involving same-sex love, the rights of women, discrimination against foreign and religious outsiders, and the struggles between the classes are all relevant in contemporary society. Theory, both consciously and subconsciously, has the potential to explain and define the world. However, the limitations of theory actually raise more questions and leave loose ends about where society stands in terms of gender, sexuality, foreignness, and capitalism, which in itself is another positive aspect of theory's potential.

In order to understand the interpretive power of literary criticism, we must begin by examining the beginnings of theory and how it changed as society has shifted and progressed. Beginning with New Criticism and liberal humanism, the attempt to find answers within a work, outside of a social context, suggests that there is a singular meaning that will be understood and applicable, regardless of where a work is written or read. The notion that a literary text can reflect a universal human experience is still a cornerstone of literary study today, but it is also too restrictive and confining. The need for truths (plural) rather than truth (singular) paved the way for those French theorists of the 1950s and 1960s who contextualized theory. Philosophers and cultural anthropologists such as Claude Lévi-Strauss, Roland Barthes, Jacques Derrida, and Michel Foucault demanded that other voices and other agents, *outside* of the text, have a profound effect on determining different meanings.[1] Barthes's 1967 essay "The Death of the Author" provided the crucial pivot point between structuralism and post-structuralism, which opened the door for the reader, the author, and society to make demands of the text and impose their own meanings on it. As a result, in the twenty-first century, numerous voices have a say about the meaning and interpretation of a text, none incorrect or absolute.

The variety and validity of such diverse interpretations prove the post-structuralist quandary in which twenty-first-century scholars now find themselves, because of theoretical limitations: if all viewpoints are valid, how can any singular viewpoint be true? Barthes's 1971 essay "From Work to Text" solidifies the idea that it is the "interdisciplinarity" of the text, its place in a wider "frames of reference" that provides its meaning; it is not the "work" in isolation that provides meaning, but the "text" in context (155-56). In short, structuralists and post-structuralists determined that meaning must come from the text *in context*, but the definition of the context itself has no fixed and permanent meaning. Theories that center around the reader, the author, the history, and the culture all stem from mid-twentieth-century literary philosophy and provide diverse meanings to literature for a variety of readers.

It is with the question "How can so many viewpoints be accurate?" that I wish to start the search for critical answers to the problems posed in *Merchant*. The individual, social, and global conflicts that plague the twenty-first century mirrors the events that engulf Portia, Antonio, Bassanio, Shylock, and the rest of the Venetians in the play. The problems that the characters experience in commerce, love, and social acceptance have stretched across oceans, borders, and even time to be just as relevant and applicable in contemporary, Western society as they were in the fictional Italy and real-life England of the late sixteenth century. This chapter investigates the address of modern-day problems through an examination of *Merchant*, as well as the play's limits in providing full answers to social questions because of the disparate theoretical explanations that can be and are applied to it by contemporary readers. *Merchant*, perhaps more than any other Shakespearean play, has at its core acutely modern issues such as the nature of the relationship between

---

[1] Lévi-Strauss's *Structural Anthropology* opened the doors for structuralism in the humanities. Foucault's *The Order of Things: An Archaeology of the Human Sciences* serves as a groundbreaking text on shifts in social discourses across time and place. Barthes's "The Death of the Author" and Derrida's *Writing and Difference* offer the next step, post-structuralism, but also offer commentary on the movement between the theories themselves.

Antonio and Bassanio, the amount of control held by Portia in her own destiny, the required social standing to "fit in" Venetian society, and the view of the religious "Other" as the villain. These issues are reflective of similar complementary contemporary debates within queer theory, feminism, postcolonialism, and Marxism. However, as theory shifts, contemporary understandings and interpretations also change, and often clash with one another, making the play both a source of answers as well as further questions.

Queer Theory, Antonio and Bassanio, and Same-Sex Rights

Queer theory does not have the same emphasis on normal and "deviant" that it initially did when the school of thought first formed in the 1990s. Foucault's chapter "The Perverse Implantation," from *The History of Sexuality*, discusses how same-sex relationships came to be condemned as "perverse" because of hegemonic and linguistic categorizations that were put in place by dominant power structures. From Foucault's study, the use of terminology such as "gay," "straight," or even "queer" evokes an identity that fluctuates between acceptable and unacceptable based on how a society evaluates sexuality and the terms used to signify homosexuality.[2] In other words, to be "gay," a word that began as a synonym for "noble, beautiful, excellent, or fine" ("Gay," OED), might be acceptable, but to be "queer," which originally meant "strange, odd, peculiar, eccentric" or "of questionable character; suspicious, dubious," ("Queer," OED) is not, at least in terms of sexuality. There is an inherent fluidity within definitions that the queer theorist seeks to highlight in order to refute the associations that accompany a singular term within a society. Even the term "queer" suggests an instability and continuous change by which theorists attempt to reconfigure the terms that define and evaluate those with non-normative sexualities. "Queer" is a word that has long gone out of fashion in the mainstream to describe or insult homosexuals. The term "queer" denotes something that is out of ordinary, abnormal, and

---

[2] Since Foucault's *The History of Sexuality*, a wealth of queer theory scholarship has been produced by such noted scholars as Judith Butler in *Gender Trouble*, Jonathan Dollimore in *Sexual Dissidence: Augustine to Wilde, Freud to Foucault*, and Eve Kosofsky Sedgwick in *Between Men: English Literature and Male Homosexual Desire*. These critics provide a legitimate and authoritative voice for the homosexual perspective and experience in literature and established the fundamental tenets of queer theory.

therefore dangerous to the average citizen.[3] To use this word to describe the interpretations that come about from seeing life and literature through the lens of the homosexual experience is offensive and problematic to those men and women who identify themselves as lesbian or gay, or even transgender or bisexual.[4] Some theorists use the phrase "Lesbian and Gay Studies or Theory," but this term also comes with problems, namely that all lesbians and gays have a shared, common experience.

Sexual alienation within contemporary Western society has diminished and the mode of thinking that considers homosexuality "deviant" or heterosexuality "correct" has moderated. Likewise, issues and identities of bisexuality and transgender that were not a part of the theoretical package because they were not a part of the initial "gay" experience as defined by queer theory are now a regular part of sexuality studies. As can already be seen, life moves much faster than a field of study, which changes to keep up, but ultimately remains one wave behind. Queer theory, according to the *Lesbian and Gay Studies Reader* makes sexual orientation "a fundamental category of analysis and understanding," but seeks to eradicate a hierarchy of sexual preference, namely that homosexual is wrong or deviant and heterosexual is right and normal (Abelove xv).

The application of queer theory to *Merchant* provides a good foundation for interpreting non-heteronormative moments in the play. Contemporary readers can use what happens in the play, in terms of defining sexuality and sexual practice, to investigate the impact of sexual preference in modern society. Although labels such as "gay" and "homosexual" are anachronistic in the sixteenth-century play, the practices and relationships that are today labeled as such can be identified, particularly in reference to the relationship between Antonio and Bassanio. The term "homosexual" as it is used today to describe "a person who has a sexual propensity for his or her own sex" only came into common use in

---

[3] Will Fisher interrogates the term "queer" in "Queer Money" and examines how it has evolved in terms of identifying "other" sexualities from its origins in economic practices.
[4] Since the establishment of the theory in the later half of the twentieth century, little has emerged to further the study into transgender or transsexual experiences. Recent studies include: Judith Halberstam's *In a Queer Time and Place: Transgendered Bodies, Subcultural Lives* and Patricia Elliot's *Debates in Transgender, Queer, and Feminist Theory*. One important study I wish to draw attention to is Jess Battis's edited collection *Homofiles: Theory, Sexuality, and Graduate Studies*. In this collection, gay, lesbian, and transgender graduate students offer insights and investigations into how literature, theory, and scholarship intersect with and influence daily social interactions in and out of academia.

the early twentieth century ("Homosexual," OED). As a result, the information that is gained from asking basic questions about the play, and the answers that result, provide information about the appearance and acceptance of homosexuality in contemporary society rather than in Shakespeare's. Is Antonio gay? Are his actions abnormal or deviant? These considerations lead to larger questions of identity in our society: how do we define ourselves today and how are we defined by society in relation to sexuality? If Antonio is gay, what message about early modern homosexuality can we glean from the play? How can we use what we have learned to act in society and feel about ourselves, either as or in relation to homosexuals and homosexuality?

An application of queer theory to the play often results in Antonio being viewed, in a contemporary context, as homosexual.[5] The language he uses in discussion with or about Bassanio is more intimate and personal than the language of friendship, even a close one. The opening scene in which Antonio unlocks his "purse, person, and extremest means" (1.1.141) to Bassanio is reaffirmed in the trial scene when the merchant insists that Bassanio tell his new wife Portia how much Antonio loved him, and also to "speak him fair in death" (4.1.283). The language used and the emotions expressed all seem to point to a homosexual Antonio, at least by contemporary standards. But the circumstances do not provide a definitive answer. The attempt to reconfigure what is "normal" and expected must be considered in constructing Antonio's sexual identity as it meshes with the tenet of queer theory that "expose[s] the 'homophobia' of mainstream literature and criticism, as seen in ignoring or denigrating the homosexual aspects of the work of major canonical figures" (Barry 143). If Antonio is seen as gay and the protagonist of a Shakespearean play, consequently, through the lens of queer theory, homosexuals can be positive characters in mainstream literature, which is a reconfiguration of the traditional, heterosexual hero of the Western canon.

The assumption that there is a commonality in gay experience is rejected by queer theory. A question of identity is addressed through more

---

[5] There are differing views on Antonio's sexual preference, particularly in view of anachronisms, but there is a wide spectrum of possibility for Antonio's affections. In particular, see Alan Sinfield, "How to Read *The Merchant of Venice* without Being Heterosexist"; Alan Bray, *Homosexuality in Renaissance England*; Coppelia Kahn, "The Cuckoo's Note: Male Friendship and Cuckoldry in *The Merchant of Venice*"; Steve Patterson, "The Bankruptcy of Homoerotic Amity in Shakespeare's *The Merchant of Venice*"; Lawrence W. Hyman, "The Rival Lovers in *The Merchant of Venice*"; and Joseph Pequigney, "The Two Antonios and Same-Sex Love in *Twelfth Night* and *The Merchant of Venice*."

sophisticated theoretical analyses that rely on binaries and fluctuations, which, in turn, cause differences in experience and outlook. After all, heterosexuals do not share a "common" experience, so why should homosexuals? There is a great deal of reliance on potential in queer theory. Identity is a constant shuffling of a range of different roles and positions. In *Merchant*, Antonio's sexuality is largely based on his potential with Bassanio. The nature of the relationship between the merchant and his gentleman friend is unclear at the outset, but the two are quickly distinguished from the other companions in Act 1. Salerio and Solanio are set to depart from Antonio because a better, closer companion has entered:

> SOLANIO. Here comes Bassanio, your most noble kinsman,
>   Gratiano, and Lorenzo. Fare ye well.
>   We leave you now with better company.
> SALERIO. I would have stayed till I had made you merry,
>   If worthier friends had not prevented me. (1.1.59-63)

Gratiano and Lorenzo are then separated further from Antonio and Bassanio, who the others acknowledge have a more personal relationship. Once the others have left, these two men engage in a more intimate and personal dialogue than the other pairings of friends had previously in the scene, with Antonio pledging his loyalty:

> I pray you, good Bassanio, let me know it;
> And if it stand, as you yourself still do,
> Within the eye of honor, be assure
> My purse, my person, my extremest means
> Lie all unlocked to your occasions. (1.1.138-42)[6]

Antonio and Bassanio keep their intimacy private from the other companions, which would suggest, to a queer theorist, that their relationship is different from those of the male friends who otherwise populate the opening scene. However, their relationship is never identified in terms of sexuality in the play itself and thus the question of whether they are homosexual or heterosexual remains.

---

[6] These lines from Antonio are often discussed, in criticism, in terms of his queer identity. Seymour Kleinberg expresses the notion that "the echoing pun on 'purse' and 'person' suggest as 'sexual longing'" in "The Homosexual as Anti-Semite in Nascent Capitalism" (117). Suzanne Penuel observes that Antonio's words may have erotic intent, a definition of "purse" as "scrotum" also lets us read the offer in terms of parenting in "Castrating the Creditor in *The Merchant of Venice*" (260).

This opening exchange between the men also brings in questions of potentiality and fluidity that are crucial to queer theory. If Bassanio will accept, Antonio will give himself and his extremities to Bassanio. Bassanio accepts and Antonio is willing to provide a pound of his flesh. However, does this acceptance make both men homosexual? If Bassanio does not accept, does that mean Antonio is not or cannot be gay? Antonio is willing to sacrifice all for his lover, in the same way Shakespearean heterosexual lovers sacrifice themselves for their loves.[7] Based on Antonio's willingness, we can make the inference that Antonio and Bassanio are lovers, which Bassanio admits when he states that to the merchant does he "owe the most in money and in love" (1.1.134). However, there needs to be something that happens for Bassanio's sexual identity to be confirmed, in either direction: he needs to take Antonio's money to be committed to Antonio and homosexuality, or he needs to sail away to win the hand of Portia to confirm heterosexual love. Both men are sexual tabulae rasae, with no default sexual orientations, until something happens, until a commitment is made.

Identity is a complex mixture of chosen allegiances, social positions, and professional roles rather than fixed essence. If Antonio is gay, does that make the object of his affections gay as well? How is the relationship defined if one wants the consummation and the other does not? Steve Patterson's "Bankruptcy of Homoerotic Amity" argues that Antonio and Bassanio are engaged in "homoerotic friendship, or amity," rather than outright homosexual relations (9). Antonio's "frustrated" sexual desire, exhibited from the outset of the play, would suggest that it is Bassanio that is resisting sexual advances from Antonio, thus proving the merchant gay, but the gentleman not (Patterson 16). However, even this assumption is slippery. When Bassanio gives the ring to the disguised Portia, at the behest of Antonio, is he choosing his gay admirer over his heterosexual wife? Although we do not know if he has consummated his relationship with Antonio, the defiance of his wife's ultimatum would certainly suggest a conscious choice of what Antonio wants over what Portia demands. Bassanio has not consummated his relationship with his wife either; yet, Bassanio appears more straight than gay to the average reader. Homosexual and heterosexual are not fixed identities in the play, nor are they fixed in our own society. Sexual identity is based on a series of marks, roles, and potentialities – a combination of everything that is provisional, contingent, and improvisatory. There is no fixed sexual

---

[7] Romeo and Juliet and their source material counterparts Pyramus and Thisbe make the ultimate sacrifice for their heterosexual loves, just as Antonio is willing to do.

identity and terms such as "gay" or "straight" become irrelevant and obsolete.[8]

The question of what makes a man or woman homosexual or what constitutes a homosexual relationship allows us to clarify sexual parameters and identities in contemporary society. Often heterosexuality is considered the default sexuality, but is it in reality? Does homosexual experience define homosexual identity? Are the identities fixed or can they be overturned? A close, personal, and intimate, but sexless relationship between two close friends can be seen, in twenty-first-century society, as being homosexual, whereas it would have been "homosocial" in Elizabethan England.[9] In the introduction to *Between Men*, Eve Kosofsky Sedgwick attempts to reconfigure the "homosocial" as more erotic in pre-twentieth-century literature, at the same time she highlights the problems associated with calling simple male friendships homosexual in a more contemporary society. In other words, relationships were more complex than the term "homosocial" implies, and now they are less latent in terms of sexual congress than "homosexual" often suggests. For instance, the volleyball scene in *Top Gun*, a film that premiered in 1986, a year after *Between Men* was published, is often referenced for its homosexual overtones, but does not necessarily mean the scene has homosexual overtones (Engle). In contemporary society, close, personal, and emotional relations between men, such as those between *Top Gun* flyboys Iceman and Maverick, are often described in homoerotic terms. Antonio and Bassanio could certainly be early modern versions of Iceman and Maverick, and their sexual identities would still be as ambiguous as their

---

[8] Such close, personal relationships are referred to as "homosocial," particularly in reference to Shakespeare's plays. In *Between Men: English Literature and Male Homosocial Desire*, Eve Sedgwick goes further and sees homosocial relations (and homosexuality by extension) as reliant on heterosexual marriages saying that homosocial and homosexual relations are patterned on heterosexual ones.

[9] In an article discussing homosocial relations in contemporary society, "Hybrid Masculine Power: Reconceptualizing the Relationship between Homosociality and Hegemonic Masculinity," Steven Arxer discusses the hybridity of homo- and heterosexual practices in everyday situations. The term "gay" has widely been thrown around as a synonym for daft, stupid, or out of fashion, and such usage has only recently been challenged. Homosocial relations are the subject of a number of scholarly works, including but certainly not limited to: Sedgwick's *Between Men*; Pequigney's "The Two Antonios and Same-Sex Love in *Twelfth Night* and *The Merchant of Venice*"; Alan Bray's "Homosexualiity and the Signs of Male Friendship in Elizabethan England." Julie Crawford discusses female homosociality in Belmont in her article "The Homoerotics of Shakespeare's Elizabethan Comedies."

modern day counterparts because the definition of homosexuality and the theory used to explain it fall short. In 1985, Sedgwick asked the question that is yet to be answered in literature, criticism, or society: "If the relation of homosocial to homosexual bonds is so shifty, then what theoretical framework do we have for drawing any links between sexual and power relationships?" (5).

Feminist Theory, Portia, and the Perception of Powerful Women

Along with homosexual identities, the social, political, and literary identities of women have also shifted far from where feminist theory began, thus making certain ideas and tenets out-dated. The different "waves" that have changed feminist theory from the early twentieth century (retroactively applied) to the present day show a willingness to adapt and redefine the philosophy as the experience of women changes in society. What is expected of/by/for women is impossible to determine, as is the spectrum of the female experience in contemporary society. The theory's social applications are vastly different from its scholarly ones and the diverse understandings of what it means to be a feminist are diverse and disparate because of this gulf.[10] There is, however, a relatively collective, vague, and loose idea of "femininity." In the context of both "sex difference theory" and popular thought, to be feminine, according to Mary Vetterling-Braggin, is to display the psychological traits of "gentleness, modesty, humility, supportiveness, empathy, compassionateness, tenderness, nurturance, intuitiveness, sensitivity, unselfishness" (5-6). This definition does not necessarily correspond with what feminist theorists believe it means to be feminine. In fact, feminist theory rejects a universal notion of what it is to be feminine and seeks to highlight political and social conflicts within a wide range of feminist circles. These differences stem from variations in race, ethnicity, class, political affiliation, and sexual orientation. In short, what separates the ideological viewpoint of feminist theorists, in terms of what it is to be feminine, is what separates all of humanity from sharing a singular point of view – individuality.

Many theoretical considerations of feminism in *Merchant* look at Portia as an individual versus Portia as a wife and member of a wider society. Portia's potential, in drag as a man, would enable her to be "accomplished / with that [she] lacks," suggesting that to be a man is to be

---

[10] The article "Academic Feminism Against Itself" by Robyn Wiegman discusses the very divide between academic definitions of feminism and social ones.

"accomplished" and productive, but without masculinity or manly accoutrements, a woman is lacking (3.5.63). The wider society in which Portia functions is patriarchal and the feminist debate, therefore, begs the question: does Portia support the patriarchal society or does she subvert it? The struggle for Portia to be an individual who makes her own decisions, regardless of the influence of the patriarchal society in which she lives, shapes a feminist argument. On the other hand, Portia's submissive speech, her genuflecting attitude, and her cross-dressing – all to support her husband and the status quo of society – muddy the waters. She is often seen both as a defender of theoretical feminism as well as one of its greatest traitors.[11]

The disagreement about Portia partly arises from the belief that the role of women is unfixed and variable. The focus on the variety of women and the varied experiences women have across social, economic, racial, and/or national boundaries becomes a cornerstone for modern feminist theory, but also a source of debate and challenge within the feminist camp.[12] The desire to show complex and real women, with multi-faceted lives and thoughts is fundamental to understanding feminist theory and then utilizing it to challenge representations of women as "Other" or as lacking. When Portia is first introduced, she appears to be every feminist's worst nightmare: a static prize to be won who is undefined in the absence of a man and who is located in an exotic locale and pursued by suitors from all over the globe to be won as a prize (1.1.169). She backs up this vision by accepting this role, but then subverts it by barking orders at Bassanio from the moment she meets him: "tarry; pause a day or two" and "Beshrew your eyes!" (3.2.1, 14). Even after Bassanio wins her in the casket game, Portia dictates what will happen: "First go with me to church and call me wife, / And then away to Venice to your friend" (3.2.312-13). Portia makes the rules and Bassanio follows her commands. She finally gains complete control over him after he fails her test of love when he gives his ring to the "worthy doctor" at the behest of Antonio (5.1.235). In the final act, Portia

---

[11] For an idea of the vast array of attitudes toward Portia's feminism, see: Lee Lady, "Shakespeare's Women in Drag: Portia" Murray Bigg's "A Neurotic Portia"; Lisa Jardine, "Cultural Confusion and Shakespeare's Learned Heroines"; Penny Gay, *As She Likes It: Shakespeare's Unruly Women*; and Susan Oldrieve, "Marginalized Voices in "The Merchant of Venice.'"

[12] The debate about who is a feminist and what constitutes feminism can be seen in the work of Camille Paglia. Paglia celebrates difference and diversity in feminist studies, but she is likely the most critically attacked feminist today. She calls herself a "dissident" feminist, which works toward showing that there is no singular idea of feminism or who is a feminist.

humiliates Bassanio by implying he is a cuckold and finishes off the play by telling her husband and his companions what they are thinking and what they are allowed to do:

And yet I am sure you are not satisfied
Of these events at full. Let us go in;
And charge us there upon interrogatories,
And we will answer all things faithfully. (5.1.314-17)

The accusatory language highlights another facet of feminist theory that sets up a direct opposition to what Sandra M. Gilbert and Susan Gubar call "the patriarchal psychosexual context in which so much Western literature was authored" (48). Portia sees the men's role as being combative and her role as "faithful." The desire to rebel against patriarchal expectations and dictate self-identity is inherent in Portia's words. She challenges the patriarchal expectations by challenging the men, but she ultimately obeys them.

Feminist theory has gone through "three waves" and still continues to be defined and re-defined in terms of other theories. Feminist literary theory roundly rejects Harold Bloom's application of Freudian structures to explain gender roles in literature. As such, the theory itself is concerned with psychoanalysis and challenging the scientific definitions of "feminine" (Gilbert and Gubar 46). Outside of science, the cultural and social definitions of femininity and the expectations of a "woman's role" also vary, depending on the society, the location, and the environment. This links feminism closely with New Historicism and Cultural Materialism. The militant aspect of combating patriarchal stereotypes and re-appropriating definitions also gives feminist theory a Marxist feel because of the call to action that is intrinsic in such rejection. Such a rallying cry often carries with it a stigma, so that to be called a "feminist" or to believe in "feminism" can be both a compliment and an insult.[13] Because the definitions of femininity and feminism are so malleable and dependant on other ideas, concepts, and points of view, how readers and audiences react goes a long way in terms of defining Portia as a feminist or an anti-feminist.

Feminism is commonly wrapped up in attitude. Personal beliefs season reactions to Portia and form readers' individual classifications of her. If the reader considers himself to be a feminist and likes Portia, then she is

---

[13] Rhiannon Root's article "Feminism Has Negative Connotation Despite Meaning" discusses the myriad of issues surrounding "feminism" in contemporary society and the vastly differing ideas about what it is to be a feminist.

likely to be called a feminist by that reader. If a reader does not like Portia, she could easily identify the character as anti-feminist. By that same token, if a reader is not a feminist and dislikes Portia then the character will likely be thought of as a feminist, but with negative connotations. Some see Portia as strong, independent, and virtuous. Others see her as a shrew, and a lying, manipulative sneak who plays on her poor, slightly dull, pretty-boy husband. Today "feminism" has loaded connotations, that either suggests a strong, smart, independent woman or an aggressive, power-hungry, ugly, cold woman. There are countless adjectives describing Portia to be found in the media, from a number of critics, actresses, directors, and scholars. Lee Lady lists a number of adjectives he has come across in his study of Portia, which include, but are certainly not limited to: unsympathetic, spoilt, dismissive, derisive, cheerful, wry, witty, popular, and sophisticated. There is a wide variety of responses to Portia, which shows how complex a character she actually is and how diverse feminist theory has become. The attitudes Lady lists are largely excluded from academic studies, but they form the core of social feminism. British playwright Wolf Mankowitz called Portia a "cold, snobbish little bitch," (qtd. in Nathan, par. 4) while Anna Jameson refers to her as a "heavenly compound of talent, feeling, wisdom, beauty, and gentleness!" (141). Both Mankowitz and Jameson are speaking in a social context, but both have been included in academic writing. Much of the vitriolic emotion that characterizes the reaction to Portia is based on how "feminist" individual readers are and she, as a character, is.

In an aside in his chapter on feminism, Robert Dale Parker discusses the possibility that we have entered into a wave of post-feminism. Parker laments that a post-feminist wave would relegate feminism to the past. He stresses that post-feminism signals "a lamentable form of cultural consumerism" and that it reduces feminism to a "fashion" (Parker 150). However, post-feminism actually signals a forward surge in feminist thinking. The social role of women has evolved past the farthest reaches of the theory and now the theory must be re-imagined for changing times. It is in that spirit that post-feminism is the standard for today. It is not that the issues heralded in feminism have been abandoned; there are new tenets that need to be constructed to fit the circumstances of the twenty-first-century world. Certainly Portia's complexity and the inability to pin down a fixed feminist/anti-feminist definition for her by modern readers suggests there is a need for some new parameters by which to judge feminist action and feminist fiction.

Even when Shakespeare was writing, the presence and influence of women in society was increasing as they gained more influence at court and began writing their own works. The phrase *querelle des femmes* (the quarrel/debate over women) was used to describe the cultural, political, and literary debate about women's roles and women's rights in the early modern era. Even then, the vision of women and what they were capable of depended on viewpoint. Barbara K. Lewalski points out that "Elizabethan women writers were chiefly occupied with translation, while several Jacobean women wrote and often published original literary works of some scope and merit" (88). Queen Elizabeth called attention to the weaknesses and frailties of women in her speech to the troops at Tilbury and used masculine pronouns to refer to herself in order to conjure confidence in her troops. The reign of a female monarch did not necessarily herald a breakthrough in women's independence. Virginia Woolf's discussion of "Shakespeare's Sister" continues the debate about the perception of women in the Renaissance in comparison with the perception of women in the early twentieth century. Her work sets the foundation for modern feminist criticism, but also connects the questions women face today with "The Woman Question" of the 1860s and the *querelle des femmes* that originated in France during the mid-fifteenth century to answer questions about the rights of women.

The continued progression of questions surrounding the rights and capabilities of women in society have led twenty-first-century critics to a more cohesive and formed notion of feminist theory. Feminism truly is, and always has been, in the eye of the beholder and therefore slippery. Just as the questions surrounding what a woman is/was capable of or how a woman should behave in society were muddled in the sixteenth century, so are they the source of great debate today. After all, the fundamental (and almost completely baffling) question is, both in and out of the play, what is a feminist?

Postcolonialist Theory, Morocco and Shylock, & Religious Villainy

The preoccupation, in theory, with who is an "Other" moves to the foreigner in postcolonial theory. The theoretical idea of the colonized and the colonizer, as envisioned by Edward Said, has fundamentally shifted since the 1980s and the publication of *Orientalism*. Said's specific focus on how the Orient/East/Non-West "has helped to define Europe (or the West) as its contrasting image, idea, personality, experience" still holds true; however he was referring to the Orient as a former colony whereas the impressions that are being made today by foreign entities in opposition to an established national identity result not from colonies, but from adversaries (1-2).[14] No longer does the colonizer enter a country and claim it. The colonized is that country whose ideology is bent to the will of another country, the colonizer. The postcolonial practice of challenging the association of superiority and inferiority based on national, ethnic, or racial origin can be used as nations try to understand, accommodate, and accept competing ideologies, religions, and races within a singular multi-cultural society.

The postcolonial aspect of *Merchant* that resonates so well in contemporary society is the suspicion, sometimes bordering on fear or contempt, of the foreign "Other." The treatment of the Princes of Morocco and Aragon as well as Shylock addresses aspects of postcolonial theory, specifically how "Other" cultures are re-impacting European and Western culture and how the very notion of a singular and coherent Western culture has been obliterated because it has been fundamentally changed by the impact of foreign "Others" through colonization.[15] The contemporary issues surrounding postcolonialism involve a hybridity of race, religion, and origin between the West and the "Other" that has changed the identities of both.[16] This fundamental reconfiguring can either be viewed with dread or with hope. The reconfiguring of society in *Merchant* to include or exclude non-Venetians and aliens is an important part of the play and also helps to explain the changes in attitude that are happening in contemporary society. The attempt to see the "Other" – whether such a view be based on religion, race, or origin that precipitates the status of

---

[14] Christopher Hitchens comments on the quotations marks that Americans put around the "Other" when talking postcolonially in his chapter on Edward Said entitled "Edward Said: Where the Twain Should Have Met." The satire of this practice shows that we are beyond the tenets of postcolonialism as established by Said's *Orientalism* and moved on to a new phase of cross-cultural mixing and exchange that has yet to be thoroughly defined or even investigated.

[15] Postcolonialism is often called "race studies" as well, in that not all the concerns are restricted to issues of colonized and colonizer, and often the fundamental challenges imposed by postcolonialism are racially based. Although Edward Said is not the founder of postcolonial theory, his ideas were some of the most influential and formed the background for critics such as Bill Ashcroft, Gayatri Spivak, Ashis Nandy, and Robert J.C. Young. These scholars, working from the ideas introduced by Frantz Fanon, represent just a small selection of those who have made very important contributions to postcolonial studies.

[16] The use of the term "Western society" in this section comes from an over-arching notion of the "West" found in postcolonial theory. This, idea, from Said to Gayatri Chakravorty Spivak to Chinua Achebe is England, Europe, and America. The "Other" is generally used to describe the third world or any world that is outside of England, Europe, or America.

outsider – as an asset to society, rather than a danger, is an important tenet and a starting place for new studies in postcolonialism.

In the play, the suitors coming to Belmont to win Portia are risking all. It is Morocco's presence as a suitor that raises questions about the acceptance of the foreigner, both in early modern England and in contemporary, Western society. Morocco values Portia as precious and golden. He is brave and honorable, he will not break his word and he takes his loss with dignity and poise. He is, however, Muslim, which was seen as the "wrong" religion in Shakespeare's England. He therefore lacks the grace that is expected of a Christian suitor, making him an untenable and imperfect choice. But does Morocco's religion still matter today in a Western society? Contemporary readers must ask why Morocco is not the best suitor for Portia. Aside from being flattering and kind to Portia, Morocco is pompous and smug. These traits could be seen as positive signs of confidence in contemporary society. Bassanio, on the other hand, is still seen as the ideal wooer, despite his financial straits and his meek attitude. Part of the answer lies in the fact that Western society still harbors some of those fearful and prejudicial ideas that dominated English society in the late sixteenth century.

Regardless of any character traits, without Christian grace, Morocco does not fit the mold of the perfect suitor, either in Shakespeare's time or contemporary Western society. What is learned from the rejection of Morocco on the contemporary stage is that there are still lingering fears of those coming from outside an established culture to woo, particularly those whose complexions are "burnished" or whose religions are divergent from Christianity (2.1.2). Many in Western society prefer the safety of something known and familiar, while fearing those who are different or "Other." What is different now is the social context in which the play is being recreated; the Moroccos of contemporary society do not actually have to come from Morocco. There are different cultures, races, and customs already present within a diverse Western society. The interactions between races and religions can be analyzed using postcolonialism. Colonizing comes from within rather than without; it is happening in Western society by "Others" emigrating and maintaining cultural norms and standards that are not necessarily part of a Western ideology, thereby influencing the more dominant surrounding Western culture. The West is being re-colonized by the "Other" and this is where the problems arise, just as the same happens in *Merchant*.

Postcolonial theory sees such a blend as a strength. The celebration of "hybridity and 'cultural polyvalency,' that is, the situation whereby individuals and groups belong simultaneously to more than one culture" is also of utmost import as citizens of the world increasingly define themselves by more than just their nations of origin or residency (Barry 192). For example, the desire of Americans to be known both as American and Irish-/Cuban-/African-American proves this notion of blending.[17] This hybridity, however, does come with the unspoken understanding that one identity trumps another and will direct action should ideological conflicts arise: American first, Other-American second. Such dual identities can be seen in *Merchant* as can an inevitable winning of one cultural identity over another.

At first, the European suitors described by Portia in 1.2 are seen as slightly weak in spirit, emotions, and convictions. The Neapolitan prince is equine, the Palatinate is "so full of unmannerly sadness" (1.2.43), the French lord is wildly changeable, the English baron cannot understand a word Portia says, the Scottish lord is quarrelsome, and the German duke is a drunkard. Inevitably, these men leave before trying their hands at the casket game, unwilling to risk the steep penalty that comes from choosing incorrectly. They will not risk themselves, their cultures, or their heritages for Portia, because guessing wrong means being unable to carry on a family line and a cultural heritage. These suitors are all from Northern Europe, where the culture is similar to and respected by both Elizabethan and contemporary Western audiences. Because of the similarities between cultures and the mutual respect shown, no conquering or subverting needs to happen. Although there are jokes at the expenses of the European suitors, the infractions that they have are minor in comparison to the dangers caused by more exotic "Others" – "strangeness, difference, exotic sensuousness" (Said 72). Belmont and Europe can mutually co-exist, because of shared values and assumptions; however, the Muslim "Other," as represented by Morocco, is an exotic threat, because he does not share with Belmont and Portia a similar heritage, religious background, or cultural ideology. The trumping of the West over the "Other" is wrapped up in Portia's dismissal of Morocco: "let all of his complexion choose me so" (2.7.80).

Aragon best represents the tensions in a hybrid identity. While postcolonialists celebrate the potential changes that the foreign "Other" may bring to Western culture, the opposite notion, the anti-postcolonial idea, is a rejection of the Western society that allows for such a change to happen. In the play, Aragon can be seen as the representation of such

----

[17] In his 2000 article "Hyphenated Americans," Armstrong Williams warns of the divisive dangers of classifying people as "hyphenated Americans." His central argument is that it creates "tribal" conflict, through the establishment of "others" as inferior, rather than unity and cooperation.

blending and he is punished for it. His kingdom has a checkered social make-up that was viewed with suspicion by many Northern Europeans of the seventeenth century.[18] Spain was sometimes seen as the country that let the Moors into Europe in the seventh century. The Jews also had a great deal of influence in the kingdom in the late eleventh and twelfth centuries. In 1588, the Spanish Armanda failed to defeat the English, which solidified the notion of England as being a divinely chosen empire. It is important to note that England did not defeat the Armada through strength or capabilities, but as a result of inclement weather and large ships to which the Spanish were not accustomed. It is the job of the postcolonialist to recover factual histories and to dismiss those created by a dominant power – for example, reversing the widely believed notion that the English defeated the Spanish Armada through military prowess.

Aragon is unsure of his decisions, he lacks the command and presence of his Moroccan predecessor, and he is dismissed almost as soon as he enters. Aragon speaks a mere seventy-eight lines at the beginning of a single scene, while Morocco gets one hundred and three lines over two scenes. There is never any real danger of Aragon's success. He does not rank himself with the "barbarous multitudes," but to Portia and Nerissa he is (2.9.32). He does "get as much as he deserves," which is second place (2.9.35). He chooses second place silver, representative of the changeable moon, which reflects his and his kingdom's changeable status. Aragon represents both colonizer and colonized.

Religious colonization and separation represent a contemporary and particularly nasty strain of prejudice that postcolonialism combats. The "Other" that is already inside – the one not trying to gain access or even take away, but who is trying to assimilate – becomes the villain. Shylock is the domestic outsider who poses such a threat. The ruin of the "Other" in the play suggests there is no room for difference; he is an "alien" who, despite all the similarities he lists to the like-named Solanio and Salerio in 3.1, is seen as a threat to the "average" Venetian (4.1.360). His forced conversion to Christianity reiterates the idea that an outsider must conform or be punished. He is broken and dejected, but he becomes a Christian, and to Antonio and other Catholics this is cause for celebration. He has attempted to re-establish his position in Venice, not as an "alien" but as a Venetian. In doing so, he tries to establish power for himself in the city-state, only to have it thrown back at him and cause him suffering. Homi

---

[18] Aragon is Catholic, a dangerous enemy in Protestant Elizabethan England, but still less threatening than a Muslim. What is important is that Aragon is from a kingdom that went back and forth with Muslim rule in the medieval ages (before finally removing many of the Moors from the Iberian Peninsula in 1492).

Bhabha clarifies what happens to Shylock and why he becomes "not well" after his forced conversion (4.1.408):

> The social articulation of difference, from the minority perspective, is complex, on-going negotiation that seeks to authorize cultural hybridities that emerge in moments of historical transformation. The "right" to signify from the periphery of authorized power and privilege does not depend on the persistence of tradition; it is resourced by the power of tradition to be reinscribed through the conditions of contingency and contradictoriness that attend upon the lives of those who are "in the minority." (3)

Shylock's great almost-moment of power in the courtroom is shattered by the traditional power structures of the Christians and their ability to dictate law and order. The established assumption that Shylock should show mercy permeates the courtroom, as this is what any good Christian in a position of power would do in regard to a weaker foe. When Shylock refuses and tries to re-establish a new tradition, he is punished, and Christian mercy is shown to him in his forced conversion, which he deems torture. He is no longer on the periphery, but a part of the Christian tradition and within an established hierarchy.

Shylock represents the "Other" that is re-colonizing the colonizer. Frantz Fanton's discussion on the psychological impact of colonialism on different factions within a singular society helps to explain the de facto "right" and "wrong" ideology within a heterogeneous society.[19] Shylock finds himself, in the "wrong." Stephen Orgel's look at "Shylocks in Shakespeare's England" presents a particularly postcolonial view of the play in Shakespeare's time, as well as sheds light on contemporary, Western notions of the "Other." Orgel contends that Shylock's name is English rather than Jewish, which makes him an insider, rather than an outsider, and strengthens the notion that Shylock is, in fact, a functional and integral part of society. The implications of a "native" Shylock are that the social fabric of the society is more heterogeneous than homogenous, and that it is impossible to favor one idea or ideology over another. What this also does, according to Orgel's article, is make Shylock an avatar for any and all outsiders. He represents the outsider already

---

[19] Fanton's chapter "The Pitfalls of National Consciousness" in *The Wretched of the Earth* rejects the idea of national consciousness being an "all-embracing crystallization of the innermost hopes of the whole people, instead of being the immediate and most obvious result of the mobilization of the people, will be in any case only an empty shell, a crude and fragile travesty of what it might have been" (148). This is because the society is divided by classes and groups, all fighting each other.

within a society and shows how both the play and the postcolonial theory resonate today, but fall short of offering any definitive answers in terms of social acceptance or preference.

After Shylock's devastation, are contemporary readers celebrating with Bassanio, Antonio, and Portia? Which bothers twenty-first-century audiences more: that he is forced into a new identity that he does not know and hates, or that he loses his identity? These might seem like the same question, but instead they get at the heart of postcolonialism in Western society. Is it better to force someone to adopt a new identity, regardless of how they feel because it will be better for them, or to leave them with their old identity in a system that is designed to have them fail?

Throughout the play, Shylock's villainy results, in large part, from his faith. This lends an anti-Semitic reading to the play. The Jews, although a minority, were affected by popular stereotypes, as were those Christians living alongside them. Such prejudice is evidenced by the anti-Jewish writings produced in the late sixteenth and early seventeenth centuries.[20] Avraham Oz makes the contention in *"The Merchant of Venice* in Israel" that it is not Shakespeare's original attitude toward the Jews that is important, but rather how it is staged and restaged that matters in determining anti-Semitic notions in the play. While contemporary staging of *Merchant* are important, it is essential to highlight the widespread prejudice that existed around Shakespeare and imbued his work and the attitudes that dominated the majority of society. Laurence Lerner's article "Wilhelm S and Shylock" also makes the claim that it is the reproduction that is important, rather than the original intentions of the author. All of this is done to protect contemporary Western audiences from seeing the beloved bedrock of the Western canon, Shakespeare, as a religious bigot. Religious prejudice is condemned in contemporary Western ideology and therefore, such a pillar of Western society cannot go against such a fundamental idea of modern Western culture. Is Shakespeare being converted from a bigot to a defender of cultural difference, and if so, is Western society okay with this superficial reconfiguring of the author?

---

[20] Alongside *The Merchant of Venice*, other plays to feature a Jewish villain were *The Jew of Malta* by Christopher Marlowe and the anonymous *The Jew (The Practice of Parasites)*. There were also a spate of public sermons and lectures, that were printed from the 1570s up to the 1650s, that included Thomas Calvert's *Causes of the Miseries of the Jews*, Peter Heylyn's *Judaizing Christians in the 1590s*, and Nicholas Bound's *The True Doctrine of the Sabbath*. There were also ballads and songs that included "The Ballad of the Cruel Jew." What these writings prove is that the Jews were a part of the early modern English social fabric and that fear and prejudice directed at this sect was very much a part of that same society.

The attempt to expose the bias of the author is a fundamental of postcolonial theory and one that certainly needs to extend to Shakespeare.

Marxist Theory, the Venetian City-State, and Class Warfare

Of all the theories used to interpret literature, Marxism is closer to the original ideas of the founder than any other.[21] Karl Marx's beliefs that the upper-class or bourgeois determine the conditions of society for the lower-class or proletariat is the basis of contemporary class conflict and the foundation for legislation designed to reform the economics of capitalist countries. As Louis Althusser distills Marx's thinking, "the State is a 'machine' of repression, which enables the ruling classes to ensure their dominance over the working class, thus enabling the former to subject the latter" (1339). The divides between good and evil, and the rich and the poor that Marx saw as simply black and white, are a muddled shade of grey in today's capitalist countries. The fundamental tenets of Marxism explain the divisions between the classes and the covert attempts of much of literature to ensure that such a class division continues and the upper-classes remain on top of the social hierarchy. When applied to *Merchant*, we can see how Marxist theory accurately captures a hierarchical, capitalist structure whereby lives are reduced to ducats. The few benefit at the expense of the many, thus proving a cyclical pattern that re-occurs in society.[22] What remains questionable is whether the play supports or undermines the capitalist system.

Looking at how the characters in *Merchant* reflect a Marxist ideal, the representations of the theory in contemporary society can also be seen. By Marxist example, the Venetian ideology is determined by the bourgeoisie, and everything depends on the acquisition of wealth. The play and the characters within also provide an insight into how and why there are so many different villains and victims in the class struggles of the twenty-first

---

[21] Marxism as we understand it from the writings of Karl Marx has been re-jigged to be more accurate or user-friendly for societies in which the word "communism" is obscene. Amongst those who have successfully tweaked the theory are Louis Althusser, who believes many of Marx's works were misinterpreted because they are taken out of a social context, and Terry Eagleton, who brings more cultural contexts to the study, including a more psychoanalytical approach to Marxism.

[22] Marx himself quoted from the play numerous times in his works. Burton Hatlen's "Feudal and Bourgeois Concepts of Value in *The Merchant of Venice*" is perhaps the most influential Marxist approach to the play as he applies different principles of the theory to Venice and Belmont.

century. Antonio can be seen as a careless lender that gives money to risky ventures. Bassanio is just such a risky bet, as he takes the money for a wild venture without any real thought of how to pay off the debt. Finally, Portia and her "just pay thrice the sum" attitude in order to dictate law and overturn a bond is representative of the bourgeoisie (3.2.307-11). Shylock, although wealthy, represents the proletariat, as an outsider who poses financial opposition to the titular hero. He constantly battles to gain influence and status, but ultimately does not stand a chance of winning his suit or enacting any kind of lasting change. He is a middle-class businessman whose taxes bail out the risky ventures of the gentry and rival members of the proletariat. Eventually, when he asks for the terms of his bond (from the risky venture capitalists who squandered it) he is utterly defeated and removed from his camp. What is left is a Marxist vision of a seriously flawed system in which all the characters make choices based solely on their own interests and without thought of what might realistically happen in the future.

A fundamental tenet of Marxist thinking, emphasized by the adaptation of the theory to literature by Althusser, is that the spread of an ideology that favors the bourgeoisie (often through literature) drives the beliefs, actions, and emotions of the whole of society. This is true in mercantile Venice, where the acquisition of wealth is the driving factor of nearly all the characters. Antonio himself would rather die than be poor:

> For herein Fortune shows herself more kind
> Than is her custom. It is still her use
> To let the wretched man outlive his wealth
> To view with hollow eye and wrinkled brow
> An age of poverty; from which ling'ring penance
> Of such misery doeth she cut me off. (4.1.275-80)

To lose wealth and fall in status is to be miserable and "wretched," or it is to be ostracized, persecuted, and even punished. If fickle "Fortune" does not punish, then the society that puts money above all else will. The individuals in society are not to deviate form this economic framework or ideology. Autonomy and difference do not work, as we can see with Shylock. He searches for independence from the Venetian state apparatus, but inevitably cannot fight against the ideology of the ruling, upper-class and is consumed. Shylock believes, like Antonio, that to lose money is to lose life itself:

> Nay, take my life and all! Pardon not that!
> You take my house when you do take the prop
> That doth sustain my house. You take my life

When you do take the means whereby I live. (4.1.385-88)

In terms of money, Shylock follows the Venetian party line, believing that money equates life. However, what is inherent in his lines is a panic. Without money, survival is jeopardized, a realization that seems to question the very system that allows for such an equation. Shylock, although a businessman, relies more on a feudal system of bartering. He does not charge monetary interest, but asks for an exchange of material, even if it is useless, for the bond, which he calls "a merry sport" (1.3.144). Shylock is punished severely for not adhering to the capitalist system whereby money is charged for interest and nothing else. In the end, he is forced to enter the capitalist society that he has fought against throughout the play.

In keeping with the Marxist ideology, all outsiders must conform to the standards and norms as established by the ruling class, or perish in Venice. The servant Launcelot is willing to buy into the ideology of the bourgeoisie, which shows a dangerous form of ideological brainwashing that Marxism exposes and the play reflects. He actively tries to distance himself from Shylock by joining ranks with the Christian gentleman Bassanio. He is also representative of the "base" – the material means of production, distribution, and exchange. According to Raymond Williams, the base has "come to include, especially in certain twentieth-century developments, the 'productive forces'" (34). However, what Launcelot lacks, even according to his one-time master Shylock, is productivity. The servant is described as "a huge feeder" (2.5.46) and "snail-slow in profit" (2.5.47); Shylock is glad to "part with him / To one that [he] would have him help to waste / His borrowed purse" (2.5.49-51). Rather than trying to break away and be his own man, Launcelot desires to switch his indenture from one master to another, from Shylock to Bassanio. His father announces Launcelot's "great infection … to serve" (2.2.111). Launcelot's primary motivation in leaving the service of Shylock is not economic, although he does hint that he is not fed enough at the "rich Jew's" house (2.2.110). Instead, what he is abandoning is the very association with Shylock and the social stigma that comes with him.

A fundamental principle of Marxist thinking is that the bourgeoisie controls the base and instigates competition amongst those members of the proletariat responsible for economic production. This sets the terms of the superstructure, the cultural world of the society, which then also supports the bourgeoisie. This also ensures the members of the lower classes spend time fighting amongst themselves rather than taking on the real holders of wealth and power, the upper-classes. When Launcelot "leaves a rich Jew's service to become the follower of so poor a gentleman" he not only reinforces this notion, but he actively works to suppress the Jew in support of the gentleman (2.2.130-31). Shylock wants to see his former servant bring down the gentleman enemy of his household, but harbors no malice for his former servant whom he deemed "kind enough" (2.5.46). Strikingly, Launcelot actively works to subvert Shylock and take away from his household for the benefit of the aristocratic Christian and his allies – a group of which Launcelot himself will never be a part.

Gratiano represents the ideological brainwashing of the proletariat who want to join the bourgeoisie. He is a part of the dominant circle, but not near enough to the center to be a major influence on his peers, who actually influence him. Gratiano is a man who begins the play footloose and fancy-free:

> Let me play the fool.
> With mirth and laughter let old wrinkles come,
> And let my liver rather heat with wine
> Than my heart cool with mortifying groans.
> Why should a man whose blood is warm within
> Sit like his grandsire cut in alabaster?
> Sleep when he wakes, and creep into the jaundice
> By being peevish? (1.1.82-89)

Gratiano specifically does not want to end up like his forefathers who slaved for money and status and were rewarded with "jaundice[d]" and "peevish" existences. This is the mantra by which Gratiano lives, on his own terms and without concern for money. That is until his manner of thinking is altered by his social better, Bassanio:

> . . . But here thee, Gratiano:
> Thou art too wild, too rude and bold of voice –
> Parts that become thee happily enough,
> And in such eyes as ours appear not faults,
> But where thou art not known, why there they show
> Something too liberal. Pray thee, take pain
> To allay with some cold drops of modesty
> Thy skipping spirit, lest though thy wild behavior
> I be misconstered in the place I go to
> And lose my hopes. (2.2.162-71)

Bassanio acknowledges that Gratiano's behavior is a problem in polite, everyday society and thus he must change or risk jeopardizing more than his own life and reputation. He must change or he will be left behind. Gratiano wants what Bassanio has: the riches, the wife, the ability to sail to exotic destinations. Thus, he obeys all that Bassanio dictates and mimics his every move. Although he wants to be part of the bourgeoisie, Gratiano ends up married to the maid, following the directions of everyone around him, and a lodger in a strange land, hardly the dynamic Fortune 500 CEO that he might have hoped for, or even believed he could become in his alliance with Bassanio. Because he desires to be a part of the bourgeoisie, he works harder to defend the capitalist structure than the merchant himself or his upper-class companions do. Gratiano's carefree and fun-loving attitude is lost to frantic considerations about outward appearance. He also exhibits extreme prejudice and malice toward Shylock, the enemy of the state and the system, at the same time he is crudely vulgar toward and dismissive of his social inferiors – such as Lorenzo at the beginning and Nerissa at the end.[23]

The difference in the real-life application of Marxism is not that twenty-first-century Western society is post-Marxist, but rather Marxism is ever present.[24] Manifestations of acute tenets of Marxist theory can be seen everyday. Many living in capitalist, Western societies are adamant that those tenets, and Marxism as a whole, are out-dated or are stifling to the individual and the growth of the society, and yet the problems of inequality in status and distribution of wealth remain linked with capitalist ideals. Such ideas are not post-Marxist, even though many may want them to be. The ambiguity arises in questioning whether to reform such a system or start from scratch. If the answer lies in the middle, somewhere between Marxists and capitalists, which seems to be where *Merchant* itself is, Marxism argues this is actually supportive of the capitalist system and therefore anti-Marxist. It must be asked, then, is there a way to critique and reform without abandoning all capitalist principles in favor of Marxist communism and would such a reformed contemporary society look more like Venice or Portia's Belmont?

---

[23] Gratiano will not let Lorenzo speak in the opening scene, thus likening him to an ox and a "maid not vendable" (1.1.115). In the final scene, Gratiano first tries to diminish the value of his wife's gift, calling it "paltry" (5.2.158), then goes on to fear for his reputation as a cuckold, all before ending the play with a vulgar pun.
[24] One need only see how the Occupy Wall Street movement, despite it being critiqued for not changing the structures it sought to reform, changed the public discourse in a Marxist fashion. Terms such as "Occupy," "the 99%," and "the 1%" are used not just by scholars and politicians but by individuals in schools, on social media, in newspaper editorials, on blogs, and in comic strips.

Conclusion

The resurgence of *Merchant* on stage, in print, and in the cinema over the last decade results from the ability of all and sundry to find meanings in the play that fit individual ideologies and expectations. With each bespoke reading comes alternate interpretations and thus, disagreements in meaning, that ultimately beg the question: is there a singular set of values or morals from which all pull in order to interpret and judge? This is also the question upon which literary theory is built. The lack of a clear, distinct, and definite set of questions and answers, and the ability to fit the work to any and all visions, explains why the play is so popular today. I have shown my theory students Trevor Nunn's version of *Merchant* in class and asked them to compare it with Michael Radford's version with Al Pacino as Shylock. About half the students in the classroom feel that Goodman's Shylock is much more sinister and blood-thirsty than Pacino's. They did not reach the same conclusion as each other or James O'Rourke, who states Nunn's version "was entirely sympathetic to Shylock" and that the Christians were "equal to Shylock in ruthlessness" (392). How could they have gotten it "so wrong"? It is because of their personal theories? What they value in life and what they believe are grafted on to the play and theory supports any and all sides. *Merchant* supports an idea, almost no matter what, and supports it through the use of loose theory. The question then becomes, is this good or bad for the play? Is it good or bad for theory?

O'Rourke also states "The original effect of *The Merchant* cannot be recreated today" (393). To which I say, absolute nonsense. Beyond the pedagogical points of interpreting and understanding, the original intent of the play was to make the audience laugh, to think, and to identify; the original effect was laughter, consideration, and agreement or disagreement. This is the intent and effect of all stage plays, to rope in the audience with something they can, in part or in whole, identify with and find a relational position. This is why the play is popular today, and ultimately, this is why we study theory.

Bibliography

Abelove, Henry, Michèle Aina Barale, and David M. Halperin. Introduction. *The Lesbian and Gay Studies Reader*. New York: Routledge, 1993: xv-xviii. Print.

Althusseur, Louis. "The State." *The Norton Anthology of Theory & Criticism*. 2nd ed. Ed. Vincent B. Leitch. New York: Norton, 2010:

1339-43. Print.

Barry, Peter. *Beginning Theory: An Introduction to Literary and Cultural Theory*. 3rd ed. Manchester: Manchester University Press, 2009. Print.

Barthes, Roland. *Image, Music, Text*. Trans. Stephen Heath. London: Fontana, 1977. Print.

Bhabha, Homi. *The Location of Culture*. New York: Routledge, 2005. Print.

Cohen, Walter. "*The Merchant of Venice* and the Possibilities of Historical Criticism." *ELH* 49.4 (1982): 765-89. Print.

Elizabeth I. "Speech to the Troops at Tilbury." *Norton Anthology of English Literature*. 8th ed. Vol. 1 Ed. Stephen Greenblatt. New York: Norton, 2009: 699-700. Print.

Engel, Charlie. "Masculinity, Homosexuality, and Military Assimilation in Top Gun." *New Comm Ave*. (Spring 2007). Web. 8 May 2012.

Fanton, Frantz. *The Wretched of the Earth*. Trans. Richard Philcox. New York: Grove Press, 2004. Print.

"Femininity, n." *Oxford English Dictionary Online*. Oxford University Press. Web. 9 May 2012.

Foucault, Michel. *The History of Sexuality: An Introduction*. Trans. Robert Hurley. New York: Vintage Books, 1990. Print.

"Gay, adj., adv., and n." *Oxford English Dictionary Online*. Oxford University Press. Web. 8 May 2012.

Gilbert, Sandra M. and Susan Gubar. *The Madwoman in the Attic: The Woman Writer and the Nineteenth-Century Literary Imagination*. 2nd ed. New Haven, CT: Yale University Press, 2000. Print.

Hitchens, Christopher. *Arguably: Essays by Christopher Hitchens*. New York: Grand Central Publishing, 2011. Print.

"Homosexual, adj. and n." *Oxford English Dictionary Online*. Oxford University Press. Web. 8 May 2012.

Jameson, Anna. "Portia." *The Merchant of Venice*. Ed. Leah S. Marcus. New York: Norton, 2006. 141-45. Print.

Kleinberg, Seymour. "The Homosexual as Anti-Semite in Nascent Capitalism." *Literary Visions of Homosexuality*. Ed. Stuart Kellogg. New York: The Haworth Press, 1983: 113-26. Print.

Kosofsky Sedgwick, Eve. *Between Men: English Literature and Male Homosocial Desire*. New York: Columbia University Press, 1985. Print.

Lady, Lee. "Shakespeare's Women in Drag: Portia." *Thoughts on Shakespeare*. University of Hawaii. Feb 2002, Web. 9 May 2012.

Lerner, Laurence. "Wilhelm S and Shylock." *Shakespeare Survey*. No. 48 Cambridge: Cambridge University Press, 1995. Print.

Lewalski, Barbara K. "Re-Writing Patriarchy and Patronage: Margaret Clifford, Anne Clifford, and Aemilia Lanyer." *The Yearbook of English Studies*, 21, Politics, Patronage and Literature in England 1558-1658 (1991): 87-106. Print.

Nathan, John. "Review: Yasser: Shylock, the Middle-East peacemaker." *The Jewish Chronicle Online*. The Jewish Chronicle Ltd, 15 Oct. 2009 Web. 9 May 2012.

Newman, Karen, "Portia's Ring: Unruly Women and Structures of Exchange in *The Merchant of Venice*." *Shakespeare Quarterly* 38.1 (1987): 19-33. Print.

O'Rourke, James, "Racism and Homophobia in *The Merchant of Venice*." *ELH* 70.2 (2003): 375-97. Print.

Orgel, Stephen. "Shylocks in Shakespeare's England." *Imagining Shakespeare: A History of Texts and Visions*. Basingstoke: Palgrave Macmillan, 2003: 151-55. Print.

"Queer, adj.1." *Oxford English Dictionary Online*. Oxford University Press. Web. 8 May 2012.

Patterson, Steve. "The Bankruptcy of Homoerotic Amity in Shakespeare's *Merchant of Venice*." *Shakespeare Quarterly* 50.1 (1999): 9-32. Print.

Parker, Robert Dale. *How to Interpret Literature: Critical Theory for Literary and Cultural Studies*. 2nd ed. Oxford: Oxford University Press, 2011. Print.

Penuel, Suzanne. "Castrating the Creditor in *The Merchant of Venice*." *SEL Studies in English Literature 1500-1900* 44.2 (2004): 255-75. Print.

Root, Rhiannon. "Feminism has negative connotation despite meaning." *Daily Nebraskan.com*. University of Nebraska-Lincoln. 8 March 2010. Web. 9 May 2012.

Said, Edward. *Orientalism*. New York: Random House, 1978. Print.

Shakespeare, William. *The Merchant of Venice*. Ed. Leah S. Marcus. New York: Norton, 2006. Print.

Vetterling-Braggin, Mary, ed. *"Femininity," "masculinity," and "androgyny": A Modern Philosophical Discussion*. Totowa, NJ: Rowman & Littlefield, 1982. Print.

Williams, Armstrong. "Hyphenated Americans." *The Sundance Writer*. Ed. Mark Connelly. Boston: Wadsworth, 2010: 489-91. Print.

Williams, Raymond. *Culture And Materialism: Selected Essays*. London: Verso, 2005. Print.

"WHY THEN YOU ARE IN LOVE": HOW A CLOSE MALE FRIENDSHIP EQUALS AN ETHICAL IDENTITY IN SHAKESPEARE'S *THE MERCHANT OF VENICE*

PAUL DINGMAN

> Lord of my love, to whom in vassalage
> Thy merit hath my duty strongly knit,
> To thee I send this written ambassage,
> To witness duty, not to show my wit.
> Duty so great, which wit so poor as mine
> May make seem bare, in wanting words to
> show it,
> But that I hope some good conceit of thine
> In thy soul's thought, all naked, will bestow
> it;
> Till whatsoever star that guides my moving
> Points on me graciously with fair aspect,
> And puts apparel on my tottered loving
> To show me worthy of thy sweet respect.
> —Shakespeare, *Sonnet 26*
> (to a fair nobleman)

Shakespeare's comedy and famous problem play *The Merchant of Venice* ostensibly profiles a new early modern world built on commercial enterprise, credit, and international trade, but upon close analysis, much of the drama follows a medieval theme of romance. The basic plot is clearly based on a number of older tales from the Middle Ages. The twelfth-century tale *The King and the Seven Sages*, for example, incorporates similar situations, and the fourteenth-century Italian story, *Il Pecorone*, contains much of the recognizable plot (Bullough). The *Gesta Romanorum*, a thirteenth-century collection of didactic stories also includes identifiable elements such as the caskets challenge. Shakespeare has, of course, put his own stamp on the story. Leaving aside heavily-discussed questions as to the bard's rendering of Shylock and the ugly anti-Semitism that has haunted Europe for more than a thousand years, the present study explores the medieval spirit that Shakespeare carefully weaves into his play through the depiction of an intense loving bond between the noble, though prodigal, Bassanio and his close friend, Antonio. After briefly examining some of the broad historical currents surrounding chivalry and nobility in the Renaissance, this chapter moves on to examine how, among those currents, an enduring cultural link between noble ethics and emotional friendship finds poetic expression in *The Merchant of Venice*.

The Intellectual Background of Change

An awareness of massive change on multiple levels—political, religious, social, economic, cultural—informs the present study's exploration of elite male friendship and how it modulated with society during the Renaissance. Some of the historical changes are still not entirely understood. In his influential work, *The Civilization of the Renaissance in Italy*, Jacob Burkhardt famously argues that a sense of individuality and the private pursuit of artistic excellence in the residents of the Italian city-states lay behind much of the renewed interest in the works of Ancient Rome, leading to what has come to be known as the Renaissance. He squarely places the epicenter of the movement in Italy, amid the "genius" of its people. Historians since then have suggested that it was the friction from competing ideas and city-states or simply the immense variety of political systems on the Italian peninsula that prompted Renaissance individuality and the subsequent changes (Baron 155-75).

Discussions continue as to whether a shift in notions of individuality, art, or civics (to name only a few factors) provided the main impetus for change in the early modern period. Questions even arise over whether transformation in Europe came from within or without, for some scholars seek a primary cause for the Renaissance in greater contact with foreign cultures and exotic commodities. In her book, *Worldly Goods*, Lisa Jardine argues that the competition for expanding trade to distant regions and the acquisition of wealth from that trade prompted what we call the Renaissance. Similarly, Jerry Brotton in his provocative book, *The Renaissance Bazaar*, decides that the influx of goods and learning from the Middle East and North Africa prompted the new movement in Europe. Both of these arguments based on materialism minimize the inner role of humanism and/or the rediscovery of human dignity that Burckhardt and so many others have identified as key factors in the period. As a result, the conclusions of Jardine and Brotton are controversial.

Whatever the exact cause(s), a relatively sudden surge of adjustment is imagined by some at a particular point, e.g., 1400, 1450, or 1500, whereas others visualize a far more gradual tide. While historians generally favor an evolving view of the period, superficial views remain even among academics, often with astonishing value judgments attached, labeling all that is good, reasonable, or familiar as early modern and all that is bad, irrational, or strange as medieval. Employing flawed elastic reasoning, objectionable practices by people after the break (whenever that is) are considered residual while those displaying brilliance prior to the break are forerunners. Johan Huizinga discusses this intellectual fallacy at length in his essay "The Problem of the Renaissance" in *Men and Ideas*. To counter such views, a number of scholars starting with Charles Homer Haskins convincingly stress continuity with cultural high points in the history of Europe since the decline of Ancient Rome. They point to revivals among the Carolingians in the ninth century, the Anglo-Saxons in the tenth, the French and the Normans in the twelfth. Admittedly, these clearly important and notable movements never reached comparable levels of transformation in the era know as the Renaissance, but they certainly reflect an undercurrent of classical interest throughout the medieval period. Despite the historical work pointing to continuity, the Renaissance retains its image as the influential starting point of modernity in the popular imagination, and studies of medieval "alterity" continue at a brisk pace.

Epic poetry and romance provided the main literary mirror of noble, lay society in the High Middle Ages, and these genres continued through the early modern period, but in many ways professional drama had come to fulfill that key reflecting capacity by the sixteenth century in England. Edmund Spenser's *The Fairie Queene* (1590) belongs to the romance/epic genre, but Spenser's poetic tale is deliberately allegorical, somewhat stilted, and aimed specifically at educating the upper-classes. The popular commercial theatre, by contrast, was more vital and drew from a broader base. Performances on the growing number of stages in London garnered much attention from and to the nobility (its required sponsors) as well as the flourishing merchant class and even the commoners by the sixteenth century. This development was due in no small part to the promotion of theatre by royal prerogative of the Tudors and the accompanying suppression of ecclesiastical themes (Brockett 191-95). As a result, dramatic literature from leading playwrights of the period may serve as a central source material in understanding the culture. Richard Levin declares that the popular drama of Renaissance England "remains one of our best sources of knowledge about the popular mind of the period"

(165). Although people attracted to political power have probably always edited or manipulated their identities to a certain degree (and always will), a distinct theatrical awareness in the mentality of Renaissance—a "self-fashioning" perception—may well have contributed to the rising appetite for theatre (Greenblatt 1-11). It is likely no coincidence that a work designed to guide behavior and influence promotion at court such as Baldesar Castiglione's *Il Libro del Cortegiano* [*The Book of the Courtier*], was widely translated in Europe, including England, and read by so many (Javitch 391).

Male friendship constituted a major theme in the theatre of the times as any review of extant plays from the period will show. This fact has not escaped the notice of modern scholarship, but only a small amount of it focuses on historical investigation, and those that do generally claim an abrupt change or new attitude about friendship tied to humanism. For example in his recent book, *Male Friendship in Shakespeare and His Contemporaries*, Tom MacFaul argues that the portrayal of male friendship in Elizabethan and Jacobean theatre, far from following humanist precepts of ideal bonding with a true companion, actually (ironically) is a means of proclaiming one's singular identity in a shifting world. Following a related path but with a denser, psychological approach, Laurie Shannon asserts in her book, *Sovereign Amity*, that same-sex friendship in the Renaissance possessed a distinctive entitlement not experienced before or since.

The present study responds to the basis of these intriguing and informative views—a supposedly new focus on friendship in the period —with skepticism. Friendship among elite men had served as a popular and fascinating subject of imaginative writers for more than a thousand years in the Latin West. Drawing from Cicero and other classical Roman authors as well as established Christian ideas of brotherly love and the sense of fierce loyalty prized by the so-called barbarian tribes, medieval poets celebrated noble forms of male-male affection in works such as the anonymous *Beowulf, The Song of Roland, Amis and Amiloun*, or *The Prose Lancelot* in addition to Chaucer's *The Canterbury Tales*, Giraut Borneil's *Reis Glorios,* and Thomas Malory's *Le Morte D'Arthur*. Knightly companions fulfill important, beloved, and ethical roles in all of these tales, and ideals of male friendship contributed substantially to chivalric archetypes and life.

By taking the longer cultural view, I propose to connect early modern ideas of male friendship to medieval ones. Yes, the stages of England pulsed with exciting energy and novel ideas in the heady years of the late sixteenth century, but a connection with medieval literary themes often remained intact, if repackaged. In particular, the chivalric sense of ethical approbation toward noble friendship endured in the experimental yet wildly popular plays of Christopher Marlowe, Shakespeare, Ben Jonson, and others. This is not to say ideas of chivalric friendship and their expression in literature were not shifting in the Renaissance, along with everything else, including chivalry itself.

Chivalric Culture in Flux

The knightly ethos had to adapt to circumstances that shaped broad sectors of society following the desperate challenges of the fourteenth and fifteenth centuries. Warfare had grown in scope to consume more resources and lives than in earlier medieval conflicts. The nascent super powers of England and France along with their many allies harassed each other in a series of costly military confrontations resulting from dynastic claims to the crown. Campaigns stretched out across generations into what has come to be known as the Hundred Years War (traditionally 1337-1453). France essentially faced civil war with Burgundy for a significant portion of the hostilities, and after losing almost all territory on the Continent in the 1450s, England descended into the domestic Wars of the Roses until 1485. The savage clashes of aristocratic dynasties over control of the monarchy in England seem to have depleted the strength of many noble families.

In addition, a number of natural events caused misery across Europe from severe famines in the early part of the fourteenth century to The Black Death, a destructive epidemic that struck in 1347 and returned repeatedly to take a horrible toll on the population. Doubts directed toward both the spiritual and secular leadership likely spread in reaction to the severe sufferings from these catastrophes. A reasoned understanding of Heaven as taught by Thomas Aquinas, the intellectual champion of the Church, and others in the Scholastic community of thought seemingly failed to address the chaotic horrors occurring in the world (Smith 28-30). The knightly ruling class responsible for managing society in these difficult times found itself under palpable new pressures.

An indirect outcome of the dire events of the fourteenth and fifteenth centuries was a sharper need for labor. Since so many died from the plagues and hunger and war, especially among the peasantry, those who lived found higher demand for their work and correspondingly more options. Caution must always govern broad judgments about causes, but a middle class of professionals and merchants, though present and involved in society throughout the Middle Ages, became more numerous, prominent, wealthy, and diversified in the early modern era. Friction between members of the established aristocracy and the new commercial set could and did result, but alliances formed as well based on mutual needs and practicality.[1] Chivalry still signified the upper levels of prestige and privilege that mercantile/professional families wished to enter, and private enterprise often provided the funds for weakened houses of nobility struggling to retain their status. Interactions between levels of gentry, nobility, and the rising middle classes were unavoidable as commercial interests intersected, and friendship ideals from the noble classes crept into the resulting mix. An ethical core of ideas remained attached to ideas of elite friendship even as the accessories, the settings, and the forms of expression shifted. The characters in Shakespeare's plays reflect these developments, particularly Antonio and Bassanio.

The Noble Love of Antonio and Bassanio

While the protagonists in *The Merchant of Venice* do not ride forth into the forest to seek adventure or do battle with lance and sword, they do possess a number of the virtuous, knightly qualities depicted in romances of the twelfth and thirteenth centuries. For one, Antonio and Bassanio share a deep affection that drives the dramatic plot but leaves some modern readers and directors nonplussed. They may be at a loss over what to make of it. Consequently, many theatrical productions—to their loss—minimize the friendship. Since Tyrone Guthrie's production at Canada's Stratford Festival in 1955, homosexual desire between Bassanio and Antonio has been available as a motivation to explain the attraction (Edelman 56-7). Guthrie thought it made the relationship "logical" and that without it, Antonio becomes "an entirely uninteresting 'good' man" (Edelman 57). After Guthrie's staging, many directors have interpreted the characters' strong friendship as homosexual desire, complete with displays of physical affection (embraces, kisses, etc.) between Antonio and Bassanio; audiences may now even expect it. Michael Radford's 2004 film, *Shakespeare's Merchant of Venice*, follows the pattern of male-male desire for these characters. In the movie, Jeremy Irons (Antonio) and Joseph Fiennes (Bassanio) share a passionate kiss and lounge on a bed suggestively together as they discuss plans and share confidences.[2]

---

[1] The *Paston Letters* graphically depicts the struggles and the associations between classes in fifteenth-century England.

[2] A.O. Scott completely ignores the implication of homosexuality in his 2004 review of the film (*New York Times*, December 29, 2004). This strangely follows

Onstage versions such as the recent Broadway run in 2010 also include displays of physical affection between Bassanio (David Harbour) and Antonio (Byron Jennings). Such efforts, while intriguing from a modern standpoint, veer sideways from medieval and early modern association of close male friendship with nobility and ethics.

But, the friendship of these two characters must be addressed if one is to understand the play because male-male affection serves as the initial, albeit mysterious, concern of *The Merchant of Venice*. Antonio, the title character, speaks of a strange ailment he suffers from in the opening lines:

> In sooth, I know not why I am so sad.
> It wearies me, you say it wearies you.
> But how I caught it, found it, or came by it,
> What stuff 'tis made of, whereof it is born,
> I am to learn.
> And such a want-wit sadness makes of me,
> That I have much ado to know myself. (1.1.1-7)[3]

Antonio's lament resembles the lovesickness described in several romances of the medieval era featuring good knights in pain from a mysterious malady.[4] Lancelot's affliction over Guinevere is likely the most well-known, but the pattern in descriptive language appears over and over again. Shakespeare himself uses a similar vocabulary of melancholy for love-struck characters in other works, e.g., Orsino in *Twelfth Night*, and Troilus in *Troilus and Cressida*, to name only a few. In *The Merchant of Venice*, steeped in mercantile considerations, Salarino and Solanio immediately suggest that commercial anxiety is to blame for their friend Antonio's unhappiness, but the diversified Antonio insists otherwise, saying "my merchandise makes me not sad" (1.1.46). Here, an important contrast comes into view that begins to define his character in a positive way: Antonio is troubled not by a preoccupation with business and profits but by something more profound. Solanio hits upon it when he follows up with "Why then you are in love" (1.1.47). Antonio's denials of "Fie, fie" do not quite convince.

---

the pattern of stage reviews since Guthrie's production, according to Edelman (56-60).

[3] This essay uses the the Folger Shakespeare Library's 1992 text of *The Merchant of Venice*, as edited by Barbara Mowat and Paul Werstine.

[4] See, e.g., the Yvain character in *Yvain* or *The Knight with the Lion* who is wounded by love and falls for Laudine, the wife of his enemy, or Palamon and Arcite in Chaucer's *The Knight's Tale*, or any number of knights in the stories of Marie de France.

But if he is in love, the question becomes with whom? Shakespeare provides no direct answer, but Bassanio is the only credible candidate in the play. As we will see, modern critics sometimes view this love as a tension, a source of emotional or even sexual rivalry with Portia, but in doing so they miss another, older aspect that is also important for interpretative history. The intense friendship Antonio expresses for Bassanio marks him as a virtuous man in medieval/early modern terms just as Bassanio's affection for Antonio brands him noble, for as Cicero (and others) teach, true friendship only touches the good.[5] Whether desire contributes to the attraction at some level remains an open question, but the implied ethical signification in the close friendship is crucial to understanding the characters and the play.

Once Gratiano and the others depart, an intimate scene of shared confidences and promises develops between the two companions with Bassanio declaring, "To you, Antonio / I owe the most in money and in love" (1.1.137-8). This line establishes their amity but also casts their relationship, like so many in Shakespeare's Venice, in terms of debts and bonds. The metaphor is not entirely misplaced for these two, nor is their meeting without an agenda. Too much largesse on Bassanio's part, another classic chivalric trait, has left the young nobleman's estate financially "disabled" and led him to request a substantial loan—another substantial loan—from his dear friend, Antonio. The advance, Bassanio says, will enable him to "get clear of all the debts I owe" (1.1.141). No doubts nor recriminations ensue; rather, warmth and goodwill imbue the exchange.

Antonio, his earlier gloom apparently forgotten in Bassanio's presence, asks only one stipulation of his companion before providing full support: whether the proposed enterprise lies "within the eye of honor" (1.1.144). Such phrasing constitutes a nod to the chivalric ideals of virtue in which honor is always paramount, for the reference was no anachronism in Shakespeare's time but a serious cultural component. Chivalry, the ethos tied to the Middle Ages, arguably reached its zenith in the Renaissance. Arthur Ferguson has argued that many of the foundations of chivalry had "crumbled" by the sixteenth century, but he also admits how seriously many contemporaries valued knightly ideals at that time (5-10). Likewise, Huizinga writes of a chivalric mentality growing exhausted, brittle, and illusory by the mid-fifteenth century (61-125). Maurice Keen and many others have challenged Huizinga's interpretation (219-37). As with the larger Renaissance itself, judging the degrees of cultural change to

---

[5] See Cicero's highly influential treatise from the first century B.C., *De Amicitia*, which was well-known throughout the Middle Ages and the Renaissance.

chivalry is exceedingly difficult. Fewer dukes or kings led columns of knights in battle, true. Yet, orders of chivalry such as the Knights of the Garter and the *Toison d'Or* retained respect throughout the early modern era. Crusading efforts to re-conquer the Holy Land declined, but crusader-type alliances, e.g., at Lepanto, still formed in order to meet the threat of the Ottomans. Tournaments, those hallmarks of knightly prowess, continued during the sixteenth and seventeenth centuries with greater protections for participants (better armor, blunted weapons, etc.) and an exponential increase in pageantry (Young 74-100). Diplomacy often became the overriding rationale for these lavish government events in the Renaissance. Early modern scholar Paul Oskar Kristellar acknowledges the retention of many elements of medieval civilization even as humanist ideals spread, with the stipulation that a greater focus on secular concerns slowly emerged in the period (18-20). Chivalric society certainly had to adjust to new conditions, and knighthood as a governing ideal faded over time, but the process was exceedingly slow. As a result, several recognizable features of elite male friendship endured within the broader developing culture and literary arts of the Renaissance, and a chivalric sense of integrity surely remained an immense concern for aristocratic men and women in the early modern period.

So, with the overarching principle of honor in place, Antonio states that he will do his "uttermost" to aid Bassanio, even though he himself must borrow the requested money, since his current "fortunes are all at sea" (1.1.184). Antonio is wealthy, and his credit in Venice is considerable, but a real possibility of danger exists, and of course all the danger is realized (and then some) as the play progresses. So, the main plot turns on this early agreement between close friends, but Shakespeare also takes care to create an ethical sense around these two characters by demonstrating the clear trust each has for the other. Antonio's willingness to hazard both his credit and himself—"my purse, my person"—for his beloved companion raises his honor in particular.

Perceiving the Ethical Dimension in the Play

Other characters in the play's early scenes, by contrast, rate lower on the ethics scale, and while Shakespeare wins much acclaim for his naturalism, morality nevertheless remains an important concern in his plays (McGinn 175-86). Among Bassanio's other friends, Gratiano seems good enough and has certainly much to say but manages only to "speak an infinite deal of nothing" (1.1.121). Solanio and Salarino similarly appear superficial or at least ineffectual. Lorenzo may fare best in an estimation of values at the beginning but only because he speaks the least, remaining a sort of attractive blank. Jessica feels morally torn between her familial "blood" and her attraction to a young man of different customs who would never win the approbation of her father. Likewise, the servant with the Arthurian-inspired name, Lancelet, wavers humorously between two devils, one his repugnant master, the other an inner "fiend" who prompts him to run away and seek employment elsewhere. Even Portia, far from her moral triumphs in the end, comes across as petulant, impatient, and a bit spoiled in Act 1, ridiculing her suitors and chaffing under restrictions imposed by her father's will. The playful, open talk with Nerissa, her maid, suggests a sympathetic character in the Lady of Belmont (and Nerissa), but the basic inequality of the mistress-servant relationship stalls any specific identification of it with inherent goodness or nobility. Any maid should care for her mistress, and any mistress should be able to confide in her maid. Furthermore, no direct danger presents itself for either of the two female characters to sacrifice for or otherwise protect the other.

Shylock is portrayed worst of all on the moral measure, obsessed with money and old hatreds as his Act I aside speech about Antonio, the Christian merchant, shows:

> How like a fawning publican he looks!
> I hate him for he is a Christian,
> But more for that in low simplicity
> He lends out money gratis and brings down
> The rate of usance here with us in Venice.
> If I can catch him once upon the hip,
> I will feed fat the ancient grudge I bear him. (1.3.41-47)

Some struggle to defend the Shylock character in *The Merchant of Venice* as a sympathetic villain shaped by the ill will of Christian society around him and harboring a valid complaint against Antonio (Bullough 454-55, Edelman 6-45). The 2004 film directed by Michael Radford provocatively removes all but the first line of the above speech, thereby coloring Shylock in less malicious tones, and many stage versions over the centuries have similarly made at least some cuts to the bitter aside (Edelman 113). The full speech as it appears in the text of the play constitutes a compelling counter-argument to such views, however, for the playwright would hardly provide this disturbing glimpse into the character's psyche if no moral judgment against Shylock were intended, however tempered by later glimpses of suffering and hurt. Shakespeare employs similar tactics to reveal the inner minds of Edmund in *King Lear* and Iago in *Othello*—blatant evildoers with few redeeming traits or apologists.

Beyond Shylock's unmistakable anti-Christian attitude (especially troubling in the overwhelmingly Christian society of Elizabethan England), Shakespeare takes special care to stress a miserly aspect in the referenced aside. Hoarding wealth carried a general negative impression from older times, for misers and usurers were widely scorned (or worse) in the Middle Ages. Disgust for misers sprang from *New Testament* teachings as well as many religious orders of monks or knights (e.g., the Knights Templar) that demanded its adherents give up all wealth upon entry for spiritual enlightenment.[6] Moreover, since *largesse* or generosity was one of the prominent, defining elements of chivalry—along with prowess, loyalty, courtesy, and franchise—knights supposedly held misers in a heightened form of contempt (Keen 2). So by skillfully tapping cultural archetypes of the medieval era, Shakespeare sets up an ethical disparity on multiple levels between Antonio and Shylock. Audiences would interpret the former's deep friendship with Bassanio favorably and the latter's fixation on money adversely. One could argue that these views are simply part and parcel of an encompassing religious prejudice that the playwright furthers (perhaps unconsciously), but the signals are too intentional, specific, and well-placed. Shakespeare always finds intriguing ways to render his characters early on; the practice is a trademark of his (Brockett 195). In *The Merchant of Venice*, he does so by invoking cues from the world of chivalric romance to strengthen first impressions, shading characters in contrasting moral tones for a sharper dramatic effect. These subtle indicators in the play, however, also help us as historians to understand how leading playwrights in the English Renaissance could communicate indirectly to audiences.

The cordial conversation of Bassanio and Antonio about a loan request stands as a stark contrast to Antonio's later discussion of terms with Shylock. Before fixing the details of the bond, the two men spar darkly over past treatment, usury, and religious elucidation. Here, the idea of friendship appears only in parody, and hostility simmers throughout their poetic speeches to one another. Shylock, for example, declares to Antonio "I would be friends with you and have your love," but he immediately belies this seemingly amiable statement with "Forget the shames that you have stained me with," (1.3.149-50). By repeatedly reiterating the perceived wrongs done to him by the merchant, it becomes clear that Shylock intends no real affection for Antonio but only a chance to

---

[6] The mendicant friars pushed this idea to its limits, though it is ironically true that some monasteries and orders as a whole often became quite rich in the medieval era.

humiliate his Christian rival and perhaps to do him mortal harm. By contrast, Antonio does not bother to feign any fondness toward Shylock, and although this may rightly offend our modern multicultural sensibility, the merchant at least represents himself truthfully. Antonio makes no apologies for his denigrating treatment of Shylock in the past, e.g., calling the Jewish man a "dog" for his excessive usury practices and religion, affirming in response to Shylock's charges of ill conduct that "I am as like to call thee so again, / To spet on thee again, to spurn thee, too," (1.3.140-1). All Antonio wants from Shylock is the necessary money to help his beloved Bassanio; for that, the merchant will "break a custom" in regards to borrowing and even seek a loan from an unsavory source. Neither wishes to nor attempts to reach any sort of genuine accord, but Antonio's honor reveals itself in his forthright approach while Shylock dissembles for effect.

As the action of the play moves forward, the ethical examination of the characters deepens as they have to meet new challenges, an indication of early modern drama drawing from morality plays (Brockett 139-40). In *The Merchant of Venice*, Antonio and Bassanio each undergo tests— difficult tests—just as knights do in various romances, but neither Venetian falters in his devotion for the other and both ultimately succeed. Mary Beth Rose intriguingly argues that the endurance of hardship became more important than the active components of battle to the heroic identity in the Renaissance as part of the "gendering" of heroism (xii-xvii). To a certain extent, though, weathering hardships had always been part of the chivalric/heroic identity in twelfth-century romances or similar older sources. For example, Shakespeare likely pulled the caskets challenge that Bassanio faces from a combination of popular medieval stories such as Boccaccio's *Decameron* or the *Gesta Romanurum*. Bassanio chooses rightly in the high-stakes trial to win his lady Portia's love in *The Merchant of Venice*, but he could never have embarked on his errand to Belmont had Antonio not first provided the means. Also, once he gains his bride and her fortune in Belmont, Bassanio rushes back to Venice to try to rescue his friend and benefactor from the teeth of Shylock's gruesome bargain.

For his part, Antonio must endure a series of misfortunes while maintaining a sense of honor. His beloved friend's departure is the first ordeal. During the farewell, Antonio bravely tells Bassanio not to worry about Shylock's threat and to take whatever time is needed for the courtship with Portia. "Slubber not business for my sake" and "Be merry" are Antonio's words of advice, but the words alone do not reveal his pain. Shakespeare crafts the leave-taking scene as a description by Salarino to

Solanio in order to show Antonio's emotions and his efforts to cover them up. Salarino reports the parting as achingly difficult for the merchant:

> And even there, his eye being big with tears,
> Turning his face, he put his hand behind him,
> And with affection wondrous sensible
> He wrung Bassanio's hand – and so they parted. (2.9.48-51)

Cultural ideals of male emotion intertwine with nobility in Antonio's behavior during this scene. The one proves the other according to traditional models of chivalry, i.e., only those of high honorable bearing could be capable of feeling friendship to such a degree; it is a signifier of nobility. Antonio does not wish to trouble or burden his friend, so he hides (or at least tries to hide) his reaction from Bassanio, suffering the burden with courage alone. To underline the effect, Shakespeare then has Solanio sum up Antonio's friendship with Bassanio: "I think he only loves the world for him" (2.9.52).

As Bassanio's fortunes rise in Belmont, Antonio's founder in Venice. With his ships overdue and reported lost, the Christian merchant cannot pay the debt he owes. Shylock has Antonio arrested for defaulting on the bond and gleefully prepares to collect his grisly payment, "the pound of flesh." Antonio tries twice to talk with his uncompromising enemy but refuses to fall to begging for his life, announcing, "I'll follow him no more with bootless prayers" (3.3.22). Always honorable, Antonio does not blame Bassanio, nor ill fortune, nor even Shylock for his bleak situation. He accepts the circumstances calmly, "with a quietness of spirit"—as men of integrity should, as knights were expected to do—resigning himself to death. He does, however, extract some contentment from suffering for his friend's sake in a medieval tradition of sacrifice. Antonio's thoughts in jail turn only to his beloved Bassanio and the hope of seeing him a last time.[7]

The ethical axis then shifts to Belmont and pulls the noble Bassanio back to Venice to defend his companion. No doubt emerges as to whether or not he will go. A less virtuous man might ignore the news now that he had won the wealthy, beautiful Portia and her extensive estate, or at least delay a few days (an hour?) to enjoy the marriage bed, but Bassanio leaves as soon as the offstage wedding ceremony concludes. Upon his entry in Venice, he immediately offers to pay Antonio's elapsed monetary debt twice over. Shylock, however, remains implacable and doggedly persists in his demand to cut the flesh personally from his enemy, Antonio.

---

[7] Antonio's state is one that shows up often in Shakespeare's sonnets to his fair male friend, e.g., *Sonnet 29*.

Bassanio promises his body, "my flesh, blood, bones, and all" before his friend comes to harm, but Antonio rejects this rash course, arguing that he is "meetest for death" and that if one of them must die, Bassanio should live (4.1.113 and 4.1.117).

Portia then arrives and famously solves all the problems by turning the legal screws back on an obstinate Shylock, but she also fulfills the larger ethical equation in the play. Bassanio and Antonio's close friendship extends to her from two sides, and she enters into it, no longer a young woman who merely complains or mocks others. How does this transformation happen? First, and most important overall, she falls in love with Bassanio. Next, and directly related to the friendship theme, Portia's love for Bassanio translates into concern for those he loves. When Salerio brings the fateful letter to Belmont telling of Antonio's state, Portia reacts in sympathy with her intended husband before even knowing the details, "I am half yourself, / And I must freely have the half of anything / That this same paper brings to you" (3.2.258-60). She has joined the friendship unconsciously and becomes further ennobled by it. When she learns of the dire threat and the high esteem in which all hold Antonio, Bassanio especially, Portia considers Antonio in her mind:

> I never did repent for doing good,
> Nor shall not now; for in companions
> That do converse and waste the time together,
> Whose souls do bear an equal yoke of love,
> There must needs be a like proportion
> Of lineaments, of manners, and of spirit;
> Which makes me think that this Antonio,
> Being the bosom lover of my lord,
> Must needs be like my lord. If it be so,
> How little is the cost I have bestowed
> in purchasing the semblance of my soul
> From out the state of hellish cruelty! (3.4.10-21)

She befriends Antonio without ever meeting him, for she reasons that he must be as pleasing to her as Bassanio. Continuing the thought, Portia resolves to act on her realization and try to rescue the man so like her beloved husband. Her inspired success at the court in Venice demonstrates the reach or the enhancement of her abilities when engaged in a worthy enterprise: true friendship.

Love Triangle or Loving Triad?

Despite the victory and the new arrangement of Bassanio, Antonio, and Portia, a few matters, e.g., the surrender of Portia's ring, still need to be worked out late in the comedy. Tension over the ring and Bassanio's support of his friend at the trial has led some scholars to interpret Antonio and Portia as rivals for Bassanio's emotional attention or even his sexual desire. Drama thrives on struggle, so modern theatrical artists may predictably advance the notion of an emotional contest—any contest—with a winner (Portia) and a loser (Antonio). Strangely, psychoanalytical critics often claim a similar friction between Bassanio's friend and his wife, one comparing Antonio to Shylock as characters forced "outside" to live unhappily alone at the end of the play (MacCary 168-70). Radford's aforementioned film version adheres to this alienated final image of Antonio, even inventing/adding a scene of the title character sadly wandering Portia's darkened house in Belmont alone near the end. Despite the heroic successes of Antonio and Bassanio in the play, another critic emphasizing competition oddly declares their friendship a bankrupted "failure" by the end (Patterson 10). Lastly, some gender/queer theorists see a heterosexist tradition to reevaluate by suggesting a homosexual relationship between the two male lovers disrupted by and in conflict with the new wife. One of these, Arthur Little, bizarrely interprets Antonio's willingness to suffer a violent death for Bassanio at the edge of Shylock's blade as a symbolic displacement of hymeneal blood (Menon 216-24).

Shakespeare's text, however, provides little actual support for these views stressing competition. Portia saves Antonio, after all, and clearly welcomes him into her home "notwithstanding" his connection to the ring dispute. The target of her trick is really Bassanio, whom she gives a difficult if not impossible choice over the ring, an echo of the original caskets decision. This time, however, Portia has merely assembled a ruse. Her ploy still makes a point and has an important effect, though, for it draws Bassanio, Antonio, and herself into a new joint pledge involving the ring—symbolically another marriage. Interestingly, the first, traditional wedding occurs hurriedly and offstage in Act 3, diminishing its significance. At Portia's direction, Antonio volunteers himself as the "surety" for this more important ceremony of commitment in Act 5. Predictably, Radford's movie version makes the surety guarantee sound like a threat to keep Antonio in line, but that interpretation works against the spirit of the comedy's conclusion and also against logic. Portia could easily have suggested/demanded the merchant depart at this juncture, thereby removing her supposed rival from the field, but the Lady of

Belmont instead deliberately includes Antonio in the union. The harmonious friendship from the play's beginning is forged anew with three loving companions instead of two.

A strikingly similar formalized triad of best comrade, husband, and wife occurs in *The Prose Lancelot* with Galehaut, Lancelot, and Guinevere. Although largely disregarded by modern scholarship (except as a source for Malory's fifteenth-century collection of Arthurian romances) and little known by today's readership, the anonymously authored *Lancelot* is a rich, influential, and absorbing tale of chivalry. In the thirteenth-century French tale, Lancelot forms a deeply emotional bond with another knight named Galehaut, and the two travel together sharing adventures, trust, and company as their joint fame and love for each other grows. Later, after noting his friend in distress over Guinevere, Galehaut arranges for Lancelot and the queen to meet discreetly. Galehaut and Guinevere seal a marriage-like accord to share Lancelot between them in their respective roles as companion and paramour. Galehaut charges the queen "*que vos li donés vostre amor et que vous le prenés a vostre chevalier a tous jours et devenés sa loiax dame a tous le jors douniés tout le monde*" [that you give him your love, and that you take him as your knight forevermore, and become his loyal lady for all the days of your life] (Micha 115 / Lacy 146). In return, Galehaut asks Guinevere "*que vous me donrés sa compaignie*" [to grant me his companionship] (Micha 116 / Lacy 146). In answer, the queen takes Lancelot's friend by the hand and tells him "*Galahot, je vous doing cest chevalier a tous jors*" [Galehot, I give you this knight forevermore]. Together, the three create an ideal triangle in perfect balance for the best of earthly knights. The *Prose Lancelot* presents this alignment of elite male and female love around Lancelot as the pinnacle of chivalric virtue, one still discernible in Shakespeare's works centuries later. An understanding of this older three-tier model from medieval times provides an interesting alternative to the supposed competition between Portia and Antonio over Bassanio. Establishing a happy coalition of three at the end not only completes the comic vector of the play but also expresses a beneficial cultural arrangement recognizable in the sixteenth century but perhaps obscured in the twenty-first. Lastly, gender theory critics wishing to destabilize how we understand intimate relationships in the past (or the present) may well have new options to examine in that regard.

The emotional structure of these positive male-male-female triad relationships in *The Prose Lancelot* and *The Merchant of Venice* differs from one of the basic compositions of domineering homosocial male desire described by Eve Kosofsky Sedgwick in her well-known work,

Between Men. The competition of two powerful males to claim a less powerful female defines the emotional pattern Sedgwick wishes to examine and expose in her book (the passionate rivalry of Palamon and Arcite with each other over the passive Emily in Chaucer's *The Knights's Tale* makes for a good chivalric example of her argument). While Sedgwick raises interesting points about power, the basis of heterosexuality, and sexual politics in her analysis, the asymmetrical triangle of men "trafficking" in women that she asserts does not fit snugly for all literary cases or models. Portia rescues Antonio for Bassanio and herself in *The Merchant of Venice* with an active plan that she launches and carries out, so it could be said that she "trafficks" in one man for another to achieve a noble outcome. The same might also be said of the agreement Guinevere and Galehaut reach over their beloved best knight in *The Prose Lancelot*. Sometimes, a loving relationship in literature between two men and a woman really does approach a happy ending for all three.

The ring episode also combines the monetary and chivalric themes in *The Merchant of Venice* for the band represents shared bonds of service and prosperity owed to each member of the successful trio at the end. After the resolution in court, the Duke of Venice commands Antonio to "gratify" his legal benefactor, the disguised Portia, telling the merchant "For in my mind you are much bound to him" (4.1.425). Antonio agrees and admits that he "stands indebted, over and above, / In love and service to you evermore" (4.1.432-33). The language of obligation that Shakespeare employs here skillfully invokes a financial connotation as well as an older, medieval sense of loyalty or homage.

The layering continues when the question of giving Portia's ring in tribute arises. Bassanio hesitates over relinquishing it to the supposed doctor of law, saying "There's more depends on this than on the value," but eventually gives it up at Antonio's request (4.1.455). Upon returning to Belmont, however, Portia clashes with her new husband over the loss, and Bassanio defends himself in chivalric terms: "I was beset with shame and courtesy / My honor would not let ingratitude / So much besmear it" (5.1.233-35). The controversy over the lost ring is strikingly reminiscent of medieval romances, e.g., Chrétien de Troyes' *Yvain*. In that tale, the title character loses his mind when he breaks his promise to return by a certain date to his new wife, and she withdraws her love from him in response, demanding the return of a ring she gave him as a token. Half of the romance deals with the heroic if tardy Yvain's recovery and redemption.

No madness or quest is needed in Shakespeare's play to resolve the situation, though; Portia unravels the passel of confusions easily "like the mending of highways in summer." Besides the removal of guilt for her husband and Gratiano, her rewards in Act 5 include excellent commercial news for Antonio regarding his argosies. She reports with mysterious, almost *deus ex machina* knowledge that three of the merchant's supposedly lost ships have arrived safely to port. Again, Radford's film eliminates this section, likely as a means to undercut Antonio's position further at the conclusion and depict Portia as the unconditional winner of their "duel" over Bassanio's affections. In Shakespeare's original full text, however, Portia salvages Antonio's material losses after saving his life, drawing the merchant to her in love and responsibility as she already is drawn to him. The combination of monetary obligations with older forms of ethical commitment anchored in medieval honor, i.e., protection from physical harm, signal a deliberate cultural modulation by the playwright from the tropes of pure medieval romance but one still firmly tied to notions of chivalric virtue. With ring returned, identities revealed, loves proven, and finances confirmed, Bassanio, Antonio, and Portia are each bound to one another contentedly on multiple levels.

Shakespeare's portrayal of friendship in *The Merchant of Venice* retains the moral/emotional tone handed down from the Middle Ages. With the help of his companion, the nobleman in the play marries a beautiful, principled, rich damsel and wins her land and love as just reward for his ethical conduct. Clearly, however, something is different: a merchant fulfills one of the traditionally chivalric roles, a woman enters the realm of high friendship, a legal battle achieves victory rather than an armed conflict at the end, and wealth pours to the heroes from commerce as much as from property.[8] Shakespeare also renders his male companions in a more understated manner, e.g., Antonio turning his head away to hide a tear, than would be usual for medieval epic or romance where knights routinely faint and sob over each other.[9] Whether a more restrained approach to emotion was a stylistic choice or indicative of a wider cultural shift, the Bard of Avon nevertheless shows us how intense feelings between men could be and how important they are to an heroic identity in the Renaissance.

Shakespeare and other leading playwrights of early modern England turned their poetic skills to the subject of ethics and male friendship as those ideas expanded into broadening layers of early modern society.

---

[8] Literary precedents exist for female characters to become true friends of knights in the Middle Ages, e.g., Lunette, in *Yvain or The Knight with the Lion*, earns the friendship of the hero as does Guinevere in *The Prose Lancelot*.

[9] King Arthur habitually collapses over missing or lost comrades in tales from the Middle Ages. The *Lancelot-Grail Cycle* and the *chansons de geste* are full of these emotional episodes.

Given the commercial nature of theatre in London, we have to assume they were giving audiences what they wanted, whether in the large public theatres or the smaller private halls. As creative writers, Marlowe, Shakespeare, Jonson, and their contemporaries tinkered with the theme of friendship, peppering their lines with classical images and humanistic allusions, pulling in references from the changing urban world around them, deliberately making connections between the past and the present. Yet, the chivalric sense of strong emotions defining an ethical friendship—as transmitted through medieval romance and epic—still endured as a central model in the dramatic literature of the times.

Bibliography

Anonymous

Early English Versions of the Gesta Romanorum. Edited by Sidney J.H. Herrtage. London: N. Trübner & Co., 1879.
The New English Bible. Oxford Study Edition. New York: Oxford University Press, 1976.
Lancelot. Edited by Alexandre Micha, Vol. VII. Genéve: Librairie Droz, 1980.
Lancelot (Prose Cycle): Lancelot Grail: The Old French Arthurian Vulgate and Post-Vulgate in Translation. Edited by Norris J. Lacy. New York: Garland Publishing, 1993-1995.
The Song of Roland. Translated by Frederick Goldin. New York: W.W. Norton, 1978.

Authored

Aelred of Rievaulx. *Spiritual Friendship.* Translated by Mary Eugenia Laker. Washington, DC: Cistercian Publications, 1974.
Baron, Hans. *In Search of Florentine Civic Humanism: Essays on the Transition from Medieval to Modern Thought.* Volumes I and II. Princeton, NJ: Princeton University Press, 1988.
Boswell, John. *Same-Sex Unions in Premodern Europe.* New York: Villard, 1994.
Bullough, Geoffrey. *Narrative and Dramatic Sources of Shakespeare.* New York: Columbia University Press, 1957.
Bray, Alan. *Homosexuality in Renaissance England.* London: Gay Men's Press, 1982.

Brockett, Oscar. *History of the Theatre*. 5th edition. Boston: Allyn and Bacon, 1987.

Brotton, Jerry. *The Renaissance Bazaar*. Oxford and New York: Oxford University Press, 2002.

Castiglione, Baldesar. *The Book of the Courtier – Norton Critical Edition*. Ed. Daniel Javitch, Trans. Charles Singleton. New York and London: W.W. Norton, 2002.

Chaucer, Geoffrey, *The Knight's Tale*. Ed. J.A.W. Bennett. London: Harrap, 1974.

Chrétien de Troyes. *Yvain or The Knight with the Lion*. Trans. Ruth Harwood Cline. Athens, GA: University of Georgia Press, 1984.

Cicero. *Cicero – De Senectute, De Amicitia, de Divinatione*. Ed. T.E. Page. Trans. William Armistead Falconer. Cambridge: Harvard University Press, 1959.

Clark, Sandra. *Renaissance Drama*. Malden, MA: Polity Press, 2007.

Dingman, Paul. "Ethics and Emotions: A Cultural History of Chivalric Friendship in Medieval/Early Modern Times." Diss. University of Rochester, Rochester, 2012.

Edelman, Charles, ed. *The Merchant of Venice* (Shakespeare in Production series). Cambridge and New York: Cambridge University Press, 2002.

Ferguson, Arthur B. *The Indian Summer of English Chivalry*. Durham, North Carolina: Duke University Press, 1960.

Greenblatt, Stephen. *Renaissance Self-Fashioning from More to Shakespeare*. Chicago and London: Chicago University Press, 1980.

Hallam, Elizabeth. *The Wars of the Roses*. New York: Weidenfeld & Nicolson, 1988.

Haskins, Charles Homer. *The Renaissance of the Twelfth Century*. Cambridge: Harvard University Press, 1927.

Huizinga, Johan. *The Autumn of the Middle Ages*. Trans. Rodney J. Payton and Ulrich Mammitzsch. Chicago: University of Chicago Press, 1996.

—. *Men and Ideas*. Trans. James S. Holmes and Hans van Marle. Princeton, NJ: Princeton University Press, 1959.

Hyatte, Reginald. *The Arts of Friendship*. New York: E.J. Brill, 1994.

Johnson, Paul. *The Renaissance: A Short History*. New York: The Modern Library, 2000.

Jonson, Ben. *Bartholomew Fair* in *Jonson: Three Comedies*. New York: Penguin, 1983.

Kay, Dennis. *William Shakespeare His Life and Times*. New York: Twayne Publishers, 1995.

Keen, Maurice. *Chivalry*. New Haven and London: Yale University Press, 1994.

Kelley, Michael. *Flamboyant Drama*. Carbondale: Southern Illinois University Press, 1979.

Kipling, Gordon. *The Triumph of Honor – Burgundian Origins of the Elizabethan Renaissance*. The Hague, Netherlands: Leidin University Press, 1977.

Kristeller, Paul Oskar. *Renaissance Thought and Its Sources*. Ed. Michael Mooney. New York: Columbia University Press, 1979.

Levin, Richard. *New Readings vs. Old Plays*. Chicago and London: University of Chicago Press, 1979.

Loades, David, ed.. *The Tudor Chronicles: The Kings*. New York: Grove Weidenfeld, 1990.

Logan, Terence P. and Denzell S. Smith, eds. *The Predecessors of Shakespeare*. Lincoln, NE: University of Nebraska Press, 1973.

MacCary, Thomas W. *Friends and Lovers – The Phenomenology of Desire in Shakespearean Comedy*. New York: Columbia University Press, 1985.

MacKenney, Richard. *Sixteenth Century Europe: Expansion and Conflict*. Houndmills and London: MacMillan Press Ltd, 1993.

Macfaul, Tom. *Male Friendship in Shakespeare and His Contemporaries*. Cambridge: Cambridge University Press, 2007.

Malory, Thomas. *Complete Works*. Edited by Eugene Vinaver. 2nd Edition. New York: Oxford University Press, 1971.

Marlowe, Christopher. *Edward the Second*. Ed. Charles R. Forker. Manchester, UK and New York, NY: Manchester University Press, 1994.

McGinn, Colin. *Shakespeare's Philosophy*. New York: Harper Collins, 2006.

Menon, Madhavi, Editor. *Shakesqueer*. Durham and London: Duke University Press, 2011.

Mulgan, Catherine. *Renaissance Monarchies, 1469-1558*. Cambridge: Cambridge University Press, 1998.

Painter, Sidney. *French Chivalry*. Ithaca, NY: Great Seal Books, 1961.

Patrides, C.A. *Premises and Motifs in Renaissance Thought and Literature*. Princeton, NJ: Princeton University Press, 1982.

Patterson, Steve. "The Bankruptcy of Homoerotic Amity in Shakepeare's *Merchant of Venice*" in *Shakespeare Quarterly*, Volume 50, No. 1 (Spring, 1999), 9-32.

Perry, Curtis and John Watkins, eds. *Shakespeare and the Middle Ages*. Oxford and New York: Oxford University Press, 2009.

Rose, Mary Beth. *Gender and Heroism in Early Modern English Literature*. Chicago: University of Chicago Press, 2002.

Sedgwick, Eve Kosofsky. *Between Men – English Literature and Male Homosocial Desire*. New York: Columbia University Press, 1985.

Shakespeare, William. *The Riverside Shakespeare*. Edited by G. Blakemore Evans. Boston: Houghton Mifflin, 1997.

—. *The Sonnets*. Edited by William Burto. New York: Penguin, 1999.

—. *The Merchant of Venice*. Ed. Barbara Mowat and Paul Werstine. New York: Washington Square Press, 1992.

Simpson, James. *Reform and Cultural Revolution*. Oxford, UK: Oxford University Press, 2002.

Shannon, Laurie. *Sovereign Amity*. Chicago: Chicago University Press, 2002.

Smith, Lacey Baldwin. *This Realm of England: 1399-1688*. Boston and New York: Houghton Mifflin Company, 2001.

Warner, Michael. "Homo-Narcissism, or, Heterosexuality" in *Engendering Men – The Question of Male Feminist Criticism*. Ed. Joseph Boone and Michael Cadden. New York: Routledge, 1990.

Young, Alan. *Tudor and Jacobean Tournaments*. London and Dobbs Ferry, NY: Sheridan House, 1987.

THE GENRE OF FEMALE FRIENDSHIP
IN *THE MERCHANT OF VENICE*

REBECCA OLSON

In 2010, the Second City Network posted a series of Shakespeare-themed "Sassy Gay Friend" videos on YouTube. Most of the sketches open mid-tragedy: Ophelia ponders murky waters, Desdemona awaits Othello atop her wedding sheets, Juliet holds the happy dagger to her chest. Enter Sassy Gay Friend (Brian Gallivan), who exclaims: "What. What. *What* are you doing?" With a flick of his salmon-hued scarf, he then rewrites Shakespeare by giving the heroine just the dose of common sense, saucy wit, and tough love her flagging spirit requires. Post-sassy intervention, Shakespeare's tortured women are giggling, loving their hair, and even ready to date again.

These funny adaptations are problematic: take, for one, their consistent message that the female characters are "stupid bitches" that require the guidance of a stereotypically flamboyant gay friend. Yet in the great tradition of parody these videos also quietly underscore something we might too easily take for granted about familiar cultural phenomena. What "Sassy Gay Friend" humorously exploits is the rather obvious but often overlooked fact that Shakespeare's tragic heroines tend to lack the camaraderie of women of their own station and age. Sassy Gay Friend takes it upon himself to be the "BFF" ("best friend forever") that Ophelia, Desdemona, and Juliet don't have.

Although female friendship is prevalent in Shakespeare's comedies, the female characters in his tragedies and late romances tend to be relatively isolated in worlds primarily dominated by men. As Carole McKewin points out, "In the tragedies, where the patriarchal world is more oppressive, women are sometimes able to do more, but they talk less to each other" (127). The exception would seem to be plays such as *Othello* or *Antony and Cleopatra*, in which a faithful servant or waiting lady acts as a confidant and seems genuinely invested in her mistress's plight—indeed, is willing to die for her. For modern readers, these relationships, which are typically defined by witty exchanges and emotionally charged dialogue, read very much like friendship. However, while a mistress and her waiting-gentlewoman certainly *could* be friends, we should not overlook the ways that these relationships are marked as socially asymmetric within the plays. Furthermore, it seems significant that however sympathetic Emilia or Charmian may be, neither prevents her mistress's demise. In contrast, companions of more comparable social standing of the heroine, such as Mrs. Page in *The Merry Wives of Windsor*, devise or participate in plans intended to save their friends and kinswomen.

These are sweeping generalizations, but I offer them at the outset of this chapter to call attention to the apparent connection between Shakespeare's representations of female relationships and his dramatic genres. If we were to separate Shakespeare's plays into the categories "heroines with intimate companions of equivalent social standing," "heroines without," and "no central heroine to speak of," we would be left with groups of plays that more or less correspond with the traditional genres of comedy, tragedy, and history. And just as is the case with the typical delineations of genre ("ends with marriage and the expectation of life," "ends with death," and "about a historical British King"), we are also left with plays that defy easy categorization: namely, problem plays and romances.

This chapter attends to what I think of as the "girlfriend problem" in *The Merchant of Venice*. Although the play's tragic overtones—which push it toward the "problem play" genre—are typically attributed to its anti-Semitic treatment of Shylock, especially in the trial scene of Act 4, Portia's social isolation from women of equivalent rank may also set the stage for the drama's anticlimactic, if technically comedic, conclusion. To make this claim, I rethink Portia's seemingly easy relationship with her waiting-gentlewoman Nerissa. In a play centrally concerned with male friendship and what we might think of as "bondship," the role of Portia's confidante, servant, and accomplice calls for greater scrutiny. Specifically, we need to rethink the standard assumption that the women are in fact friends—and see themselves as such. As I explain, the play lends itself to a more cynical interpretation of their hierarchical relationship, one that could cast a shadow on the dual nuptials with which the play concludes.

Shakespeare's Waiting-Gentlewomen

Whereas most of Shakespeare's comedic heroines enjoy the company of sympathetic sisters, cousins, friends, and attendants, many of Shakespeare's tragic heroines appear isolated from other women: this list includes Lavinia in *Titus Andronicus*; Calpurnia and Portia in *Julius Caesar*; Gertrude and Ophelia in *Hamlet*; Lady Macbeth in *Macbeth*, and Cressida in *Troilus and Cressida*. We might extend the list of isolated heroines to also include characters in the late romances: Imogen in *Cymbeline* has a lady attendant, Helen, but the latter speaks only two lines; and *The Tempest*'s Miranda—certainly the most geographically isolated female character in Shakespeare—has only a hazy memory of women waiting upon her in her infanthood (1.2.46-47). In all of these plays, a paucity of female interaction would seem to underscore other kinds of loss—not only of an absent mother figure (as is more often than not the case), but also familial or romantic relationships with men or a previous, and seemingly better, way of life.

If the absence of female companions helps to communicate a degree of bleakness in Shakespearean drama, what might the *presence* of female companions on the contrary suggest, either about a play's fictional world or even the heroine herself? Furthermore, how might the social station of her companion signify something even more specific? At the crux of my investigation is whether or not the relationships between heroines and their waiting-gentlewomen (Desdemona and Emilia in *Othello*; Julia and Lucetta in *The Two Gentlemen of Verona*; Olivia and Maria in *Twelfth Night*; and Portia and Nerissa in *The Merchant of Venice*) function in ways that are parallel to comedic "BFFs" who are of more apparently equivalent social status (cousins such as Beatrice and Hero in *Much Ado About Nothing*, for example, or Helena and Hermia in *A Midsummer Night's Dream*). The relationships between mistresses and their waiting-gentlewomen in Shakespeare are often characterized by seemingly mutual affection and the exchange of intimate confidences, not unlike those we see between characters such as Hermia and Helena at the start of *A Midsummer Night's Dream*. Might Shakespeare suggest, though, that the inherently hierarchical nature of the mistress/servant relationship sways that affection?

Critics have been quick to downplay the social discrepancies between Shakespearean heroines and their waiting-gentlewomen, reminding us that Elizabeth I's own attendant ladies were noble and pointing out that the marriages of characters like *Twelfth Night*'s Maria suggest that Shakespeare's fictional equivalents were similarly high-ranking (Draper 255-58).[1] When it comes to Shakespeare's female characters, even subtle

---

[1] More recently, Laura Gowing has argued that although queens and princesses, like kings and princes, may have "indulged in the creation of private personas for friendship," the "fantasy of common ground was belied by the real dangers of intimacy between monarchs and commoners" (138).

hierarchical differences could potentially impact our understanding of their dynamic, for two main reasons. First, social asymmetry would seem to undermine the possibility of "likeness," which was frequently represented as a crucial element of friendship—or at least, male friendship—in the period. Second, because the marriages of waiting-gentlewomen are consistently represented by Shakespeare as creating avenues for treachery against a heroine, plays like *The Merchant of Venice* could leave at least some audience members less than optimistic about the future relationship between a mistress and her married attendant.

The part of the waiting-woman in Shakespeare is often a substantial one, apparently by design: as John Draper observes, twelve of these ladies have speaking roles, and they are usually Shakespeare's own additions to a story (256, 258). Critics have provided a range of reasons for the popularity of these figures in Shakespearean drama. Draper points out that their inclusion can be a convenient staging decision, for dialogue with a confidante allows the heroine to inform the audience of her "inmost thoughts" (256). These parts can also be highly entertaining; as David Evett notes, the relationships between Shakespeare's heroines and their attendants are "marked by an element of sheer fun" (160). Others have considered Shakespeare's female attendants in the context of actual Tudor practice. Elizabeth A. Brown, for example, uses the strategic function of Elizabeth's Privy Chamber as a lens for rethinking Shakespeare's depiction of Cleopatra's ladies: "An examination of the presence or absence of an extensive network of family members, courtiers, advisors, and servants who provide support for and validation of power reveals a surprising strength of Elizabeth's use of her Privy Chamber and a corresponding weakness in Cleopatra's use of her household as a strategy of power" (131). More than simply a plot device or opportunity for comedic relief, then, the dramatic figure of the waiting-gentlewomen could alert early modern audiences to larger structures of power both within the play and without.

What is clear is that the relationships between Shakespearean heroines and their servants—and perhaps especially their waiting-gentlewomen—provide a striking contrast to what we see between male characters in the plays. As Evett observes, although Shakespeare provides fewer examples of female-female service relationships, in those relationships, "mutuality and familiarity are the norm": "The exchanges among the Princess of France, Juliet, Hero and Beatrice, Desdemona, and Cleopatra and their female attendants are almost uniformly cheerful, good-natured, mutually supportive—models of ideal mastery, ideal service" (160). This "female mutuality," as Evett puts it, is quite different from what we see in

Shakespeare's male-male service relationships, in which upbraiding and insolence frequently appear.[2] One way to look at it, then, is that Shakespeare's women are better "masters" than men in the domestic domain.

Although Evett is right that the lady/waiting-gentlewomen relationships in Shakespeare are consistently genial, it is also true that these warm feelings do not prove effective at preventing disaster. Characters such as Emilia or Charmian are willing to die for their mistresses, but interestingly, they do not or cannot prevent their mistress' deaths. Indeed, one of the most troubling things about female servants in Shakespeare is their propensity to unintentionally advance a villain's schemes. The most obvious example is *Othello*'s Emilia, who procures Desdemona's handkerchief for her husband Iago and consequently undermines a mistress for whom she appears to have genuine affection. This dynamic is even more obvious in plays which include a variety of female relationships: just as female service relationships help cast light on male service relationships in plays such as *Antony and Cleopatra*, as Evett argues (161), female service relationships can also provide a contrast to a play's representation of female friendship. For example, in *Much Ado About Nothing*, Hero's waiting-gentlewoman Margaret plays a role, if unwittingly, in Don John's treacherous plot to slander her lady, while Hero's cousin Beatrice actively participates in the friar's plot to remedy the situation. Beatrice asks her suitor Benedick to avenge Hero's honor; Margaret's affection for Borachio, on the other hand, is what leads to Hero's misfortune. Although Margaret is eventually exonerated by Hero's father Leonato as being involved "against her will" (5.4.5) in the plot against Claudio, she nonetheless strikes many readers as not entirely innocent: her alleged wearing of her mistress's clothes at Borachio's behest and her willingness to be addressed as "Hero" while in a passionate embrace does raise questions about her level of agency in the affair (3.3.127; 5.1.221-22).[3]

As Evett explains, when such betrayals on the part of female servants occur, "it is always at the behest of some man" (161). In this way, the waiting-gentlewomen in Shakespeare's tragedies would seem to call our attention to serving women's divided loyalties, especially when they are (as Emilia is) married or (perhaps like Margaret) hope to be. The compromised loyalty of the attendant lady is a real problem, for although waiting-gentlewomen are not the only female characters who betray other women in Shakespeare's plays in order to please a male character, their

---

[2] Evett locates a potential origin of this model in the 1549 *Book of Common Prayer*'s gendered representation of service; see *Discourses of Service* (180).

[3] All quotations from Shakespeare's plays are from *The Norton Shakespeare*.

betrayals do seem to have more dire or lasting consequences. For example, Helena in *A Midsummer Night's Dream* threatens the happiness of her friend Hermia when she reveals the latter's plan to elope, an act that one might read as more overtly antagonistic than Emilia's theft; even so, at the end of *Midsummer* Hermia still marries the man of her choice *and* gets to stay in Athens. It does not seem a coincidence that Shakespeare's comedies provide us with such examples of women torn between loyalties to their female friends or mistresses on one hand, and to their spouses or potential spouses, on the other: these plays are centrally concerned with the larger social effects of marriage. Even someone as powerful and strong-willed as Titania in *A Midsummer Night's Dream* ultimately reneges on her promise to another woman at her husband's insistence. Occasionally male characters, too, find themselves in similarly conflicted positions: Benedick does, after all, challenge Claudio at Beatrice's request, despite the fact that he and Claudio are close friends and fellow soldiers.

Portia and Nerissa

Again and again, then, Shakespeare's plays illustrate the kinds of social negotiations and renegotiations between same-sex friends that betrothal requires, but these negotiations may be more pronounced when it comes to women. Laura Gowing observes, "More so for women than for men, a fondness for one's own sex may have existed as an opposition to marriage long before heterosexuality and homosexuality are supposed to have been invented" (138). As she explains, in a patriarchal system marriage is assumed to "absorb [women's] whole identity," something female friendship could threaten (138). In *The Merchant of Venice*, the character Jessica provides an illustration of how alienating marriage could be: although we might expect her, as the Christian wife of Lorenzo, to befriend women in her new community, she remains as socially isolated in Belmont as she was in Venice. For example, although Graziano entreats Nerissa to "bid her welcome," that welcome is not included in the script, and her only direct exchange with Portia is a brief farewell (3.2.236; 3.4.42-44). In fact, only a sixth of Jessica's lines in the final three acts of the play are spoken when other female characters are even onstage.

Given how powerfully marriage was perceived to shift a woman's social priorities, it is perhaps not surprising that the marriage of a trusted servant would provide even more opportunity for dramatic conflict than that of a friend. *The Merchant of Venice* provides us with an unusually extended look at this problem; whereas female servants in Shakespeare's plays tend to be either already married or are hastily married or betrothed in a final scene, Portia and Nerissa's joint engagement happens relatively early, in Act 3. What this means is that the audience sees the two together onstage during a transformative period in their relationship. Interestingly, even though they transcend gender hierarchies during this period by appearing in the Venetian court as youths, they nonetheless retain their class positions: Portia plays the lawyer, and Nerissa, his clerk. Through the course of the scene, however, Shakespeare reminds us of their impending positions as wives, especially when Antonio and Bassanio refer directly to the women they have left in Belmont (4.1.277-87). The trial scene interrupts not only Portia's marriage, but Nerissa's as well, and this interruption creates a space in which the women, as well as the audience, might contemplate what their newfound unions will mean for their own mistress/servant relationship.

On the surface, *The Merchant of Venice* would seem to be among the best examples of the happy relation between ladies and their servants in Shakespearean drama. Portia's relationship with Nerissa—one of Shakespeare's original additions to his main source (Draper 259)—is portrayed, from their opening scene together, as full of mutual affection and respect.

When we first see Nerissa and Portia, the latter is bemoaning her "little body's" weariness in a speech that recalls Antonio's expression of "sadness" at the start of the play. Just as Antonio's friends provide possible explanations and increasingly teasing banter, Nerissa responds to her lady with a line that establishes her as practical, astute, and perhaps gently mocking: "You would be, sweet madam, if your miseries were in the same abundance as your good fortunes are; and yet, for aught I see, they are as sick as surfeit with too much as they that starve with nothing. It is no mean happiness, therefore, to be seated in the mean. Superfluity comes sooner by white hairs, but competency lives longer" (1.2.3-8). Here, it is Nerissa, and not Portia, who is presented as the longer-winded, something that may be significant when we consider that Portia actually has the most lines in the play. Portia's appreciation for Nerissa's rhetoric—and her acceptance of her attendant's chastisement—is evident in her next line: "Good sentences, and well pronounced" (1.2.9). From this point in the scene their patterns of speech inverse: Nerissa provides a one-line quip ("They would be better if well followed") to which Portia replies with a thirteen-line, metaphor-rich defense that also conveniently informs the audience of her father's death and the casket scheme, a lottery system that will, in his absence, determine her future husband. The women then go on to discuss Portia's suitors, landing eventually on the subject of Bassanio.

It is hard not to read the characters' back-and-forth wit, the mirroring of their language patterns, and the ease with which Nerissa chides her lady (as well as the ease with which Portia takes it) as anything but friendly, despite the fact that the women do not, at least on the surface, always agree. Portia, for example, does not confess personal attraction for Bassanio, despite Nerissa's prompting (1.2.100). Nerissa, when pressed to commiserate with Portia about the casket scheme, chooses instead to take Portia's father's side (1.2.23-29). Yet these examples hardly seem like genuine conflict: the easy explanation for evasiveness or debate between the women is that like many good friends, they can read between one another's lines. That is to say, Nerissa may very well comprehend Portia's personal motives for appearing somewhat neutral about her most promising suitor, while Portia understands that Nerissa's position requires that she play devil's advocate. Although one could imagine a production in which the women were not affectionate, and perhaps even adversarial, from the start the characters' lines more obviously lend themselves to a relationship that is both friendly and comfortably intimate.

The mutuality of the affection between Portia and Nerissa appears even stronger when set in contrast to the relationship between Julia and her waiting-gentlewoman Lucetta in *The Two Gentlemen of Verona* (c. 1590), which would seem to be its earlier prototype (Draper 257). Lucetta, like Nerissa, teases her mistress, provides counsel regarding potential suitors, and is taken into her lady's confidence (see, in particular, *Two Gentlemen* 1.2 and 2.7.1-7). The conversations between Lucetta and Julia, however, are marked by consistent demands on the latter's part, and include more overt, if apparently lighthearted, references to the nature of their relationship. In their first scene, for example, Lucetta presents Julia with a love letter from Proteus; Julia refuses to look at it and then, regretting that decision but unwilling to lose face, becomes highly impatient with her servant, whom she repeatedly calls back for spurious reasons. "Is't near dinner-time?" she asks at one point, to which Lucetta responds, "I would it were, / That you might kill your stomach on your meat / And not upon your maid" (1.2.67-69). In comparison, Nerissa comes off as relatively autonomous—more like a companion than a maid—and her part is, perhaps accordingly, also more sustained. In *The Two Gentlemen of Verona*, Julia refers to Lucetta as a "table," or tablet, which can assist her in forming her cross-dressing plan (2.7.3), but she ultimately travels without her servant, who is never seen again. Nerissa, on the other hand, accompanies Portia in drag to Venice and pays a large role in the play's conclusion.

Yet Portia's sustained relationship with Nerissa might also be fruitfully compared to that of Jessica and Lancelot within *The Merchant of Venice*. Although Lancelot is obviously not an attending woman, his interactions with Jessica do provide a glimpse of another version of a cross-class relationship, for Lancelot is in service first to Jessica's father Shylock, and then to her new husband's friend Bassanio. When the audience first sees them together, Jessica expresses regret that Lancelot is fleeing her father's house, but acknowledges that it is "hell" (2.3.1-2). The pair show obvious affection, or at least appreciation, for one another: Jessica says that his presence alleviated some of her home's "tediousness," and Lancelot in turn refers to his master's daughter as a "most beautiful pagan; most sweet Jew" (2.3.3-11). Their relationship continues after they both arrive in Belmont, where Lancelot assures Jessica that she is damned (3.5.12). Their back and forth banter to some extent recalls that of Portia and Nerissa, but it has more of an edge, especially on the side of the utterly frank servant: we might even see the forthright Lancelot as the play's closest equivalent of a sassy gay friend, someone who freely shares his opinion and apparently enjoys his companion's defensive response. Compared to these brief but dynamic exchanges between Lancelot and Jessica, those between Portia and Nerissa seem more one-sided than they may at first appear.

However, the idea that Portia and Nerissa are in fact friends has yet to be seriously contested. Theodora A. Jankowsi observes that "much evidence attests to Portia and Nerissa's affection for each other," but does not provide examples (156). Evett, who calls Nerissa Shakespeare's most "extensive" of Shakespeare's waiting-gentlewomen, acknowledges that her relationship with Portia includes a "certain amount of amiable mockery, even of conspiracy," but concludes that it is "without malice" (161). Draper deems Nerissa an "expert confidante" (257). Norman Nathan reasons that Nerissa's social rank is high enough to make it possible for the women to be "true friends," and that they are "devoted to each other as are the merchant and the lord" (56). In this way, he explains, Shakespeare uses the relationship between Portia and Nerissa to parallel the play's central male friendship. Nathan is right that as a gentlewoman-attendant, Nerissa would be of higher social standing than a character like Juliet's nurse, something that her marriage to Graziano—Bassanio's peer—seems to confirm.

Yet, like the Princess's attendant ladies in *Love's Labour's Lost* or Maria in *Twelfth Night*, who also marry (or plan to marry) at the plays' conclusions, Nerissa is obviously not of equal rank as her mistress, or she would not be in the latter's attendance. More helpful, then, is Corinne S. Abate's nuanced view of Nerissa's friendship with Portia. Nerissa, she argues, is a more influential character than critics have acknowledged, for she teaches Portia by example to distrust men and to become an empowered wife. Abate also claims that the result of the casket test is effectively orchestrated by Nerissa, "whose partial and biased interest in what happens to her mistress may account for her careful arrangement of Portia's marital future to a man who is most decidedly not Portia's financial equal" (283). I find this reading persuasive, not only because it is more sensitive to the class distinctions between the women than most, but also because it suggests that Nerissa's intentions are more self-serving than is generally assumed. Although Abate herself sees Nerissa as a friend from whom Portia learns to look for love in marriage (297), we can also read Nerissa's support of Bassanio's suit, and encouragement of Graziano's to her, as an attempt to adjust, even slightly, the social differences between herself and her mistress.

In fact, although Nerissa's playful dialogue with Portia would seem to mark her as a "BFF" in the comedic tradition, the script nonetheless exposes the asymmetry of their social positions and thus provides opportunities for the audience to question the depth and sincerity of their mutual affection. This is something the 2010 Oregon Shakespeare Festival (OSF) production (dir. Bill Rauch) emphasized by occasionally straining the rapport between Portia and Nerissa. In their initial exchange, for example, Nerissa was seen busily engaged in attendant/household duties while her restless mistress lamented her overwhelming "weariness." In this way, the production made the inequity of their positions immediately visible, and consequently painted the aristocratic Portia (Vilma Silva) as somewhat insensitive to Nerissa's relative lack of "good fortunes."

Such insensitivity was even more apparent in Act 2. In what is arguably Portia's ugliest moment in the script, she dismisses her suitor the Prince of Morocco with the following line: "A gentle riddance. Draw the curtains, go. / Let all of his complexion choose me so" (2.7.78-79). Because Nerissa was played by a black actress (Dawn-Lyen Gardner), the OSF production underscored the racism of this line and simultaneously highlighted the class difference between Portia and her (offended but silent) attendant. After Portia's nasty couplet Nerissa winced, visibly stung, before resuming her cheerful demeanor. The production thus demonstrated that because she occupied the role of gentle-woman attendant, even the intelligent and forthright Nerissa had to bear such a painful comment without objection. By making this line a slight not only to the absent Morocco but also the onstage Nerissa, the production used the speech to provide a suggestive counterpoint to the aggressive racist taunts directed at Shylock throughout the play and to highlight the pervasive xenophobia in the script. This moment ultimately called attention to the way Belmont functions in the drama as a place where outsiders come, go, and stay—sometimes uneasily. What seemed particularly fresh about the OSF production is that it included Nerissa—Portia's right-hand-woman—among those outsiders.

This creative decision is supported by later lines in the script, to which I now turn. After both women are betrothed, Portia herself repeatedly calls attention to her higher social status. What is particularly interesting is that Portia's most direct references to Nerissa's status as servant occur in the context of her observation of the intense loyalty that defines Bassanio's friendship with Antonio. On one hand, we might see Portia as therefore drawing a line of comparison between her relationship with Nerissa and the male friendship central to the play. More likely is that these speeches indicate just the opposite: that is to say, that they convey her own sense of social isolation.

Portia on Friendship

I have referred to the relationships between characters like Beatrice and Hero as "friendship," but it is true that the word is rarely used by Shakespeare's female characters to refer to another female character; instead, a "friend" is often a perceived political ally of the opposite gender, or even a lover.[4] One question to ask, then, is how to identify friendship between female characters when they do not, as Hermia does, themselves define it as such (3.2.217). In Shakespeare's plays, friendship between female characters would seem to be communicated through witty exchanges, moving examples of blank verse, and, perhaps especially, the unfolding of confidences. But what if the rapt companion is more or less a captive audience? Should we read Julia's description of Lucetta as her "table wherein all [her thoughts] / Are visibly charactered and engraved / to lesson [her]" (2.7) as indication that their relationship is comparable to that of Hermia and Helena, who have shared hours of "counsel" (3.2.199)?

To answer the question of whether or not Portia and Nerissa are friends as we understand that concept today, we should look at Portia's own understanding of friendship ideals, as articulated in speeches prior to her appearance at Shylock's trial. Of all the characters in the play, it is Portia

---

[4] In *Othello*, for example, Desdemona's refers to her promise to speak to Othello on Cassio's behalf as a "vow" of "friendship" (3.3.21); Bianca, upon being presented with Desdemona's handkerchief, jealousy suspects that Cassio must have some "newer friend" (3.4.176).

who defines friendship most articulately: according to Laurie Shannon, "we receive much evidence of Portia's specific cognizance of the ideals of Renaissance friendship for which this play is so well known, although it is usually the exchanges between Bassanio and Antonio that evidence the play's engagement with amity" ("Likenings" 17). What is especially relevant to my argument is that Portia advances the Renaissance theory that friendship requires likeness. Shannon explains: "While the speeches of Bassanio and Antonio copiously evidence his familiarity with conventional friendship tropes, Shakespeare's scripting of Portia's 'female' gaze at it and her affect-ation of its forms mark the play's real improvisation on the popular discourse of doubled selves" (17). If Portia does see likeness as a requisite for true friendship, as indeed she expresses, it would seem unlikely that she herself would define her relationship with her servant Nerissa as such.

By way of example, and before turning to Portia's most extensive discourse on friendship, I want to point out an earlier passage in which friendship figures large. Shortly after Bassanio has chosen the correct casket and he and Portia profess their love for one another, Lorenzo, Jessica, and Salerno arrive in Belmont with messages about Antonio's predicament in Venice. "Is it your dear friend that is thus in trouble?" Portia asks Bassanio (3.2.290). He responds:

> The dearest friend to me, the kindest man,
> The best-conditioned and unwearied spirit
> In doing courtesies, and one in whom
> The ancient Roman honour more appears
> Than any that draws breath in Italy. (3.2.290-95)

Portia—herself named for a famously honorable Roman—wants to know how much is owed to the Jew. When answered, she delivers a speech in which the word "friend" consistently reappears:

> Pay him six thousand and deface the bond
> Double six thousand, and then treble that,
> Before a friend of this description
> Shall lose a hair thorough Bassanio's fault.
> First go with me to church and call me wife,
> And then away to Venice to your friend;
> For never shall you lie by Portia's side
> With an unquiet soul. You shall have gold
> To pay the petty debt twenty times over.
> When it is paid, bring your true friend along.
> My maid Nerissa and myself meantime

Will live as maids and widows. Come, away,
For you shall hence upon your wedding day.
Bid your friends welcome, show a merry cheer.
Since you are dear bought, I will love you dear.
But let me hear the letter of your friend. (3.2.298-313)

Given Portia's repeated allusions to Bassanio's "friend" or "friends" in this speech (which may be an early instance of the kind of echoing Portia and Bassanio will later invoke with the "ring" dialogue in Act 5), it seems significant that she refers to Nerissa instead as "my maid." First, her decision to call Nerissa "my maid" emphasizes the contrast between Bassanio's rich social life in Venice (he will "bid [his] friends welcome" and "show a merry cheer") and her own lonely wait (as a "widow") for his return. However, it is noteworthy that "friend" is not the only word that appears more than once in close proximity in this speech: "maid" appears twice in the sentence "My maid Nerissa and myself meantime / Will live as maids and widows." By repeating that word, Portia underscores her admirable willingness to delay consummating her marriage, and thus remain a "maid," until the conflict with Shylock is resolved. In other words, if Portia's reference to Nerissa as "my maid" suggests that their relationship is somehow inferior to that between Bassanio and his "true friend," we could also read the reference as a way that Portia, in a line that reminds us of her own impending subjugated position as a wife, advertises that she is willing to make sacrifices for her new "lord" (3.2.171). She may choose to call Nerissa her "maid" at this moment chiefly for the opportunity the pun provides for her own self-presentation.

However, we might also read Portia's reference to her "maid" as her first verbal response to something that happens about one hundred lines earlier in the scene: Nerissa's betrothal. When Portia is told that Nerissa agrees to marry Graziano, pending the marriage between "her mistress" and Bassanio, Portia appears to express surprise: "Is this true, Nerissa?" (3.2.208). Nerissa's answer, "Madam, it is, so you stand pleased withal," is at the very least a performance of deference, to which Portia—not typically one to lack for words—does not in dialogue respond. Of course, Portia could embrace Nerissa or otherwise physically communicate her approval at this moment, but the script itself makes a range of reactions available. When Portia, who has not actually voiced her assent to the marriage, then calls Nerissa her "maid" later in the scene, she reminds us that Nerissa still answers to her. In this way, Portia calls attention to their social asymmetry even at the moment that Nerissa is about to enter another hierarchical relationship by becoming Graziano's wife, a relationship that could very well threaten the loyalty previously shown to her mistress. She will not be Portia's—or anyone's—"maid" for long (and indeed, the play famously ends with a reference to her "ring").

Portia delivers the play's most eloquent treatise of friendship two scenes later, when Lorenzo praises Portia for her "godlike amity" in her husband's absence. Her response begins with a description of the special dynamic between "companions" that would seem to apply to her relationship with Nerissa as much as it does to that between Antonio and Bassanio, for the women also "converse and waste the time together" (3.4.12). However, here, as in 3.2, Portia concludes her observations on Bassanio's friendship by directly referring to Nerissa's status as an attendant:

> I never did repent for doing good,
> Nor shall not now; for in companions
> That do converse and waste the time together,
> Whose souls do bear an equal yoke of love,
> There must be needs a like proportion
> Of lineaments, of manners, and of spirit,
> Which makes me think that this Antonio,
> Being the bosom lover of my lord,
> Must needs be like my lord. If it be so,
> How little is the cost I have bestowed
> In purchasing the semblance of my soul
> From out the state of hellish cruelty.
> This comes too near the praising of myself,
> Therefore no more of it. Hear other things:
> Lorenzo, I commit into your hands
> The husbandry and manage of my house
> Until my lord's return. For mine own part,
> I have toward heaven breathed a secret vow
> To live in prayer and contemplation,
> Only attended by Nerissa here,
> Until her husband and my lord's return. (3.4.10-29).

Portia's observation that friendship requires "a like proportion / Of lineaments, of manners, and of spirit" is in line with a popular Renaissance ideal, which could be traced to Aristotle and Cicero (Shannon, *Sovereign Amity* 128). We also see this idea, for example, in *A Midsummer Night's Dream*, when Helena says that she and Hermia were "like to a double cherry: seeming parted, / But yet an union in partition, / Two lovely berries moulded on one stem" (3.2.210-12). Interestingly, having speculated on the similitude of her fiancé and his extraordinary friend, Portia then informs Lorenzo of her plan to depart for a convent, "only attended by Nerissa here"—a line that, once again, calls attention to Nerissa's position in her employ. Although one could argue that this is part of Portia's cover—she and Nerissa are in fact traveling to Venice—I think that the phrase "attended by Nerissa here" does remind playgoers that Nerissa, as an attendant in service, is not ultimately "like" her mistress in the way she imagines Antonio to be like Bassanio; that is to say, in "lineaments," "manner," and "spirit."

For early modern audiences, the women's social differences would certainly render friendship more difficult. As Shannon puts it, "The central importance of equality to perfect friendship in Aristotle and Cicero rendered affectionate linkage across boundaries of rank an imperfect approximation at best" (*Sovereign Amity* 128). This would appear to be true for women as well as men: it is a difficulty she sees expressed, for example, in Amelia Lanyer's "Description of Cooke-ham." Although she acknowledges that Lanyer's poem may not reflect the true range of "cross-class companionship" in the period, it does, she claims, call attention to the problem of reconciling rank in friendship (131). In the aforementioned speech, Portia herself focuses more on the physical and behavioral likeness between friends ("lineaments," "manners," and "spirit") than their social equality. Even so, the fact that her "friend" speeches include phrases that remind us that Nerissa is her servant indicates that she does not see their relationship as parallel to that between Bassanio and Antonio. In short, it is possible that Portia acknowledges the class differences between she and Nerissa more than critics have.

Such sensitivity to rank would be in line with Portia's character, for she frequently invokes the language of hierarchy. A particularly noteworthy example occurs when she and Nerissa return to Belmont, where they will reconcile with their husbands. When comparing the eclipsing of a candle's light by the moon, she observes:

> So doth the greater glory dim the less.
> A substitute shines brightly as a king
> Until a king be by, and then his state
> Empties itself as doth an inland brook
> Into the main of waters. Music, hark. (5.1.92-96)

It is hard not to read Portia's political analogy as more or less self-referential; she will presently resume control of her estate from her own "substitute," Lorenzo. Certainly Nerissa seems to pick up on the parallel: "It is *your* music, madam, of the house" (5.1.97, emphasis mine). "Nothing is good, I see, without respect," Portia responds, "Methinks it sounds much sweeter than by day" (5.1.98-99). Nerissa, in the last line she speaks directly to Portia in the play, then observes, "Silence bestows that virtue on it, madam" (5.1.100). This sets Portia up for another analogy, this time involving birdsong, which concludes with "How many things by season seasoned are / To their right praise and true perfection!" (5.1.106-07). We might assume that it is the female characters which are now in season and will presently be "seasoned" via the ring plot. Portia and Nerissa, restored to their feminine garb, are also back to their "true perfection" as women. But in these lines, and especially her observations about the crow and the nightingale, which are defined by their difference from other birds, Portia also seems to be calling Nerissa's attention to natural as well as political hierarchies (5.1.101-05). Nerissa's lack of articulated response could suggest something unsettling about the future of their relationship and the extent to which she, once no longer a "maid," will support Portia the wife.

Female Friendship and Genre

The Merchant of Venice's treatment of Shylock is the obvious reason to consider the drama a problem play or "soured comedy"; the intensity and discomfort of the trial scene can easily upstage the ring plot and so-called happy ending of the final act (Hale 195). The presence of Shylock's now-Christian daughter Jessica during that final act further reminds the audience of what the Venetians have taken from the "rich Jew." At the same time, as I have argued, *The Merchant of Venice* also varies from traditional comedies in the way it dramatizes exchanges between women, and Portia and Nerissa in particular. To that end, the few and rather formal exchanges between Jessica and Portia throughout the play (in the OSF production their interactions were downright tense) may further contribute to the audience's uneasiness with the play's comedic ending.

It is, in fact, in the romances and so-called problem plays in which we see some of Shakespeare's most interesting examples of female relationships, some of which appear to be friendship and others, perhaps simply friendly. These (often newfound) relationships assist in bringing about the conclusive union or reunion of husband and wife (as do the bed tricks in *Measure for Measure* and *All's Well that Ends Well*). Even *The Winter's Tale*'s Paulina, perhaps the most complex example of a lady attendant in Shakespearean drama, eventually orchestrates the reunion between Leontes and Hermione. What is particularly interesting to me about these female alliances is that although they may be mutually beneficial, they are not always characterized by mutual affection or jovial complicity. I do not think, for example, that we would call *Measure*'s

Isabella and Mariana "friends": their personal goals dovetail, yet they appear to have little else in common.

Nerissa and Portia may also provide an example of women working together not chiefly out of shared affection, but rather because they are useful to one another, and thus correspond with a larger shift in Shakespeare's representation of female friendship in the latter part of his career. As McKewin observes, "Although Shakespeare's comedies offer the richest variety of women's private scenes, the development of those conversations from the early to the later comedies shows a diminishing of the counter-universe" (126). This "counter-universe," she explains, is a space of relief from male oppression and is exemplified by *As You Like It*'s Arden. As Valerie Traub has illuminated, these early comedies also demonstrate a greater range of female intimacy than the later plays. Encouraging scholars to think beyond moments of cross-dressing to identify sites of lesbian desire in the work of Shakespeare and his contemporaries, she identifies an early modern tradition of representing "femme-femme" love as a "viable and dramatically compelling, if ultimately untenable, state," and locates examples in *Midsummer*'s Helena and Hermia and *As You Like It*'s Celia and Rosamond (170). Portia's relationship with Nerissa—which does include cross-dressing as well as intimate conversation—would seem to provide a similarly rich entry point for addressing the nuances of female intimacy in Shakespeare's works.

Interestingly, despite the widespread assumption that Portia and Nerissa's relationship is a close and affectionate one, and despite the fact that the homosocial relationship between Bassanio and Antonio is frequently described as erotic, the possibility that Portia and Nerissa could be lovers has been left largely unexplored. This may in part be explained by the fact that influential accounts of early modern male friendship such as Alan Bray's were not thought to apply to women's less political and visible relationships, an assumption that has come under increasing scrutiny (Gowing 131). Indeed, Jankowski observes that *Merchant*, like *Much Ado About Nothing* and *Twelfth Night*, raises a "specter of woman-woman eroticism," especially in light of Nerissa's duties as Portia's personal attendant, but points out that the degree of their intimacy could range from "minimal" to "intense" (155-56). Furthermore, she explains, Nerissa's relatively large part, combined with the dearth of male servants in Belmont, suggests that Belmont "is a female community whose male presence (those who try for Portia's hand) is transitory" (155). It is therefore tempting to see Belmont, whose still-authoritative patriarch is deceased, as a version of McKewin's "counter-universe." Yet such views of Belmont are inevitably focused on Portia's perspective. To what extent, we might ask, can Belmont really offer Nerissa, as servant, a satisfying release from oppression? And does she even appear to appreciate her position in a community in which male presence is only transitory?

In *The Merchant of Venice*, a play in which characters are forced to make impossibly difficult decisions and their loyalties toward one another are consistently tested, the subtle tensions between Portia and her waiting-gentlewoman deserve to be taken seriously. Although she is clearly opinionated and prone to what Evett calls "admirable mockery," Nerissa is also highly politic: it is hard to imagine her freely giving Portia a piece of her mind her mind à la Sassy Gay Friend. Portia's relationship with Nerissa reveals that her character is more domineering, and ultimately less sympathetic, than she is frequently taken to be, and in this way she also defies generic expectations for comedy. In fact, I am often surprised by the affection Portia elicits from modern audiences, given not only her explicit racism, but also her tendency to willingly prolong the discomfort—to the point of torture—of other characters. Still, even *The Oregonian*'s review of the 2010 OSF production, one that, as I have explained, seized some of the script's opportunities to complicate her character, proclaimed that the play should more accurately be called "The Bride of Belmont." As Marty Hughly, the paper's theatre critic, explains:

> For it is Portia, given a wonderfully shaded depiction by Vilma Silva, whose beauty and wealth inspire suitors, whose charm and goodness attract the truly loving Bassanio, whose famous disquisition on mercy (plus a little specious logic) saves Antonio at trial, and whose forgiving nature wraps up the play's guiding ideas of love, loyalty and charity in a sweet romantic bow. (par. 11)

I suspect that in the end, playgoers' perception of Portia's "charm and goodness"—and in turn their satisfaction with the play's comedic ending—has much to do with her lively onstage interactions with Nerissa, the only major character in the play who does not at some point express abhorrence for what we might broadly call "otherness" or otherwise inflict suffering on another character. In addition to Portia's xenophobic attitude toward her suitors, such instances include the Christian's racism toward Shylock, Shylock's antipathy for the Christians, as well as more subtle moments of expressed miscegenation.[5] One of the best things we can say about Portia, in other words, is that Nerissa likes her. I think we should question even that.

---

[5] See, for example, Kim F. Hall's account of the play's "wrought nexus of anxieties over gender, race, religion, and economics" (94).

Works Cited

Abate, Corinne S. "'Nerissa Teaches Me What to Believe': Portia's Wifely Empowerment in *The Merchant of Venice*," in *The Merchant of Venice: New Critical Essays*. Eds. John W. Mahon and Ellen Macleod Mahon. New York: Routledge, 2002. 283-304. Print.

Brown, Elizabeth A. "'Companion Me with My Mistress': Cleopatra, Elizabeth I, and Their Waiting Women," in *Maids and Mistresses, Cousins and Queens: Women's Alliances in Early Modern England.* Ed. Susan Frye and Karen Robertson. New York: Oxford UP, 1999. 131-45. Print.

Draper, John W. "Shakespeare's Ladies-in-Waiting." *Neophilogus* 49 (1965): 255-62. Print.

Evett, David. *Discourses of Service in Shakespeare's England*. New York: Palgrave, 2005. Print.

Gowing, Laura. "The Politics of Women's Friendship in Early Modern England." In *Love, Friendship and Faith in Europe, 1300-1800.* Ed. Laura Gowing, Michael Hunter, and Miri Rubin. Basingstoke and New York: Palgrave, 2005. 131-49. Print.

Hale, John K. "Does Source Criticism Illuminate the Problems of Interpreting *The Merchant* as a Soured Comedy?" in *The Merchant of Venice: New Critical Essays*. Eds. John W. Mahon and Ellen Macleod Mahon. New York: Routledge, 2002. 187-97. Print.

Hall, Kim F. "Guess Who's Coming to Dinner? Colonisation and Miscegenation in *The Merchant of Venice*." In *The Merchant of Venice*. Ed. Martin Coyle. New Casebooks. New York: St. Martin's Press, 1998. Print.

Hughley, Marty. "Theater Review: Problem Play 'Merchant of Venice' less of a problem in OSF production." *The Oregonian*. Online Posting. Oregonlive.com, 19 June 2010. Web. 31 January 2012.

Jankowski, Theodora. *Pure Resistance: Queer Virginity in Early Modern English Drama*. Philadelphia: University of Pennsylvania Press, 2000. Print.

McKewin, Carole. "Counsels of Gall and Grace: Intimate Conversations between Women in Shakespeare's Plays." In *The Woman's Part: Feminist Criticism of Shakespeare*. Ed. Carolyn Ruth Swift Lenz, Gayle Greene, and Carol Thomas Neely. Urbana: University of Illinois Press, 1980. 117-32. Print.

The Merchant of Venice. Dir. Bill Rauch. Oregon Shakespeare Festival. Elizabethan Stage/Allen Pavilion, Ashland. 19 Sept. 2010. Performance.

Nathan, Norman. "Portia, Nerissa, and Female Friendship." *Topic: A Journal of the Liberal Arts* 7 (1967): 56-60. Print.

Shakespeare, William. *The Norton Shakespeare*. Ed. Stephan Greenblatt et al. New York: Norton, 2008. Print.

TheSecondCityNetwork. "Sassy Gay Friend: Hamlet." Online posting. YouTube, 17 February 2010. Web. 31 January 2012.

—. "Sassy Gay Friend: Romeo and Juliet." Online posting. YouTube, 28 March 2010. Web. 31 January 2012.

—. "Sassy Gay Friend: Romeo and Juliet." Online posting. YouTube, 8 March 2010. Web. 31 January 2012.

Shannon, Laurie. *Sovereign Amity: Figures of Friendship in Shakespearean Contexts*. Chicago: University of Chicago Press, 2002.

—. "Likenings: Rhetorical Husbandries and Portia's 'True Conceit' of Friendship," *Renaissance Drama* 31 (2002): 3-26. Print.

Traub, Valerie. *The Renaissance of Lesbianism in Early Modern England*. Cambridge: Cambridge University Press, 2002. Print.

"I MAKE IT BREED AS FAST":
PATERNAL AND FINANCIAL ANXIETY
IN *THE MERCHANT OF VENICE*

HORACIO SIERRA

This chapter proposes one more motivation for better understanding Shylock's cruelty: his anxieties about having been cuckolded. The nearly absolute scholarly silence on cuckoldry in *The Merchant of Venice* belies the various references to it in this perennially problematic comedy. There is no literal reading of Shylock as a cuckold. Rather, Shylock is cuckolded through verbal innuendo, rumor, imagery, double entendre, and subtext. What makes these cuckoldry rumors so rich are their textual ties to the condemnation of Shylock's business practices and contextual links to Renaissance-era ideologies, in theology, politics, and literature, about usury. Early modern conceptions about usury originate in classical prohibitions of the practice based on its unnaturalness as it relates to biological propagation. Simply stated, making babies and making money is not the same thing. Shylock's inability to be sure of the former fuels his desire to succeed in the latter. As this study argues, we can understand Shylock's desire to exact his bond as a hyperbolic, psychosexual manifestation wherein he paradoxically battles and embodies anti-usury polemics. Shylock displaces the unease he feels about Jessica's paternity and the Venetian community's hypocritical denigration of his business by conflating financial regeneration and biological reproduction. Given that the play is so concerned with issues of financial and biological propagation, religious difference and conversion, and non-normative gender roles, I find that a closer study of Shylock's possible betrayal by Leah, an erstwhile wife mentioned only once by name in the play, can provide rich rewards for those who want to continue considering ways that Shylock can be better understood.

The intention of this work is not to force a handful of lines into a narrow interpretation of the play. Rather, it opens the door for a discussion about yet another way for coming to terms with the vexing character of Shylock. In a post-Holocaust era, most readers and viewers of the play latch onto any sympathetic rendering of Shylock so as to delimit Shakespeare from being yet another anti-Semitic author. From Shylock's stirring "If you prick us, do we not bleed?" (3.1.47) speech to his final pathetic acquiescence to sign the deed after expressing that he is "not well" (4.1.391) the text offers us ways to redeem Shylock from an inclusive, humanist perspective. Although Shylock's lines and the Christian elite's hypocrisy are conduits for viewing Shylock with some empathy, the lack of background information about him makes him all the more malleable as a character – for better or for worse. After all, "what distinguishes Shylock from the other characters of the play is a representational void, or an absence. It is, of course, a roaring absence, full of stage presence. We do not know whence . . . he came from, or how he came by his present occupation or wealth" (Oz 100). The character of Shylock offers valuable gaps and loaded silences. The explicit mentions of and subtle allusions to cuckoldry that abound in the play present us with the opportunity to consider how the persecuted Jew of Renaissance Europe can be a placeholder for anxious expressions about cuckoldry, usury, and corporeal capitalism.

The play's title character, Antonio, can be viewed as a foil to Shylock in this proposition since he neither charges interest nor articulates fears about his nonexistent offspring. Antonio's queer acceptance of his childlessness contrasts with Shylock's doubts about being Jessica's father. Scholars ranging from David Hawkes to Marc Shell have commented upon how the play creates tense ties between money and the body, but have not gone so far as to link it to Shylock's fears regarding Jessica's paternity. I showcase how this drama questions Shylock's fatherhood and reflects concern about conflations of love and money while simultaneously interrogating early modern angst over capitalism's reliance on usury and the body.

The Evidence

The audience is first invited to doubt Shylock's paternity in Act 2 when Jessica bids goodbye to Lancelot and asks him to deliver a letter to Lorenzo. Lancelot teases Jessica about her vexed relationship with Christian men. His farewell begins as follows: "Adieu. Tears exhibit my tongue, most beautiful pagan, most sweet Jew. If a Christian do not play the knave and get thee, I am much deceived" (2.3.11-13).[1] The multiple

---

[1] This essay uses the the Folger Shakespeare Library's text of *The Merchant of Venice*, as edited by Barbara Mowat and Paul Werstine.

valences of "get," which could mean to either possess or to beget, is further complicated if one goes with the Second Folio reading of the play, "If a Christian *did* not play the knave and get thee, I am much deceived" (emphasis mine). Whereas the first version anticipates Jessica's elopement with Lorenzo, the alternate edition's past tense, "did not play the knave," easily slides into the reproductive meaning of "get" as in her having been begotten by a Christian father rather than the Jewish Shylock. The implications underpinning these two versions can be jarring. The replacement of one verb for the other creates mercurial instability about Jessica's past and future relationships with Christian men.

Admittedly, Jessica's response vouches for her belief in a biological link to Shylock, "Alack, what heinous sin is it in me / To be ashamed to be my father's child! / But though I am a daughter to his blood, I am not to his manners" (2.3.15-18). However, Jessica's brief, couplet-length soliloquy after seeing Shylock for the final time begins her corporeal removal from his grasp and symbolically encourages the audience to once more consider the idea of Shylock's cuckoldry: "Farewell, and if my fortune be not crossed, / I have a father, you a daughter, lost" (2.5.55-56). When we consider the status of women in early modern Europe as property of men, by transferring her body's ownership from Shylock to Lorenzo, Jessica emasculates Shylock by negating his disapproval of this transaction. Furthermore, the clandestine nature of this act mirrors that of cuckoldry wherein the body of Shylock's woman, in this instance his daughter's instead of his wife's, is being physically claimed by another man, both times through assumed sexual union. If Shylock believes that the cuckoldry rumors are true he could still hold on to Jessica as a façade to cover up for his embarrassment and to claim her as an adopted daughter that he can barter on the marriage market. Jessica's elopement deprives him of the ability to employ her as chattel in a homosocial triangle that would cement his friendship with a man of equal or better status within the Jewish community. Robbed of being able to exert paternal control, Shylock's fury becomes all the more enraged after Jessica flees in the middle of the night and leaves him no recourse for employing his daughter as capital.

When Jessica sells the turquoise ring prized by Shylock because it reminds him of his early days with Leah, she disowns her father's claim over her. This act of disengagement is as much a rejection of Shylock's obsession with monetary exchanges, since she trades it for a trivial object, a pet monkey, as it is a confirmation and celebration of her bastard status. Perhaps intrigued by Lancelot's suggestion, Jessica revels in the freedom of no longer having any parents and relishes having "lost" a father as much as she does Shylock having lost a "daughter." Because she barters the ring her mother gifted Shylock, Jessica symbolically divorces her parents and underscores more anxieties about Shylock's paternal claim to her.

The ring as a signifier for the state of marriage and the value of fidelity opens the door for more readings of the play's cuckoldry leitmotif. Jessica trades Shylock's ring for a monkey, a popular symbol for sexual ribaldness, wantoness, and lechery. Considering the exchanges of rings in the Act 5 between Portia and Bassanio and Nerissa and Gratiano, respectively, as metaphors for faithfulness in the midst of accusations of infidelity, as well as the last bawdy pun on "ring," one can imagine the removal of this souvenir of Shylock and Leah's relationship as a poignant reminder of his cuckolded status.

Shylock shares his grief over the loss of the ring with Tubal: ". . . it was my turquoise; / I had it of Leah when I was a bachelor: / I would not have given it for a wilderness of monkeys" (3.1.110-12). Even in the midst of his anger, frustration, and humiliation, Shylock's references to the ring offer a movingly sentimental side of the man commonly referred to as "the Jew." The implication is that he attaches fond memories to the ring. He "had it of Leah" when he was a "bachelor," which could signify their courting, pre-marital phase: the days of innocence, the days before she wronged him. He focuses on the trade with monkeys, once again creating the image of animalistic behavior, and affirms his affection for Leah and the ring despite the possibility that she has betrayed him. There is no direct mention of Leah's death, she is simply absent. Did Leah also abandon Shylock? Was their relationship filled with strife once they were married? After all, in the Old Testament Leah was Jacob's first wife, the wife he didn't want, and we see how Shylock identifies with Jacob in his conversation with Antonio in Act 1. The gaping absence of information about Leah is puzzling and paradoxically unhelpful and fruitful in this analysis.

Throughout the play, Shylock's masculinity is publicly challenged by other characters. For example, Solanio and Salerio vividly report the public nature of Shylock's humiliation with their account of Shylock's agonizing cries over the loss of his daughter and jewels. Venetian boys are said to taunt him with cries of "his stones, his daughter, and his ducats" (2.8.22). Shakespeare's bawdy employment of "stones" as slang for testicles performs a verbal castration of Shylock. By having what the audience might imagine as ostensibly Christian and virile young men mock Shylock, Salerio's testimony reasserts the embarrassment that a cuckolded man experiences when word gets out about their wife's sexual transgression. Readers of the comedy must remember that this scene is reported and not acted on stage unless a director chooses to mime the actions of this report as a reenactment. Because of Solanio and Salerio's obvious hatred of Shylock, their tale could simply be the act of propagating rumors to solidify stereotypes that continue to sully Shylock's reputation. As such, the pair's tale complements Lancelot's unsubstantiated allegations that Jessica is not Shylock's daughter. The combination of Lancelot's private misgiving and Solanio and Salerio's public slander create an atmosphere of gossip and surveillance surrounding Shylock's personal life.

The Christians' mockery of Shylock continues when he laments his daughter's betrayal and cries "My own flesh and blood to rebel!" (3.1.29). Shylock's incredulity is instantly met by Salerio's cruel rejoinders. First he makes a puerile joke about Shylock's sexual appetite, "Out upon it, old carrion! Rebels it at these years?" (3.1.30). By denying Shylock the obvious reference to his daughter's elopement, Salerio increases the punch of his lewd double entendre by referencing Shylock's sexuality. This sexuality is rendered unmanageable if not impotent when Salerio proclaims that there is a vast disparity between Shylock's and Jessica's bodies: "There is more difference between thy flesh and hers than between jet and ivory; more between your bloods than there is between red wine and Rhenish" (3.1.32-33). The syntactical placement of Salerio's comparisons place Shylock in the realm of dark shades and Jessica in the sphere of lighter hues. Because the prurient gag precedes the more emotional and racially tinged comment about the pair's complexion and blood lineage, the lines once again invite us to imagine that Shylock has been cuckolded. The implication is that Shylock's dark, Semitic features were not passed on to Jessica.

M. Lindsay Kaplan argues that during the early modern period "Jewish women are not distinguished racially from Christians" and that "the sincerity and efficacy of their conversions are not called into question" (19). Kaplan then posits that Jessica's "whiteness is established as a fact before her conversion and predicts its success" without mentioning the possibility that she might be the daughter of a Gentile father (21). Because Judaism was widely seen as a racial identity during the Renaissance, particularly in Inquisition-era Spain, even converts such as Jessica would be regarded with suspicion and subject to surveillance. Her "whiteness," commented upon by others in the play who note her "fair" skin, stands in contrast to her father's alleged darkness, which is representative of popular depictions of Jews as "physically unmistakable, with red or black curly hair, large noses, dark skin" during the Medieval and early modern era

(Adelman 79). Jessica's ability to pass may be thanks to her white Christian paternity. As such, her desire to become a Christian is easier than if Shylock, whose skin is propagandistically described as "jet," were ever to desire such a conversion.

Provocatively enough and within the same racial vein, a Nazi-era production of *Merchant* commissioned by the Vienesse Gauleiter Baldur von Schirach and orchestrated by Lothar Müthel in 1942 included a bastardized Jessica. In this purposely polemical performance, Jessica "emerged as a product of the adultery of Shylock's wife with a non-Jew" in order to conform with Nuremberg laws that would have prohibited her marriage to the "Aryan Lorenzo" (Grunberger 371). The anti-Semitic elements of Shakespeare's work cannot and should not ever be denied. For what other reason would the Nazis have sponsored a production of the play even if they had to insert some new plot lines? Even when considering the reprehensible reasons for such a genealogical thread emerging in the play, we can wonder if the re-write was inspired by a reading of the play that already lends itself to such an appropriation of the text. If we imagine the inclusion of such a development, the lines highlighted in this essay become all the more poignant. But, as intriguing as the overall idea is, this is not what Shakespeare did. The truth is more enigmatic.

Within a more appropriate early modern contextual consideration of Jessica and Shylock's racial designations, John Foxe's caustic *Acts and Monuments* (1563) contains a section wherein he lambasts Jews for their lack of faith in Christ being the Messiah. Foxe utilizes the word "infidelity" to describe their belief system:

> this is that unbeliefe, which being more noysome then any pestilenct botch, may rightly & properly be called the Jewish Infidelitie, & seemeth after a certaine maner their inheritable disease, who are after a certaine sort from their mothers wombe, naturally caned through perverse frowardnes, into all malitious hatred, & contempt of Christ, & his Christians. (qtd. in Achinstein 103)

The fact that Foxe's popular text employs the word "infidelity," which by the early sixteenth century already denoted both a want of religious faith as well as disloyalty to a lover, amplifies a discussion that views Shylock, as the stereotypical Jewish villain, and in turn, Leah, personifying larger prejudices linking Jews to all manners of deceit: from rejecting Christ as the Messiah to sexual impropriety.

Following similar racist ideologies, the widespread anti-Semitic discourse of the early modern era was not above linking Jewish usury to illicit sexual practices. Samuel Purchas, an English cleric who is best known for publishing compilations of travel narratives, includes the following description of Venetian courtesans in his 1617 edition of *Pilgrimage*:

> The beastly trade of Curtizans, and cruell trade of Jewes is suffered for gain, these paying a yeerely rent for the heads they weare, besides other means to racke & wracked them in their purses at pleasure, they being used as the spunge-like Friers, to sucke from the meanst, to bee squeezed of the greatest. (165)

Although not the only moneylenders of the early modern era, Jews were the standard personification of the practice. Elizabethan England's reliance on capital and interest as a conduit for social mobility was becoming increasingly indispensable to the burgeoning middle class and even the aristocratic old guard. This comparison to courtesans underscores the unnatural conflation of sexual relations and money that created the popular perception of usury as such a detestable practice.

The link between Judaism and usury was almost indelible in the Middle Ages and the early modern period. The terms were used synonymously by preachers, poets, and politicians. At the turn of the sixteenth century, the Venetian Senate described Jews as "grossly enjoying usury from the blood of our Christian subjects" and "enrich[ing] themselves through Christian blood" (Shatzmiller 47). The executive branch's language clearly links usury and the body. The religious invective volleyed against Jews speaks to a mercantilist society's unease about their reliance on money-lending and interest when it is in the hands of an Other. Consequently, racial and religious differences become a gateway for voicing fears about such codependency.

Leaving behind historical contexts once again, we can focus on the most explicit reference to Shylock's cuckoldry in the drama, which occurs through Lancelot's rumor-mongering when the young lovers are gathered at Belmont and he reiterates his idea about Jessica's illegitimate link to Shylock so that she can escape having "the sins of the father" laid on her:

> LANCELOT. There is but one hope in it that can do you any good; and that is but a kind of bastard hope neither.
> JESSICA. And what hope is that, I pray thee?
> LANCELOT. Marry, you may partly hope that your father got you not, that you are not the Jew's daughter.
> JESSICA. That were a kind of bastard hope, indeed: so the sins of the mother should be visited upon me.

LANCELOT. Truly then I fear you are damned both by father and
mother: thus when I shun Scylla, your father, I fall into Charbydis, your
mother: well, you are gone both ways. (3.5.4-13)

Note how Lancelot once again utilizes the reproductive sense of "got" in
this exchange as he continues to slander Shylock. Because he has been a
longtime servant in Shylock's household, Lancelot may have been privy to
family gossip. Of course, such assumptions are unsubstantiated in the text.
The allusion to Charbydis, a whirlpool from Homer's *Odyssey* personified
as a female sea monster, plays into the idea of the horrific nature of
disloyal women. Furthermore, the phrase Lancelot uses, "I fall into,"
intimates sexual indiscretions in respect to entering the female anatomy,
hinting at her mother's looseness. Could one go so far as to suggest that
Lancelot, following in the footsteps of his Arthurian namesake, has slept
with Leah, and is perhaps Jessica's biological father? His sexual promiscuity
has already been confirmed with his impregnating of a Moorish servant in
the household. The interracial and interfaith nature of the liaison, much
like the threat of Morocco marrying Portia, speaks to other such illicit but
not uncommon occurrences. The possibility is tantalizing, particularly if
we consider that Lancelot is listed as a clown in the *dramatis personae* and
in some direction prefixes throughout several editions of the play, and
such characters, if we think of Feste in *Twelfth Night*, often speak a truth
that is absent in the mouths of others.

Regardless, Lancelot's closeness to Shylock and his family may give
him some grain of truth to work from regarding Shylock's biological link
to Jessica. If Judaism was conceived of as a race and not the more fluid
cultural identity some view it as today, the play's repeated attempts to
differentiate Jessica from Shylock serve to persuade the original audience
that Jessica's betrayal of her father is acceptable even in such patriarchal
times because it removes her from her Jewish heritage. Lancelot's offering
of another reason to accept her elopement clings to racist ideologies that
seek to remove as much Jewishness from Jessica as possible. However,
since Jewishness is inherited through the matrilineal line as alluded to in
the Mishnah, which deals with the validity of marriages according to
halakah and the religious standing of offspring thereof, if Jessica has
another biological father, even a Christian father, she would still be a Jew.
Hence, the "sins of the mother," that is being Jewish, will be "visited
upon" her. The Nazis, in their denial of Jewish traditions consequently
failed in their Nuremberg Laws-appropriation of *Merchant*.

Janet Adelman comes closest of all the scholars closely studying
Jessica's parentage to surmise that Shylock may not be her father. When
referencing Lancelot's "knave" line, Adelman posits that Lancelot's

"assumption that the only way out for Jessica is to have been begotten by some other father is so deeply embedded in him (and so endemic to the culture in which his author operates) that it occurs in a muted form even here, while he is ostensibly serving as the agent of her escape" (71). However, Adelman then elides such a possibility by discussing the replacement of Shylock with the new father figure of Lorenzo and arguing that the pun on "get" in 2.3 and the wordplay with "marry" in 3.5 underscore that "neither marriage nor conversion will fulfill her hope that her father got her not" (72). Yet, there is so much evidence to the contrary. One cannot forget that the play peters out with the strangely comedic Belmont scene wherein character after character jokes about rings, female anatomy, fidelity, and cuckoldry. So much so that within one hundred lines of the play's conclusion Gratiano asks, "What, are we cuckolds ere we have deserved it?" (5.1.284)

Another plot point that is often overlooked and augments this chapter's analysis of the drama's cuckoldry leitmotif is the fact that Shylock has to borrow money in order to lend money. Shylocks admits that he "cannot instantly raise up the gross / Of full three thousand ducats" (1.3.56-57). He must borrow the funds from Tubal. We presume Tubal will not charge his religious brother interest as Jewish tradition insists, but we must note that the degree of Shylock's vengeful desires is so high that he is borrowing money he does not have. Hence, his financial insufficiency can be seen as an impotence that forces him to use the strength of another man just as his wife may have relied on another.

Witnesses and Deductions

I suggest that Shylock's anxieties about being publicly taunted as perhaps not only a cuckold but also impotent fuel his desire to charge interest as a way of producing some kind of tangible legacy in the world. Hence, a long-seated fear of Leah's sexual improprieties would be just one more reason to kindle his desire for revenge on the Christian majority with Antonio as the target. Following the precepts of psychoanalysis's understanding of schemas in relationship to moral development, we could consider the possibility that Shylock's long-standing resentment about Leah's infidelity has resulted in an encapsulation: an underdeveloped schema that has failed to be integrated with an adult's mature moral schema. Shylock's rancorous outlook on life has been (de)formed by fears stemming from more youthful days. Shylock ruthlessly produces money from money and cannot see the forest for the trees when he tries to substitute regenerative finances with a pound of Antonio's flesh and fetishistically insists on the bodily manifestation of interest in lieu of his ability to know about Jessica's parentage.

Primary Witness: Antonio

Antonio, the play's title character, acts as the perfect foil to Shylock in this proposition since he neither charges interest nor has fears about his nonexistent offspring (or even alludes to hoping for any). Antonio's queer acceptance of his seemingly interminable bachelorhood is a constructive contrast with Shylock's fears and embarrassment about his negligible claim to being Jessica's father. The distinction is positive because Shylock displaces his paternal unease when he substitutes financial regeneration for biological reproduction. Although we see him as sullen and despondent in the play's opening line when he laments "I know not why I am so sad" (1.1.1), his depression does not turn into anger. Rather he selflessly aides the man he loves, Bassanio, in pursuit of a woman, Portia, even if it means that he cannot have an exclusive romantic relationship with him. Hence usury, by way of Shylock's bizarre bond terms, is a hyperbole of anti-usury polemics manifested through this antagonist's attempts to combat his emasculated public persona. In a stretch worthy of Lee Edelman's queer negation of reproductive futurity, Antonio's opposition to earning interest could even be read as a defense of his non-heteronormative decision to not procreate. His justification of lending money without interest, a losing bet for a capitalist, can be linked to his aforementioned death drive. Antonio's survival is championed by the audience not only because of Shylock's ruthless dealings but also because he would be a martyr for capitalism. Such a crass martyrdom bodes well for a superior positioning of Antonio's queer nonchalance when it comes to procreating, in comparison to Shylock's manic desire to breed metal in lieu of children and his desire to produce flesh by the mutilation of the merchant's body.

However, Antonio is not entirely without concern for the livelihood of the next generation. By arranging that Shylock's money will come to Jessica and Gratiano after her father's death, Antonio shows compassion once again for heteronormative coupling and its assumed regenerative potential. Antonio stands in sharp contrast to Shylock's unceasing desire to breed interest in place of children. Furthermore, Antonio's love for Bassanio is portrayed as unconditional. Anthony's first step in showing a maturity that recognizes his inability to possess Bassanio comes when he invests in Bassanio's bid to win Portia. Admittedly, his insistence that Bassanio give the ring to the lawyer finds Antonio regressing. However, after Portia forces Antonio to publicly recognize that he can no longer meddle in her marriage, he agrees to be the couple's "surety" (5.1.252). This ultimate recognition of Bassanio's independence is antithetical to Shylock's maniacal reaction to being unable to control Jessica.

Antonio's Christian namesake, Saint Anthony of Padua, was known for his forceful exhortations against usury in his defense of the poor. His opposition to the practice was commonly cited in anti-usury tracts published outside of the Church. One of the many legends about Saint Anthony's life that is still circulated among clergy and lay followers of his Order includes the story of his preaching at the funeral of a money-lender. Saint Anthony claimed that the man should not be buried in consecrated ground because he was already being punished in the afterlife for his career as a usurer. When the money-lender's body was opened, his heart could not be found. It was inside his "coffers" (Huber 60). Besides the link to the equally childless and possibly queer Antonios of *Twelfth Night* and *The Tempest*, this Italian merchant could not have a better patron saint in respect to his opposition to lending money at interest.

Antonio's rejection of Solanio and Salarino's fears about the fate of his ship-bound mercantile treasures as the reason for his unease at the beginning of the play underscore what little concern he has for his finances. Kenneth Gross explains that Antonio's "pathological generosity" refuses to "acknowledge the reality of chances, gifts, and exchanges" in the commercial world (49). Shylock, who relishes the opportunity to invest, gamble, and prosper is his diametrical opposite. Whereas Antonio has no interest in reproduction or gleaning profit from lending money to his customers, Shylock wants his "breed for barren metal" to multiply. The merchant's employment of the term "breed" could hint that Antonio recognizes the anxiety that plagues Shylock in his craving for money and flesh.

Despite Antonio's romantic feelings for Bassanio, this early modern queerness is far from today's world of legally sanctioned same-sex marriage and child-rearing. Antonio does not express interest in having children. The only investment one can see him making in reproductive futurity is via a homosocial triangle wherein he unites Bassanio and Portia, whom we assume will have children. If he were to get anything out of this investment it is the loyalty and gratitude Bassanio should show the merchant for risking his life on his behalf. No doubt Antonio has such sentiments in mind with his desire to be close to the soon-to-be unavailable Bassanio. Nonetheless, Antonio's insistence on not charging interest when he lends money is mirrored by his lack of interest (pun intended) in biological reproduction. When Antonio's hopes of survival ebb, immediately preceding Portia's entrance into the courtroom, he morosely accepts his impending death in symbolic language that once again speaks to his comfort in not being a father: "I am a tainted wether of the flock, / Meetest for death. The weakest kind of fruit / Drops earliest to the ground, and so let me" (4.1.116-18). A wether is not a young pre-pubescent lamb but rather a mature, castrated ram. Like the neutered ram, Antonio is "weak" and "meetest for death."

In a world hostile to the lives and desires of gay men and women, Antonio has internalized society's violent homophobia and consented to his death sentence. If Shylock sees usury as regeneration, productivity, and livelihood, Antonio's rejection of both financial and reproductive interest showcase him embracing a queer negation of reproductive futurity. Borrowing from Edelman's postmodern definitions of queerness as representing not only an identity for those who reject or are excluded by heteronormativity, but also as a site of being "the social order's death drive: a place, to be sure, of abjection expressed in the stigma, sometimes fatal" where "queerness attains its ethical value precisely insofar as it accedes to that place, accepting its figural status as resistance to the viability of the social" (3), we see Antonio as an early modern embodiment of counter-cultural norms in respect to financial and biological reproduction, even as it stems from a nihilistic perspective. Such a cool acceptance of death can see be seen when Antonio faces the prospect of having his flesh carved by Shylock with measured resignation: "I shall hardly spare a pound of flesh / Tomorrow to my bloody creditor" (3.3.36-37).

Recalling Solanio and Salerio's report of Shylock's cries about having lost "his stones, two rich and precious stones," we recognize how the bawdy humor morphs into a glimpse of the psychological anguish Shylock feels over his lack of potency and paternity. In contrast to Antonio's self-identification as a neutered "wether," Shylock's public loss of his daughter and his riches is a final blow against his masculinity for which he feels he must avenge himself. Shylock cannot accept his tainted status like Antonio can. David Hawkes's study of usury in English Renaissance literature finds that some usurers were portrayed as homosexual "primarily to connote sterility" while "even heterosexual usurers are deprived of their wives or daughters in many Renaissance plays, as if to stress the divergence between usury and the natural production of the family" (162). Such a poignant observation dovetails with this reading of Antonio as Shylock's psychosexual capitalist foil. Shylock's Leah is absent and Jessica runs away from him. Without any woman with whom to sleep or control, Shylock is as female-deprived as Antonio.

Many scholars of *Merchant* have discussed Shylock's desire to cut off a portion of Antonio's "fair flesh" as an allegorical, and, some argue, physical, circumcision. James Shapiro, in *Shakespeare and the Jews*, has well articulated the competing Christian discourses surrounding Saint Paul's references to a "circumcision of the heart" and early modern deconstructive explications of circumcision as either a literal sign or a symbolic signification of man's Covenant with God. Shapiro notes that "Shakespeare's contemporaries used circumcision as a metaphor for castration" (114). Thus, we must remember that when Shylock first outlines the bond he vaguely requires "an equal pound / Of your fair flesh, to be cut off and taken / In what part of your body pleaseth me" (1.3.161-63). It is only during the trial scene that the audience learns the flesh will come from near Antonio's heart. Historians have shown that during the Renaissance, the word "flesh" was consistently used in place of "penis," particularly in the Bible (Shapiro 122). Because Renaissance-era Christians saw circumcision not only as a physical sign of religious otherness but also as a form of emasculation, those who read the "fair flesh" as an allusion to Antonio's genitals see him coolly accepting this forced castration, since he is already comfortable with being a man who generates neither financial nor biological interest. In this regard, Antonio is opposed to the anxious Shylock who transfers his fears of being cuckolded by Leah unto others, particularly Antonio. This projection renders itself as a monomaniacal obsession with Antonio's flesh, which when considered as his external reproductive organ, casts Shylock as wanting to rob Antonio of any chance he might have to procreate if he so ever desires. Another way to understand how the "fair flesh" is a literal desire to cut off Antonio's genitalia is by way of considering Shylock's displacement of his anxieties. The fantasy-induced conflation of circumcision and castration positions Shylock as wanting to emasculate another man just as he has been. After all, Jewish men were often derided in early modern polemics as feminine because they were circumcised.

Antonio's first conversation with Shylock in the play revolves around the two's differing views on usury. After Antonio acknowledges that he will break his own rule about neither lending nor borrowing "upon advantage" (1.3.61), Shylock defensively cites a Biblical precedent for enjoying personal gain through investments in regeneration. He relates the story from Genesis 30 about Jacob's deal with Laban. While grazing Laban's sheep, Jacob proposes that he will take only the multi-colored lambs born that year as compensation for his work. Laban agrees to the proposition. Believing that offspring appear like whatever the mother was looking at during the moment of conception, Jacob strikes the ground with multicolored branches. His plan is a success and, according to Shylock, the "parti-colored lambs" were Jacob's "way to thrive, and he was blest; / And thrift is blessing if men steal it not" (1.3.96-98). Several scholars of the play have commented on Shylock's choice for Biblical support and his sophistical attempts to legitimize usury. Antonio picks up on Shylock's exploitive interpretation of this parable with his rebuttal:

> This was a venture, sir, that Jacob served for,
> A thing not in his power to bring to pass,
> But swayed and fashioned by the hand of heaven.
> Was this inserted to make interest good?
> Or is your gold and silver ewes and rams? (1.3.99-103)

Antonio claims that Jacob was working through Heavenly providence and that this story is a faulty rationalization for Shylock's autonomous decision to practice usury. Antonio deflates Shylock's conflation of flesh and money by highlighting the difference between "gold and silver" and "ewes and rams." This contrast hews closely to the popular support limitations against usury enjoyed in the Medieval and early modern eras. Shylock ignores the obvious disparity (coins are not livestock) by sarcastically denying his ability to answer Antonio's questions: "I cannot tell; I make it breed as fast" (1.3.104). Of course, money cannot breed itself. Only life can. David Hawkes asserts that Shylock's cynical aside presents "a new kind of hermeneutic, one that bestows determining power on the image" (89). Shylock's transference of his anxieties to the marketplace signifies the limits of such representation. Antonio highlights the absurdity of Shylock's employment of the Old Testament parable, but Shylock cannot, or refuses to, acknowledge that the spirit and letter of genuine biological reproduction is incommensurable and consequently antithetical to financial investments and returns. Although I do not argue that images of usury are necessarily functioning metonymically as symbols of cuckoldry, the link between the unnaturalness of lending money at interest and illicit sexual relationship is common. Morris Tilley's seminal work on proverbs in sixteenth- and seventeenth-century England showcases just such a link with the following Renaissance-era example: "An usurer is one that puts his money to the unnatural act of regeneration, and the scrivener is his bawd" (694, U28).

In the same vein of Antonio's effort to get Shylock to acknowledge this difference, Medieval positions on usury, which shaped early modern unease with the practice even when it was legalized and taken out of the jurisdiction of Church Courts, were influenced by Aristotle's dictum in Book 1, Chapter 10 of *Politics*, explaining why usury is the most unnatural form of acquisition. Aristotle begins his discussion of lending money at interest by noting that the natural form of acquisition stems from flora and fauna since it is "the business of nature to furnish subsistence for each being brought into the world" as this is "shown by the fact that the offspring of animals always gets nourishment from the residuum of the matter that gives it birth" (28). Aristotle transitions into a discussion of retail trade and household management as forms through which individuals acquire goods and, more importantly, material for subsistence. By placing censure on simple retail trade because "the gain in which it results is not naturally made [from plants and animals], but is made at the expense of other men" (28), Aristotle does not hesitate to offer a stern reprimand of those who lend money at interest. In fact, his language is stark and unbending:

> The trade of petty usurer is hated most, and with most reason: it makes a profit from currency itself, instead of making it from the process [i.e. of exchange] which currency was meant to serve. Currency came into existence merely as a means of exchange; usury tries to make it increase [as thought it were an end in itself]. This is the reason why usury is called by the word we commonly use [the word *tokos*, which in Greek also means "breed" or "offspring"]; for as the offspring resembles its parent, so the interest bred by money is like the principal which breeds it, and it may be called "currency the son of currency." Hence we can understand why, of all modes of acquisition, usury is the most unnatural. (29)

Such conceptions have their origin in what Diana Wood calls "the sterility doctrine." Because the composition of money as a precious metal allowed it to be seen as a store of wealth, it was this specific "metal content which gave rise to the very important idea of the sterility of money" (84). This sterility doctrine fueled the denunciation of usury throughout Classical and Medieval times. This classical interpretation of usury's deviance clearly hinges on ideas of biological reproduction. Children should not be clones of their parents. Although the terms breeding, usury, propagation, and reproduction are discrete they are often used interchangeably. As such, there are clear parallels between Aristotle's language and that of Antonio when he asks Shylock ". . . For when did friendship take / A breed for barren metal of his friend?" (1.3.130-31) The differences between these terms are all the more fluid in the mind of a paranoid character such as Shylock. Unfortunately, Shylock's chaotic view of what can and cannot breed is marred by his fears over who has and has not begotten Jessica.

This heated exchange between Antonio and Shylock possesses more undercurrents relating to the theme of marital duplicity. Shylock's first reference to Jacob notes the influence his mother had in his success:

"When Jacob grazed his Uncle Laban's sheep – / This Jacob from our holy Abram was / (As his wise mother wrought in his behalf) / The third possessor; ay, he was the third –" (1.3.79-82). According to Genesis 27, Jacob's mother, Rebecca, mislead her husband, Isaac, into making Jacob his heir. Hence, the idea of a wife's deceiving her husband over her child is introduced into the play before any of the aforementioned cuckoldry references.

Shell notes how Shylock confuses himself with Jacob since the First Folio edition of the play reads, "This Jacob from our holy Abram was / As his wise mother wrought in his behalf, / The third possessor; I, he was the third" rather than the more commonly printed version of "ay, he was the third" (52). Shylock pauses and corrects himself about his sacred connection. Shell's astute observation allows us to follow this link and remember that Leah, Rachel's sister and the woman for whom Jacob was husbanding the ewes, is also the name of Shylock's former wife. Hence, Shylock's desire to generate money in lieu of his ability to be certain about having sired Jessica gains more traction. Shylock's bastardization of language and meaning in respect to his interpretation of Jacob's story finds the verbal usury working within his larger, albeit latent, psychosexual confusion between financial generation and sexual reproduction.

Kenneth Gross expands on W. H. Auden's explication of the play's focus on money as "a symbol of man's dependence on the world" to assert that in the play's landscape, "money ideally should be a means of social glue, a vehicle, for some, of love" (46). Such an amalgamation of the tangible and the abstract has the potential to corrupt an individual's perspective of their relationships with others. Shylock's inability to employ money as a way to garner respect and friendship has already failed miserably. If one keeps in mind that Thomas Wilson's 1572 *Discourse Upon Usury* argues that "God ordeyned lending for maintenaunce of amitye, and declaration of love, betwixt man and man: wheras now lending is used for private benefit and oppression, and so no charitie is used at all, as thoughe there were no God to judge, nor lyfe to come" (N7r), Shylock's lending of money has in fact created nothing if not more acrimony and bitterness between him and Venice's mercantile community. He has fulfilled the stereotype of Jewish usurers as godless and uncharitable.

When we consider that Shylock has been deprived of respect from the Christian community, the security of having fathered his daughter, and, ultimately, the power to arrange Jessica's marriage, we can understand some of the integral components that fuel his desire to exact interest *and* flesh from his oppressors in the name of the love he is denied. Facing an unsympathetic court, Shylock ardently insists on pleasing his "humor" (4.1.44) and to "have" (4.1.101, 104) his "bond" (4.1.213). Is the "bond" Shylock calls for simply used in the legal sense to refer to a deed? The first recorded usage of this term in the English language dates only to 1592 according to the Oxford English Dictionary. Or might he employ a second valence for the term? One which refers to a covenant between two or more persons and has an etymologic origin as early as the 1300s? Shylock's estrangement from society, coupled with his wifelessness and insecurity about being Jessica's father, leave him hopelessly hopeful about forming intimate ties with the Christian majority. With Jessica now converting to Christianity, he has been robbed of any pretense of familial allegiances and ties. After all, the initial conversation between Shylock and Antonio shows the former wanting to "be friends" and "have" the "love" of the merchant (1.3.149) even in the face of Antonio's admission that he will spit on and spurn Shylock once again. After such a rebuff, Shylock details the terms of his "bond . . . in a merry sport" (1.3.157).

Shylock's fixation on Antonio's flesh amounts to a monomania worthy of the sadistic protagonists of Edgar Allan Poe's "Berenice" and "The Tell-Tale Heart." Even when Bassanio offers Shylock six thousand ducats for the three thousand the bond calls for, he insists on Antonio's flesh: "Were in six parts and every part a ducat, / I would not draw them; I would have my bond" (4.1.87-88). His singular focus on the merchant's body underscores his desire to extract flesh, even a useless part, in his manic quest to engender respect and vitiate by embarrassment. Hence, Antonio's flesh is a crossroads of many of the play's anxieties as it relates to fears about usury, interracial socializing, homoerotic relationships, and uncertainty about paternal status. Drew Daniel's excellent examination of Antonio's masochist impulses complements such a reading of Shylock in the way that he employs Richard Halpern as a model "for thinking through overdetermination that is not a lateral profusion of equally likely causes but a bottleneck in which multiple components of lived social subjection equally in play (to norms of sexuality, to economic practices, to civil laws) are routed through an organizing trait whose particular qualities allow suspension between conflicting, mutually incompatible rationales" (217). The lack of a thoroughly organized epistemological understanding of Shylock's motivations underscores the need for closely reading text, context, and subtext to recognize how characters such as Shylock and Antonio function within early modern appreciations of money, amity, sexuality, and paternity. Just as Antonio's melancholia can be attributed to repressed sexual desires, Shylock's insistence on the merchant's flesh calls attention to misgivings about his own sexual potential.

Secondary Witnesses: Jessica and Lancelot

Jessica's ethnically exogamous elopement is not one bereft of financial concerns. She absconds with Shylock's wealth in order to supply her own dowry to the gentile Lorenzo. After Jessica gilds herself with more ducats, Gratiano remarks that she is "a gentle and no Jew" (2.6.53). Having furnished herself with a dowry, Jessica begins the conversion process from Jew to Christian. Barren metal makes way for marriage and, one assumes, reproduction. Because this scene conflates love and money as key connections between Jessica and Lorenzo, we can see that the psychosexual amalgamation of financial and biological propagation are closely linked not only in Shylock's mind but also in the world view of many characters.

Jessica's desire to escape the joyless Shylock is understandable. He is portrayed as a curmudgeon and spoilsport who, before he leaves the house to meet with the Christians in 2.5, warns Jessica to lock the house's doors and windows and ignore the sounds of music on the street so that ". . . not the sound of shallow fopp'ry enter / My sober house" (2.5.36-37). Shylock's fear of Jessica and his household being penetrated by Christians is mirrored in his warnings to lock up the house. Adelman argues that when Shylock's exhorts Jessica to close off the house's openings he embodies the "emphatically coded masculine" presence "in a world that identified the closed body with the masculine body" (131). Shylock wants to create a façade and reality of impenetrability when it comes to his home, his possessions, and his family. A fear that another man has penetrated his wife would underscore and heighten the symbolic importance of his final advice for enclosing Jessica within his home, as it once again connects bodily safety with financial terms: "Do as I bid you. Shut doors after you. / Fast bind, fast find– / A proverb never stale in thrifty mind" (2.4.54-56).

James Shapiro's *Shakespeare and the Jews*, which is indispensable to studies of *Merchant*, offers a provocative read of Jessica's Jewish signifiers that invites the common reading of Shylock as her biological father. Shapiro notes that in place of the male marker of Judaism, circumcision, Jewish women in fifteenth-century northern Italy wore earrings as a sign of their faith. He admits that this practice was short-lived and not widespread, but offers the prospect that it finds its echo in *Merchant* when Shylock finds out about Jessica's elopement and cries "I would my daughter were dead at my foot, and the jewels in her ear" (3.1.86-87). Shapiro claims that "Shylock fantasizes that his converted daughter returns, and through her earrings is reinscribed at last as a circumcised Jewess" (120). Firstly, we must remember that this is a report of Shylock's reaction and not a verbatim transcript. Secondly, one can envision another reading of this fantasy. If we are to take Solanio's report of Shylock's reaction as gospel, then his employment of "would," the subjunctive form of "will," underscores the fantasy fulfillment he desires. He wishes for his daughter's death. He wishes for his wife's fidelity so that Jessica might be a full-blooded Jew.

Remembering Shylock's employment of Jacob as a model for his business practices, Bernard Grebanier astutely notes in *The Truth About Shylock* that the usurer gets his comeuppance when praising Jacob since Jessica's jewel-riddled elopement mirrors Rachel's stealing of her father's images when she and Jacob run away in Genesis 31: "the sentiment is that the girl was appropriating her dowry as she fled in the welcome arms of matrimony . . . are we not expected to be lenient toward them when the absconder is a character with whom we sympathize?" (242). Several scholars and even casual viewers of the play notice an exponential increase in Shylock's desire to cut off Antonio's flesh after Jessica has eloped. The correlation between the hurt he experiences and the amount of pain he wants to enact on others is clear.

Jessica's arrival at Belmont is caustically acknowledged by Gratiano who marks her as Lorenzo's "infidel" (3.2.223). Jessica stays on the periphery of the scene, which revolves around news of Antonio's imminent trial, save for when she references Shylock:

> When I was with him, I have heard him swear
> To Tubal and Chus, his countrymen,
> That he would rather have Antonio's flesh
> Than twenty times the value of the sum
> That he did owe him. And I know, my lord,
> If law, authority, and power deny not,
> It will go hard with poor Antonio. (3.2.296-302)

Sensing her alienation from the Christian majority in Belmont, Jessica once again attempts to distance herself from Shylock by citing Tubal and Chus as *his* countrymen rather than individuals with whom she would be related to by religious, racial, or blood ties. Despite her act of distancing herself from Shylock, Portia does not engage with Jessica but rather turns to Bassanio and asks if the letter is in reference to his friend. One wonders how the actor portraying Jessica might react: steady interest in Antonio's plight or despondence that she has not been fully welcomed by the mistress of Belmont. In fact, Bassanio welcomes only Lorenzo and Salerio by name (3.2.225), to which Portia does in kind (3.2.231).

Jessica's confidante, Lancelot, as already discussed, is an indelible element in this analysis of *Merchant*. The scene wherein Lancelot comes upon his father, Old Gobbo, is interpreted by many as a distracting one that is sometimes cut from productions of the play (C. Edelman 130). Yet this father-son relationship, the only one in the comedy, acts as a foil to the father-daughter relationships of the drama. The clown's erratic prose soliloquy finds him vacillating between staying with or leaving Shylock. He quotes his conscience and the "fiend" at his side, allowing the audience a glimpse into his complex-in-the-style-of-a-funhouse mind. Before his father enters, he disparages him by hinting that he was not "honest" because he "smack[ed]" and "had a kind of taste" for lechery (2.2.15-19). Given his father's penchant for immorality, he would rather be known as "an honest woman's son" (2.2.16). Like Jessica, he wants to disown his father, coincidentally enough, in the same scene where he contemplates quitting Jessica's father. Unlike Jessica, Lancelot is bemused and perhaps charmed by his father's dotage as well as his visual impairment and accepts his return as a father as a prodigal one.

This reunion occurs only after Lancelot has tested Gobbo, whom he recognizes as his "true begotten father" (2.2.34-35). The clown's usage of "begotten" anticipates his ambiguous employment of "get"/ "got" when he speaks with Jessica in the subsequent scene and in 3.5. Here we see the unmistakable recognition of "begotten" being utilized to mark a biological fathering. Gobbo is unaware that he speaks of Lancelot about Lancelot. The clown asks "Do you know me, father?" (2.2.67) and repeats the same call for recognition when his father denies knowing him, "Do you not know me, father?" (2.2.71). Gobbo's literal blindness prefigures the audience's vision of Shylock's metaphorical blindness in respect to Jessica's authentic parentage. Lancelot reverses a popular proverb and tells Gobbo that "It is a wise father that knows his own child" (2.2.74-75) before he sweetly kneels in front of his father and asks for his blessing. What can initially be read as one of Lancelot's malapropisms becomes poignant in light of Shylock and Jessica's ambiguous biological link. The play's continual attacks on Shylock meshes with an interpretation that reads this line as another jab at the Jewish character's foolishness with regard to his status as cuckolded man who has no biological child to speak of. This scene immediately precedes Lancelot's talk with Jessica, thus paternity is fresh on his mind in Act 2.

It is once again Adelman who comes nearest to exploring Leah's possible betrayal when discussing the theme of religious and racial conversion in respect to Lancelot and Jessica's conversation during the play's second act. Adelman observes that "Lancelot's solution can save her only by invoking the infidelity of her mother. The end of *Merchant* is full of cuckoldry jokes and thus of a barely concealed anxiety about the mother's place in the making of children" (67). The link between children and their mother is always more secure than that with their father. Jessica can be assured that Leah is her mother just as Lancelot is safe in assuming that Margery is his mother. Each child's identity is staked through the matrilineal line and whatever sexual relations the mother had with men. Lancelot publicly accepts Gobbo as his father after they have both identified Margery as their tie. Gobbo's blindness is a literal opposition to the metaphorical sightlessness of Shylock in respect to Jessica's paternity.

Final Verdict

As the play reaches its conclusions in luxurious Belmont, Shakespeare does not demonize wealth or capital. Portia and Bassanio inherit her patrimony. The comedy's reprimands do not go after such a normative succession of wealth, but rather Shylock's unnatural attempt to breed barren metal in an attempt to recover from Leah's illicit but natural betrayal. Lorenzo and Jessica's marriage will be blessed with inheritance once Shylock dies, but this has yet to occur by the end of play. Jessica's scant lines in the final scene mark her as an outsider. Her verses with Lorenzo approach romantic banter but are rife with words of betrayal and cruelty. We wonder whether her conversions as a racial and religious Other will be successful even through the conduit of a love-based marriage and a monetary windfall. Love and money are conflated in this dizzying, mercurial play that ostensibly functions as a comedy but enters such dark territory in respect to religious prejudice, racism, and death that attempts to meld financial gain and natural love are deflated, no more so than in Shylock's pitiable attempt to utilize usury as a way to erase the shame he experiences as a cuckold and an outcast.

Bibliography

Achinstein, Sharon. "John Foxe and the Jews." *Renaissance Quarterly*. 54.1 (Spring 2001): 86-120. Print.

Adelman, Janet. *Blood Relations: Christian and Jew in The Merchant of Venice*. Chicago: University of Chicago Press, 2008. Print.

Aristotle. *The Politics of Aristotle*. Trans. and Ed. Ernest Barker. Oxford: Clarendon Press, 1946. Print.

Daniel, Drew. "'Let me have judgment, and the Jew his will': Melancholy Epistemology and Masochistic Fantasy in *The Merchant of Venice.*" *Shakespeare Quarterly.* 61.2 (Summer 2010): 206-34. Print.

Edelman, Charles. *Shakespeare in Production: The Merchant of Venice.* Cambridge: Cambridge University Press, 2003. Print.

Edelman, Lee. *No Future: Queer Theory and the Death Drive.* Durham, NC: Duke University Press, 2004. Print.

Grebanier, Bernard. *The Truth About Shylock.* New York: Random House, 1962. Print.

Gross, Kenneth. *Shylock is Shakespeare.* Chicago: University of Chicago Press, 2006. Print.

Grunberger, Richard. *The 12-Year Reich: A Social History of Nazi German 1933-1945.* New York: Da Capo Press, 1971. Print.

Hawkes, David. *The Culture of Usury in Renaissance England.* New York: Palgrave Macmillan, 2010. Print.

Huber, Raphael M. *St. Anthony of Padua: Doctor of the Church Universal.* Milwaukee: Bruce Publishing Company, 1948. Print.

Kaplan, M. Lindsay. "Medieval Constructions of Jewish Race and Gender in *The Merchant of Venice.*" *Shakespeare Quarterly.* 58.1 (Spring 2007): 1-30. Print.

Nelson, Benjamin N. *The Idea of Usury: From Tribal Brotherhood to Universal Otherhood.* Princeton: Princeton University Press, 1949. Print.

Purchas, Samuel. *Purchas his Pilgrimage; Or Relations of the World and the Religions Observed in All Ages and Places Discovered, from the Creation Unto this Present.* London. Printed by William Stansby for Henry Fetherstone. 1617. Print.

Shakespeare, William. *The Merchant of Venice.* Folger Shakespeare Library Edition. New York: Simon & Schuster, 1992. Print.

Shatzmiller, Joseph. *Shylock Reconsidered: Jews, Moneylending, and Medieval Society.* Berkeley: University of California Press, 1990. Print.

Shell, Marc. *Money, Language, and Thought: Literary and Philosophical Economies from the Medieval to the Modern Era.* Berkeley: University of California Press, 1982. Print.

Tilley, Morris Palmer. *A Dictionary of the Proverbs in England in the Sixteenth and Seventeenth Centuries: A Collection of the Proverbs Founds in English Literature and the Dictionaries of the Period.* Ann Arbor, MI: University of Michigan Press, 1950. Print.

Wilson, Thomas. *A Discourse Upon Usury.* London, 1572. Print.

Wood, Diana. *Medieval Economic Thought*. Cambridge: Cambridge University Press, 2002. Print.

"HOW EVERY FOOL CAN PLAY UPON THE WORD": ALLEGORIES OF READING IN *THE MERCHANT OF VENICE* AND *PERICLES*

JAMES NEWLIN

In Memory of Professor James Paxson

In the introductory chapter to *Allegories of Reading*, Paul de Man observes that literary formalism is never "allowed to come into being without seeming reductive" (4). For formalists, "meaning" is alternately understood as an external reference applied interpretatively to various "internal," self-reflexive features of the text or those formal features themselves are understood as "external trappings" enclosing "literary meaning and content" (4). Such a polarity of inside and outside is arbitrary, and any reading blind to the essentially figural nature of language itself will strive vainly to reconcile form and meaning:

> The attraction of reconciliation is the elective breeding-ground of false models and metaphors; it accounts for the metaphorical model of literature as a kind of box that separates an inside from an outside, and the reader or critic as the person who opens the lid in order to release in the open what was secreted but inaccessible inside. It matters little whether we call the inside of the box the content or the form, the outside the meaning or the appearance. The recurrent debate opposing intrinsic to extrinsic criticism stands under the aegis of an inside/outside metaphor that is never being seriously questioned. (5)

The proposed "serious questioning" is a never-ending interrogation. Every narrative is "primarily the allegory of its own reading," and those allegories "narrate[] the impossibility of reading" (76-77). Not only is any given reading an aporetic confrontation with incompatible meanings that can never be completely reconciled or distinguished, but any "finished" critical reading is itself a new text to be read. No text, then, can be "closed off by a final reading" (205).

It may seem off-putting to begin with Paul de Man in an essay that proposes to read *The Merchant of Venice* and *Pericles*. Like those plays, de Man's writings have also faced charges of anti-Semitism and collaboration. Yet de Man's challenge of "box"-models of interpretation is directly relevant for a play revolving around the reading and opening of three caskets. This central scene also resonates in the riddle scene that opens *Pericles*, where Antiochus's silent, nameless daughter is identified as both readable ("her face the book of praises") (1.1.15) and a casket ("were not this glorious casket stored with ill") (1.1.78).[1]

Of course, readers have long recognized the influence of a more doctrinal understanding of allegory in *The Merchant of Venice*. Barbara Lewalski, following Nevill Coghill's identification of the influence of the "Parliament of Heaven" tradition upon the play, finds patterns in *Merchant*'s "various dimensions of allegorical significance" that parallel Dante's four levels of allegorical meaning (328). This structure enables a reading that equates Bassanio with the "Love of God," Antonio with a (nearly) crucified Christ, and the forced conversion of Shylock as a prefiguration of the "final, pre-millennial conversion" of *all* Jews (334).

The concept of prefiguration is essential to understanding the thematic concerns of *Merchant* and *Pericles*. It also informs the plays' formal structures, which rely heavily on foreshadowing and repetition. Consider Erich Auerbach's distincton between figural and allegorical interpretation in the early Christian tradition: "Since in figural interpretation one thing stands for another, since one thing represents and signifies the other, figural interpretation is 'allegorical' in the widest sense. But it differs from most of the allegorical forms known to us by the historicity both of the sign and what it signifies" (54). The figures of the Old Testament are fulfilled in the New Testament; for, say, Tertullian, "*figura* is something real and historical which announces something else that is also real and historical" (Auerbach 29). For example, Joshua and Moses may each prefigure Jesus. Yet the figural tradition also involves interpretations of the concrete, historical event as a signifier of a more abstract concept at an allegorical or ethical level. Such figures can even prefigure details of the Last Judgment at an anagogical level. In Auerbach's view, this means that the medieval world developed an increasingly intangible understanding of history, where all of history—not just the events detailed in the Old Testament—"remains open and questionable, [and] points to something still concealed" (58).

---

[1] All citations from Shakespeare are taken from the Arden Third Series.

Such an understanding of scripture clearly informs *Merchant*, where a character may be read as "a second Daniel" (4.1.336). But while we need to distinguish between the allegorical method of a Tertullian versus that of a de Man, the view of history as something that is both "open" and "concealing" is not unrelated from de Man's later claims about the unceasing deconstruction performed by every narrative. With special attention to the depiction of biblical exegesis in Act 1 of *Merchant* and the return to those tropes in the casket scenes, I argue that Shakespeare depicts a similar transition from the typological allegory to something like the de Manian, metatextual understanding of reading itself as allegorical. Then, turning to *Pericles*, I read the later play as a kind of fulfillment of the earlier play's prefiguration. The two plays share many similarities at the plot-level: the familiar tropes of shipwrecks and recognition scenes, the association of women with "caskets," the overarching concerns with the exchange of women by their fathers, often through elaborate and arbitrary ceremonies involving interpretative reading, and the thematic obsession with virginity. But I am mostly concerned with reading the later play as a clarification of the concerns about reading that appear (or are allegorized) in the earlier one. We can take Gower's comments on authorship and reading as not only a manual of sorts for reading *Pericles*, but a continuation of the earlier play, so that together they frame an allegory of reading *any* of his plays.

Meanings and Readings Changed and Exchanged in *The Merchant of Venice*

In his first aside to the audience, Shylock informs us that he hates Antonio "for he is a Christian; / But more" for lending money without interest (1.3.38-9). These twin reasons are grouped into a single "ancient grudge" (1.3.43) that confuses more than equates Shylock's cultural and personal animus. The relation between the ancient grudge of Jew and Christian and the ancient grudge of Shylock and Antonio is further conflated in the depiction of biblical exegesis:

ANTONIO.   And what of [Jacob], did he take interest?
JEW.   No, not take "interest", not as you would say
                 Directly "interest", Mark what Jacob did:
                 When Laban and himself were compromised
                 That all the eanlings which were streaked and pied
                 Should fall as Jacob's hire, the ewes, being rank,
                 In end of autumn turned to the rams;
                 And when the work of generation was

> Between these woolly breeders in the act,
> The skilful shepherd peeled me certain wands,
> And, in the doing of the deed of kind,
> He stuck them up before the fulsome ewes,
> Who, then conceiving, did in eaning time
> Fall parti-coloured lambs, and those were Jacob's.
> This was a way to thrive, and he was blest:
> And thrift in blessing, if men steal it not.

ANTONIO.   This was a venture, sir, that Jacob served for,

> A thing not in his power to bring to pass,
> But swayed and fashioned by the hand of heaven.
> Was this inserted to make interest good?
> Or is your gold and silver ewes and rams? (1.3.71-91)

In *The Merchant of Venice*, meaning and explanation are nearly always described in possessive terms. Just one scene earlier, Nerissa explains that the "lottery that [Portia's father] hath devised in these three chests of gold, silver and lead, whereof who chooses his meaning chooses you" (1.2.28-29). Later, Antonio and Shylock will each qualify their disagreement as a conflict of one another's reasons: "what's his reason? I am a Jew" (3.1.52-3), "His reason well I know: I oft delivered from his forfeitures" (3.3.20-22), and so forth. This pattern of assigning blame by associating it with the other's (presumably wrong) "reason" is broken by Shylock's frenzied confession that "there is no firm reason to be rendered" (4.1.42) other than his own, individual "humour" (4.1.52). Meaning is quite literally relative in the play. Because interpretation is personalized, like property, the father's meaning can be equated with his daughter and exchanged like his daughter.

But just as daughters are exchanged by fathers to suitors, it is the goal of interpretation to transfer one's meaning to another. If Shylock's extended metaphor is inexact (the eanlings do not "directly" correspond to interest), he claims that is only because Antonio "would [not] say / Directly interest." The facts—that, following the "work of generation" and the "doing of the deed of kind," a number of "parti-coloured lambs" were born and claimed by Jacob—are not in dispute. But the meaning of the events—attributing the credit of all of these news lambs to either a "skilful shepherd" or the "hand of heaven"—*are* in dispute, because they belong entirely to the individual. Shylock's individual interpretation also claims cultural possession over the narrative and its interpretation, which fittingly follows the parable's opening claim to account for the "third possessor" (1.3.69) from "our holy Abram" (1.3.67).[2]

In terms familiar by now, Antonio qualifies Shylock's entire rhetorical strategy as an *insertion*: "Was this inserted to make interest good?" The notes in the Arden gloss lines 90 and 91 as Antonio "press[ing] further the issue of the Jew's *reading* of Scripture" (212 n. 90, Arden's emphasis) and his "questioning the Jew's *allegorical* interpretation of Scripture" (212 n. 91, Arden's emphasis). That Antonio is disputing Shylock's interpretative strategy seems relatively clear. What is interesting is that the model of allegory is not one of levels—like the Dantesque levels of literal, allegorical, moral, or anagogical—but of enclosure and penetration, like the formalist "box"-model. Though I suspect that Shylock and Antonio make an implied distinction, the "box"-model of reading can certainly coexist with the levels-model of religious allegory. Auerbach repeatedly associates the allegorical or figural meaning of an image with a "deeper meaning" (35).[3] But "deeper" meaning is not all that is found within the "box" of the biblical form; nefarious meanings may be secreted (to borrow de Man's curious phrasing) within it as well.

The questions posed in *Merchant* about reading regard how texts move and how readers move with them. Readers may look *in* to texts for deeper meanings, but the figural model also moves those meanings forward and backward. Shylock's liberties with interpretation include equating Jacob's trickery with the message "thrift is blessing, if men steal it not," including his own figure within the frame of the past events, and by coyly deferring any closed meaning ("I cannot tell") (1.3.92). By rereading Old Testament scriptures figurally, Shylock appears to be appropriating or even parodying

---

[2] A note in the Arden informs that line 80's "peeled me" is a use of the "ethical dative *me*," used to "call attention to the Jew himself, who is the real focus of this narrative" (211 n.80). But why does Shylock, who may or may not be the "real focus" of an anagogical or allegorical level of narrative, enter the *literal* level of his narrative? Shylock seems to me to be entering the frame of his narrative in order to leave something like his signature behind; if that signature is in the dative case, it indicates that the signer received a kind of gift, a new possession. At any rate, if Shylock attempts to "sign" the Jacob story, he may be identifying himself with Jacob, the "trickster," as much as asserting a kind of cultural ownership over the Old Testament. Inadvertently, this identification prefigures how he will be tricked during the trial scene (see Colley). The trial scene does not end with Shylock's signature, only the *promise* of the signature ("Send the deed after me / And I will sign it") (4.1.392-3).

[3] See also passages on 36, 45, 47, 73.

a specifically *Christian* mode of allegory.[4] What is more, this entire depiction of interpreting biblical prefiguration is itself a prefiguration of his famous promise "the villainy you teach me I will execute" (3.1.64-5). Shylock has already been taught how to read like a Christian, and reading that way can be a kind of villainy.

Antonio characterizes this reading as villainy, but he does so with what seems like a degree of discomfort. After witnessing Shylock's mastery of the trope of inside/outside and figural reading, Antonio seems to shift the trope. In an aside to Bassanio, a secreting from Shylock, Antonio tweaks the familiar allegorical model:

> ANTONIO [aside].   Mark you this, Bassanio,
> The devil can cite Scripture for his purpose.
> An evil soul producing holy witness
> Is like a villain with a smiling cheek,
> A goodly apple, rotten at the heart.
> O, what a goodly outside falsehood hath! (1.3.93-98)

The concern for the interpretation of the text's inside has now, almost metonymically, shifted to a concern for the interpreter's inside. And if that shift is "almost" metonymic, it is towards language that is "almost" metaphorical. Comparing an "evil soul" to a "villain" may, strictly speaking, be an act of synecdoche, where the evil soul is a part of the villain. If so, this shift may mark where *Merchant of Venice* begins to transition from a doctrinal, open-ended view of interpretation where the difference between textuality and history becomes increasingly negligible (as described by Auerbach) to a concern with the aporetic quality of language itself (as described by de Man). Synecdoche is, for de Man, a "borderline figure[]that create[s] an ambivalent zone between metaphor and metonymy ... creat[ing] the illusion of a synthesis by totalization" (63 n.8). The use of "like" in line 96 all but announces that the line will finish with a metaphorical construction, an unexpected "thing" standing for another as in any allegory of figural equation. Instead, Antonio associates the evil soul reading scripture with something that is not quite a metaphorical construction and not quite an equivalence: an evil soul is a part of and also a kind of a villain, but quoting scripture is not necessarily like smiling. The illusion of totalization here—this is what *all* evil souls are like—hinges on a confusion of tropes and terms.

---

[4] For an alternate reading of this passage, see Lupton, who identifies Shylock's speech as a dramatization of "a specifically Jewish hermeneutics" (124).

This kind of tropological confusion is a recurring feature for Antonio's character. Comparing an evil soul to a villain may be more accurately identified as a failed metaphor than as a synecdoche or metonym. For instance, Antonio earlier held "the world but as the world, Gratiano, / A stage where every man must play a part" (1.1.77-8). Comparing the world to the stage is certainly commonplace, but what is more interesting is the superfluity of the construction: the world is like the world, and also a stage. This verbal tic reappears in the passage excerpted above, where the stutter-like quality of the line detailing the "goodly apple" lacks a conjunction, so the image feels unnecessary (i.e. an evil soul is like a villain, an apple). The tic illuminates the contradictory quality of Antonio's logic of inside/outside. The problem of "the devil" (Shylock) reading scripture is that the devil is like an evil soul who will corrupt the inside of the scripture by placing, rather than finding, meanings there. This is like a villain who is smiling, like an alluring apple, or like virtually *anything* with a goodly outside. But Shylock is not comparable to an alluring apple with a rotten core; he does not have a "goodly outside" to begin with. Otherwise, why would Antonio spit upon Shylock?

Antonio's meaning is relatively clear: Shylock is manipulating his text. But to make that point clearly would be to decry citing beyond the "outside" of the text, the very process that makes the Jewish text a Christian text. Antonio will not admit that Shylock's text is an essentially *Jewish* text; he finds a Jew recounting the story of Jacob as suspicious as the Devil citing scripture. Shakespeare appears to suggest that the elastic meanings of figural interpretations of scripture easily beget an understanding of the "transformational" quality of *all* tropes (de Man 63 n.8). Such a negligibility of tropes, demonstrated through a quick confusion of them, is the "deeper" comment of this passage. It is one of those powerful, wonderful instances where Shakespeare writes incredibly well by appearing to write quite badly. Antonio wants to remain in possession of scripture as a Christian, yet that is precisely when the word starts getting away from him.

Antonio's struggle to make a clear meaning rhetorically clear is the inverse of his own rhetorical image: a rotten outside of superfluous images and confused tropes enclosing a goodly center. In this respect, we find that the opposite of Antonio is not Shylock (as Lewalski might propose) or Bassanio (as Sarah Kofman argues), but rather Lancelet, who understands that the "ambivalent zones" of language are the place for *play*:

> CLOWN.   It is much that the Moor should be more than reason; but if
> she be less than an honest woman, she is indeed more than I took her for.

LORENZO. How every fool can play upon the word. I think the best
grace of wit will shortly turn into silence. (3.5.37-40)

Like Antonio's use of "goodly," the passage rings with repetition. Yet
Lancelet's repetitions are puns, so their repetition is more traditionally,
aesthetically pleasing. Where Antonio's aside seemed to say too much
with the extraneous image of the apple, Lancelet seems to exclude
necessary adjectives: "it is much" what?

Though the issue at hand is quantification—how much *more* of the
Moor is there? *Another* Moor?—Lancelet plays with language's unique
powers of qualification. To be "less" than something should not be
evidence of being "more" than something else, since by definition the
second term would also have to be "less" than the initial one. But
language, "the word," is the exclusive realm where what is "more than
reason" can be expressed and one person's individual reason or meaning
can be asserted as *the* reason or meaning. What Lancelet originally "took"
the Moor for was the opposite of honest, rather than simply less than
honest.[5] Here the play upon the word that accounts for the play's
allegories of reading clarifies not just that the meanings of the given
allegories are personal, and therefore potentially arbitrary or fraudulent,
but that the form of allegory itself may be thoroughly deceptive as well.
The lesson we are to learn from Lancelet about deception and the word
was prefigured earlier by his parody of Jacob's deception of his father
Isaac in 2.2. Lancelet's transition from biblical allegory to a more
deconstructive play upon the word parallels Antonio's similar move from
familiar, biblical exegesis to tropological confusion (though Lancelet
understood that even typological allegories should be "played"). But it
also resembles a Shakespearean reunion or recognition scene, like those
seen in *Lear* and *Pericles*. The scene between Lancelet and his own father
seems to prefigure a reunion between Shylock and Jessica. But that scene
never arrives.[6]

This recurring pattern of transitioning from religious allegory to a more
secular attention to the tropes and aporias of language accounts for the
similarities between Antonio's aside to Bassanio in 1.3 and the latter's
solving of the riddle in Belmont:

---

[5] The Moor is comparable to the similarly impregnated Kate Keepdown, only
existing in the language of the play, and never the staging. See Adelman 87.
[6] See "Leaving the Jew's House" (38-65) in Adelman's *Blood Relations* for a
brilliant reading of Lancelet.

BASSANIO.   So may the outward shows be least themselves,
            The world is still deceived with ornament.
            In law, what plea so tainted and corrupt,
            But being seasoned with a generous voice,
            Obscures the show of evil? In religious,
            What damned error but some sober brow
            Will bless it and approve it with a text,
            Hiding the grossness with fair ornament? (3.2.73-80)

The passage clearly invokes Antonio's skepticism about goodly outsides and scripture cited for the devil's purposes, thus retroactively making Antonio's warning a prefiguration of the casket scene. Again, we find that the inner subject matter (discussions of religious allegory) determines the outer, formalist narrative structure (allegorical prefiguration). But the reconciliation of inner and outer, of form and meaning, is no less dangerous for characters in *The Merchant of Venice* than it is for those formalists critiqued by de Man. Bassanio solves the riddle not through any particularly special insight into Portia's inner worth, but by equating the "grossness of fair ornament" with "the word": "in a word, / The seeming truth, which cunning times put on / To entrap the wisest" (3.2.99-101). Any allegory, unless it is a failed metaphor like holding the world but as the world, is false: it insists two things that are not alike are like one another. If the riddle of the caskets is like reading, it is like deceiving and being deceived.

Unlike Morocco and Arragon, Bassanio is able to solve the riddle of the caskets because he understands that he is being deceived. Bassanio is not Paul de Man; he is not interested in querying how tropes and figures are used or understood. His first descriptions of Portia associate "her sunny locks" with "a golden fleece" (1.1.169-70). After the riddle is solved, Portia, Nerissa, and Jessica are all compared to an oddly singular "fleece" claimed by three Jasons (3.2.240). While escaping Shylock's house, Jessica "gild[s]" herself (2.6.50), equating her body with Shylock's gold well before Salanio and Salarino can chastise Shylock for the same "confused" association (2.8.12). Both the young male *and* female lovers of the play emphatically employ the trope of equating the beloved female body with gold. "First go with me to church and call me wife," Portia assures Bassanio in the play's second most unsettling contract, and "you shall have gold to pay the petty debt twenty times over" (3.2.301-6).[7]

---

[7] Stephen Orgel has noted repeatedly that "the prospects for life after marriage in Shakespeare really are pretty grim" (170). There is an anxiousness about marriage in *The Merchant of Venice*, dramatized as a nearly arbitrary exchange of women and their "rings" by men to other men, that Shakespeare elaborates upon in

Women are *like* gold and so, by the accepted tropology of the play, Morocco's choice of casket should be right. Most readers highlight Morocco's description of himself ("As much as I deserve...") to indicate why he does not deserve Portia (2.7.31). But is there any substantial difference between his description of her and the descriptions given by Bassanio and his cohorts? For that matter, Bassanio's "four winds blow in from every coast / Renowned suitors" (1.1.168) easily prefigures Morocco's "From the four corners of the earth they come / To kiss this shrine" (2.7.39-40). Morocco fails because he assumes that he is being told the truth, learning instead that "*All that glisters is not gold*" (2.7.65).

If Morocco fails the riddle by assuming the truth of one of the play's commonly accepted tropes, Arragon's "error" differs only by degree, as he accepts the virtue of what may be the play's central trope:

> that "many" may be meant
> By the fool multitude that choose by show,
> Not learning more than the fond eye doth teach,
> Which pries not to th' interior... (2.9.24-7).

Critics of Arragon's reading fault his apparent elitism and narcissism for failing to choose the "right" casket ("I will not jump with common spirits / And rank me with the barbarous multitudes") (2.9.31-2). But choosing a metal less bright than gold may in fact indicate a cautiousness not to "wear an undeserved victor" (2.9.39). The worry that an "honour / Picked from the chaff" might be "new varnished" even indicates that he may suspect the deception that Morocco did not even consider (2.9.46-8). Compared to Antonio's proverbial warnings about a devil citing scripture, Arragon's account of the trope of inner/outer reading is far clearer. There is no reason to find anything particularly "bad" about Morocco or Arragon's uncovered meanings (or at least nothing worse than what is said by the reported heroes of this play). They are just not Portia's father's meaning.

Sarah Kofman, in an extended rebuttal to the "regressive interpretation" of the play in "The Theme of the Three Caskets" (142), argues that Freud "misrecognize[s] the more general 'theme' of ambivalence" in *Merchant* (161). But if the play emphasizes the duplicitous, "dual face of all things" as its representation of meaning, those who determine which face of the Janus coin is presented at any given moment do so arbitrarily (153). Portia and her suitors alike are "hedged" by her father's "wit" (2.1.18). With this sense of predetermined, arbitrary meaning dictated as if on high (or, in this

---

Pericles, where Marina is married off to the very man who attempted to purchase her virginity at a brothel.

case, from beyond the grave) in mind, we can begin to examine the various figures of caskets in the play.

At a literal level, the caskets are small coffers holding jewels and gold. Yet "casket" naturally recalls coffins as well. The play reflects this linguistic parallel: Morocco rejects the lead casket as though he were preparing for Portia's death ("it were too gross / To rib her cerecloth in the obscure grave") (2.7.50-1); Shylock, relating Jessica's theft of a casket of jewels in 2.6, conflates his daughter with his riches and wishes "the ducats in her coffin" (3.1.82). And though it may be regressive, the play's constant emphasis on the trope of inner and outer all but demands the Freudian reading that the caskets are "symbols of what is essential in women" (111).[8]

But the caskets are also readable. And like a word that is both God and with God, the women are (tropologically speaking) both the caskets and inside the caskets, like the jewels that they are arbitrarily compared to and dissuaded from being compared to. Lorenzo says as much when he explains the ruse of the masque to Salanio and Salarino:

> She hath directed
> How I shall take her from her father's house,
> What gold and jewels she is furnished with,
> What page's suit she had in readiness. (2.4.30-34)

The gold and jewels that "furnish" Jessica indicates not only the established metaphorical substitution between the two, but also connects her with the condition of confinement within her father's house. But by opening the outside and looking within this other casket (the house has already been compared by Jessica to Hell, which, like a casket, houses the dead), Lorenzo finds that his beloved approximates a "page" and is "read"-y, an invented heteronym for ready, meaning readable (2.3.2). This page is ready to be read.

Caskets, wombs, and book covers can all enclose bodies. The bodies found within a casket or a womb are literally personal, because they are literally persons. But like Hamlet's "pregnant" replies (2.2.205), the literary body is often considered like a literal one. The personal, though figural, interpretations of the bodies of Shakespeare's pages are the life

---

[8] In what seems like an overemphatic attempt to dispute Freud's reading, Kofman claims that "Shakespeare frequently uses the word coffer, casket, or closet in a metaphorical sense, but this word never represents 'woman' or 'the essence of woman'" (163 n.7). Kofman appears to have missed or forgotten *Pericles*, where Antiochus's daughter is described as a "glorious casket stored with ill" (1.1.78).

force that generates and enables this network of shifting signifiers, not least of all through a confusion of locating meaning within or without. This shifting of form and meaning, inner and outer, culminates in the scene that seems as though it will conclude the play: the trial where the inner, deeper meaning of Shylock's bond determines whether Antonio will lose his outer flesh. For Bassanio, reading a letter recounting the events in Venice, the word is and is with Antonio: "The paper as the body of my friend, / And every word in it a gaping wound / Issuing life-blood" (3.2.263-5).

In *The Merchant of Venice*, there is no difference between a meaning and a reading, only a difference of authority granted to specific, personal readings. Like the bodies that fell from Laban's lambs, the readings in the play are the product of something we could call (de/con)ception. Figural interpretation is as subject to these transformations as any other trope. Yet there is still an inherent authority granted to *Christian* reading, meaning little more than a reading performed *by* a Christian. This is why Portia can arrive in Venice confident that the bond yet unread by her will hold a reading that will save Antonio from Shylock's knife. And though Shylock has learned how to read like a Christian—demonstrated not only in his figural reading of Laban's lambs, but in his identification of Balthasar as a figure of "Daniel come to judgement" (4.1.219)—he does not carry the Christian authority to determine the moments of transformation between reading like a Jew and reading like a Christian. In this reading, Gratiano's repeated taunts (textual repetition being a sign of both the uncertainty and arbitrariness of the Christian subjective reading in this play) seem especially cruel: "A Daniel still, say I, a second Daniel! / I thank thee, Jew, for teaching me that word" (4.1.336-7).[9]

I began this reading with the observation that, in the world of *Merchant of Venice*, interpretations can be exchanged like daughters. For Shylock, such exchanges are always thefts. Portia/Balthasar's great speech about "the quality of mercy" is often cited to qualify the anti-Semitism of Shylock's forced conversion. But it is possible that this speech also prefigures that conversion. Mercy "blesseth him that gives and him that takes," but we need not read "him" as being two separate people nor giving and taking as two separate actions. The gift of tradition that Shylock claimed in his account of Jacob's lambs, so clearly associated with the "law" that he craves in this scene, is forcibly exchanged for a gift of Christian grace that he never quite accepts (see footnote 2). The entire

---

[9] See Lewalski 340-1 for an illuminating discussion of the references to Daniel in this scene.

transaction is figured, as we may have come to expect, in the simultaneous, forcibly withdrawn "gift" to his daughter upon his death. For Jessica, like the other Christian lovers of the play, caskets are meant to be opened. Once opened, they can be replaced with the all too easily exchangeable wedding ring, a new container that is too open to actually close off and contain its contents. But for Shylock, everything is closed within one final casket, "the privy coffer of the state" (4.1.350).

Pericles and New Joys In Old Songs

Following the model of "reconstruction" established by the second Oxford edition of 1986, the Arden third series attributes *Pericles* to "William Shakespeare and George Wilkins." If that earlier edition was, in the words of one of its own general editors, a confronting of "the Shakespeare-loving public with a full-frontal challenge to its sense of propriety," the present Arden is decidedly less shocking (Taylor 320). The Oxford's "full-frontal challenge" to Shakespeareans in the 1980s is now the Arden's measured compromise: "in a postmodern age of fragmentation, any all-encompassing hegemonic explanation for the state of the text will be greeted with scepticism, [so] more limited intervention seems appropriate and is followed in this edition" (54).

The Arden's considerably toned down "appropriate" and "limited" intervention—that is, the versifying of Wilkins's *Painful Adventures*— seems to have it both ways. The Arden makes the case for collaboration on the "original" *Pericles* in the "bad" quarto of 1609 partly by invoking contemporary resistance to the "hegemonic explanation" of the (or "an" or "any") edited text.[10] Implicitly, the Arden introduction reveals that the case for collaboration is made by the (printing of the) play's errors. If confused meter and verse printed as prose prompted Malone to declare "no play of our author's [is] … so incorrect as this" in the introduction to his edition (qtd. in 11), the Arden—which largely corrects *those* errors— expects its readers to attend to "dialogue that makes little or no sense" and "gaps in the motivation of actions and events" (11). Instead of the challenge to our propriety, we may have cause for a kind of back-door bardolatry. What is "likeable" and "readable" about the play is attributable

---

[10] I am largely referring to the controversies of collaboration and textual transmission as reported by the Arden's introduction in order to better understand the Arden *Pericles* as itself a work of transmission. See also accounts of these issues in Vickers and Jackson.

to Shakespeare; what is badly written may be either corrupt *or* attributable to Wilkins.

At any rate, to this reader, the Arden's *Pericles* seems far more coherent, not only as an individual work but also as a figure in the canon, than skeptical readers may expect. Read alongside *The Merchant of Venice*, the latter play seems like a fulfillment of the earlier play's concerns for allegories and reading. Antiochus's silent daughter, identified as both readable and a casket, immediately offers a major typological connection between the two plays in the first scene. Though this scene, like the bulk of the first two acts, is commonly attributed to Wilkins, it seems to pick up where *Merchant* left off. The open caskets of *Merchant* are transformed into the uncomfortably open "book of all that monarchs do," which is safer closed than opened (1.1.95-6). Antiochus, in turn, stagily reminds us of Portia's father with his own riddle's use of (de/con)ception. In an aside he declares that Pericles "has found the meaning" (1.1.110), then claims openly that "Your exposition misinterpreting" (1.1.113). Portia's father presents a "gold casket" that is not really gold; Antiochus's father identifies the "right" reading as a misinterpretation.

Antiochus's worry about the revelation of his shame has, to borrow Freud's reading of Bassanio's speech, a forced ring (109). This forcedness particularly rings out in the nervous repetition of "found the meaning" after Pericles exits the stage (1.1.144). This forced nervousness is the sort of gap of motivation that the Arden's introduction warned us about, since it seems unlikely that *anybody* could miss the "hidden" meaning of this riddle:

> *I am no viper, yet I feed*
> *On mother's flesh which did me breed.*
> *I sought a husband, in which labour*
> *I found that kindness in a father.*
> *He's father, son, and husband mild;*
> *I mother, wife, and yet his child.*
> *How they may be, and yet in tow,*
> *As you will live resolve it in you.* (1.1.65-72)

Like a purloined letter, the crime is hidden in plain sight. The horribleness of the sin that Pericles immediately recognizes ("Why cloud they not their sights ...") parallels the dreadfulness of the writing that readers are plainly supposed to associate with reporter's errors or a lesser writer like Wilkins (1.1.75). Yet the dramatic or literary power of a reader encountering a weak text is easy to overlook. There are a number of echoes of the depiction of Shylock and Antonio's competing allegorical readings: the "deed of kind" performed between one's lambs and one's father-in-law's lambs is now "kindness in a father"; Antonio's shifting of the inner/outer trope from reading to reader invoked by resolving the riddle "in" Pericles himself. While those echoes may not indicate Shakespeare's hand, they seem thoroughly Shakespearean in the scene's entangling of transmission of interpretative meaning with the transmission of one's daughter.[11]

Books are still like caskets and caskets are still like women and, recalling *Merchant of Venice* even more directly, there are three women-casket pairings in *Pericles*: Antiochus's daughter, Thaisa, and Marina. Antiochus's daughter "is" a glorious casket, Thaisa is thrown overboard in a coffin that is "like a coffin" (3.2.53), and Marina is memorialized with a monument that, like Portia's three caskets, is complete with a verse inscription (4.4.34-43). "Marina" is a kind of "port," and Marina is a kind of *Port*ia.[12]

Recalling *Merchant*'s many prefigurations and fulfillments, the central structural device that drives *Pericles* is its repetitions. Characters sail to places where they have already been and say things that they have already said while the audience is told and shown things that it has already been told and seen. Marina's fate is not only repetitious in and of itself ("Thou was born at sea, buried at Tarsus, / And found at sea again!") (5.1.186-7), but she also "beget'st" (5.1.185) her own father in an eerie repetition of Antiochus's daughter taking on the role of "mother" (as well as wife and child) to her father, all while paralleling her mother's fate. Both are mistaken for dead, become a priestess to virginity, and both are then found by Pericles. Marina's story also repeats elements of her father's story, such

---

[11] Compare Thaisa choosing from the suitors' legible shields with the choice of the three caskets: she picks the sixth and final one, even though like the lead casket, it is far from the glossiest choice. Of course, the choice is clarified with reference to the tyrannical muse of inner and outer ("He had need mean better than his outward show") (2.2.46).

[12] The characters' names may also indicate the more corporeal understanding of Freudian reading of the "casket" imagery (disputed by Kofman). John Wilmot, Second Earl of Rochester's "On Mrs. Willis" equates "her Cunt" with "a Common shore" (20). Though "shore" is here typically glossed as "sewer," an even more repulsive image, "shore" as "port" works as a metaphor as well, where the quantity of lovers is equated with the quantity of boats docked at a popular port (rather than the comment about the quality of lovers associated with the sewer). Similarly, Bassanio's claim that "I have disabled mine estate / By something showing a more swelling port" appears to pun on Portia's name with the common slang treatment of pregnancy (1.1.123-4).

as their shared escapes from hired killers. Textual repetition is practically genetic in this play.

Yet the repetitions in *Merchant of Venice* are propelled with a clearer, narrative force. *Merchant* moves us towards the opening of the correct—as in predetermined—casket out of the three possible choices. *Pericles* not only begins with the discovery that the authorities who determine "right" meanings are corrupt, but the play also proceeds with a nearly constant accumulation of more caskets.[13] In other words, the conclusions about typological allegory are largely moot. What *Pericles* depicts instead is an allegory of its own reading; De Man's account of the "specificity" of Proust applies just as ably to *Pericles*:

> The specificity of Proust's novel would instead by grounded in the play between a prospective and retrospective movement. This alternating motion resembles that of reading, or rather that of re-reading which the intricacy of every sentence as well as of the narrative network as a whole constantly forces upon us. … This occurs by means of a process of elision, transformation, and accentuation that bears a close resemblance to the practice of critical understanding. (57)

It is perhaps not surprising that a text like *À la recherche du temps perdu*, initially translated into the Shakespearean *Remembrance of Things Past*, may share other resonances with Shakespeare.Our own movement through the text follows a similar play of retrospection and prospective motion; the play does not need *foreshadowing*, per se, because more often than not Gower simply *tells* us what will happen.

But if repetition is a mark of the play's narrative design, it also indicates its corruption. The Arden introduction groups "repetition" with "mislineation" and "metrical disorganization" as a possible indicator of a reported (and therefore corrupted) text (22). The notes dedicatedly catalog instances where textualist scholars have noted troubling repetitions: "The Oxford editors call this repetition of 2.1.35 'suspicious' and omit" (247 n.43); "Some of the repetitions of *come your ways* may be a reporter's error" (326 n.37); "Taylor and Warren treat this repetition of 123 as suspicious and assume that the first occurrence is 'contamination' from the current passage" (361 n.168); "Brooks calls this 'memorial expansion and duplication,' but the repetition is credible and stageworthy" (388n.199-200). When this plethora of repetitions is not blamed on the reporter, it is

---

[13] See Hoeniger, who attributes the play's "loose episodic design" to the expectations of the "adventures" genre (465). Hoeniger argues that the play follows Gower's original text very closely, which accounts for its repetitive structure.

blamed on Wilkins: "Wilkins tends to repeat himself" (174 n.30-1); "characteristic Wilkins repetition" (210n.23).

I do not seek to impugn the Arden, only read it. And one does not need to dispute the history of great textualist approaches to the play to wonder if perhaps the superfluity of a particular error is precisely the evidence we need to understand the presence of such an "error" as intentional. At any rate, we can always return to the word. Even if this is a bad text from a bad quarto, Gower tells us what to do with bad texts:

> To sing a song that old was sung
> From ashes ancient Gower is come,
> Assuming man's infirmities
> To glad your ear and please your eyes. ...
> The purchase is to make men glorious,
> *Et bonum quo antiquius eo melius.*
> If you, born in these latter times
> When wit's more ripe, accept my rhymes,
> And that to hear an old man sing
> May to your wishes pleasure bring. (1.0.1-14)

As a "song that old was sung," *Pericles* was always already a reconstructed text. And whereas Portia was "hedged" by the wit of the past, of the dead, readers of this play are liberated by their own wit, which supersedes the voice of the dead Gower even as he crows in Latin that "the older a good thing is, the better" (172n.10).

Gower's speeches are filled with not only acknowledgments of the audience and readers, but a sense of complicity shared with them as well. *We* are expected to make the best of a bad text that is filled with "lame feet" which Gower could never "convey unless [our] thoughts went on [his] way" (4.0.48-50). For a play that exists only in editions marred with "mislineation" and "metrical disorganization," the confession that some of the lines are "lame" cannot help but resonate with us. And is there not something uncanny about Gower's claim that he stands "i'th' gaps to teach you / The stages of our story" (4.4.8-9)? Does that not recall the Arden's forewarning about "gaps in the motivation" of the characters even as the "teaching" also prefigures the scholarship that preserve's Marina's virginity ("I doubt not but this populous city will / Yield many scholars") (4.5.189-190)? Why not read this way when Gower's speech in 4.4 begins by asking for both our pardon and "our"—meaning his *and* our— "imagination" (4.4.4-6)? Gratiano cruelly thanked Shylock for "teaching" him a word to read typologically. Our transactions with Gower are not thefts, like Gratiano's, but rather invited collaborations.

Gower's final speech is first and foremost a repetition: "you have heard / Of monstrous lust" in the case of Antiochus and his daughter, "seen" the virtuous Pericles and his family, and "may" have "well descr[ied]" Helicanus's faith and loyalty (8chorus.1-8). The verbs of what the audience or reader supposedly "does" appear to get progressively more active: we were told something, we observed something, and then we may (or may not) have concluded something for ourselves about the action on the stage or page. Gower then turns to the fate of Cleon and his wife:

> The gods for murder seemed so content
> To punish, although not done, but meant.
>   So on your patience evermore attending,
>   New joy wait on you. Here our play has ending. (8chorus.15-18)

The epilogue, after a catalog of repetitions, tells us something new: that Cleon and his family died in a fire, punished not for the actual crime, but for the intended, *meant* crime. This punishment leaves "the gods," as his own punishment left Shylock, "content." There may be another implied heteronym here. Gower's gods and Shylock are not only contented, they are content(s). In spite of the fixity of Portia/Balthasar's sentence and the play's "ending," there is substance and meaning yet to be uncovered. That is why the play "has" ending, rather than is ending (as Prospero's revels "are ending") (4.1.148). The ending is as open, exchangeable, and negligible as any of the readings that we have examined. This is an ending, it is not the ending.

"Our play" no doubt, on a literal level, attributes *Pericles* to Gower and the performers. But it clearly includes the audience, with its oft-mentioned imagination and patience, in the collective, collaborative auth*our*ship. The sound of "our" not only echoes Gower's own name, but also the *hour*glass that is invoked in his previous request for the audience's imaginative input (i.e. because "our sands are almost run," please assist the play's narrative with "kindness" to "relieve" Gower and the players of dramatizing the "pageantry," "feasts," "shows," and "minstrelsy" that one would expect following Pericles's reunion with Marina) (5.2.1-7). The synchrony between Gower, hour, and our may clarify what it means to "evermore" attend to "new joys" after this ending. An hourglass can be turned over again, just as a casket or book can be re-opened or a coin with the ambivalent faces of Janus can be flipped. Each future reading or attending to this very text may be, like a virgin in Pander's brothel, fresh but not "raw" (4.2.50). If such old songs are improved by the riper wit of "latter times," this song can improve with the individual return by any specific audience of re-readers, and by the future readings by wits riper still.

Pericles ends with a sort of benediction of re-reading, a bequeathing of the text to whomever wishes to read (or edit) it.[14]

Shakespeare may not have fit our definition of a progressive, but he seems to have been aware that the riper wits of latter times would be faced with difficulties like our need to read his plays without being heterosexist. These two plays, read together, demonstrate a clear awareness of the way that our values change and how those changes change our texts and our readings. If his texts are to live "evermore," they will have to change as well. If Shakespeare was aware of his own status as a writer not of an age, but for all time, he understood that his immortality would be indebted to the interpretative shifts applied to and found within his texts. He did not expect, or seem to want, his readers to stay content about his contents; the eternal lines are guaranteed by our play upon his words. Thus, while we may read *Merchant of Venice* as a tragedy of (de/con)ception, we can read the Shakespearean canon as a triumph of (re)conception. There is a tacit endorsement in the way these plays allegorize their own reading that we make each play *ours*, knowing full well that forever attending to his poetry—"the most rigorous" and "most unreliable language in terms of which man names and transforms himself" (de Man 19)—may reveal more about what is inside us than what is inside the text.

De Man's "box"-model of reading was familiar to Shakespeare, and it is not exhausted for us. While recent paperback, reprint editions of the Arden Shakespeare second series promised its readers a guide to "a richer understanding and appreciation of Shakespeare's plays," the back cover of the Arden third series guarantees a "*deeper* understanding and appreciation," as well as an "*in-depth* survey of critical approaches to the play" (my emphasis).[15] Yet even with the turn (or return) to the supposedly debunked inner/outer paradigm of literary analysis, one could hesitatingly call the approach of the third series deconstructive. The claimed definitiveness of the second series' "definitive edition of Shakespeare's work" is noticeably dispensed, with the third series claiming instead to be "the established scholarly edition of Shakespeare's plays." "Definitiveness" is perhaps

---

[14] See Mullaney for more on the tradition of the gift (in the Maussian sense) in *Pericles* (139). Mulaney also reads *Pericles* as a treatment of the exchange between playwright and audience, though he reads this exchange as essentially anxious.

[15] The three paperback third series editions that I consulted were *Pericles* (ed. Gossett), *Merchant of Venice* (ed. Drakakis), and *King Lear* (ed. Foakes), all of which carry the description quoted above. The second series edition that I quote from is the Arden's *Cymbeline* (ed. Nosworthy), completed in 1955 and reprinted in 1997.

beyond the reach of any mere edition, but "establishment" is something that can be asserted and reasserted, not just with third-, but with fourth-, fifth-, and other future editions. This awareness seems very much in the spirit of Gower's promise of "new joys."

In a response to the controversies surrounding the unearthed writings of de Man, Derrida made a plea in 1988 for "a reading that ought to remain as open and as differentiated as possible" ("Like" 644). An "open" reading naturally entails rereading, and near the close of the essay, Derrida asks his readers "if they still have some concern for justice and rigor, to take the time to reread" both his friend's writings and his reply "as closely as possible" ("Like" 651). Rereading is not only the "just" approach to Paul de Man's hurtful texts—Derrida remarks, echoing Bassanio's account of the letter with "every word in it a gaping wound," that his first reading of de Man's wartime writings left the feeling of "a wound" ("Like" 600)— it is also the response to the general difficulty of de Man's theoretical texts: "I know that I am going to reread him and that there is still some future and promise that await us there" ("Like" 650).

Shakespeare is often discussed this same way.[16] Shakespeare seems to expect and invite an "open" reading and re-reading of his texts as well. Sometimes those texts are like an open casket, and sometimes they are like an open case. But whether we readers feel like we are in his wake or at his trial, he assures us that with each inevitable return to his text, "new joy" will "wait" for us there.

---

[16] For instance, in Terry Eagleton's short book on Shakespeare, Eagleton famously intones that, "Though conclusive evidence is hard to come by, it is difficult to read Shakespeare without feeling that he was almost certainly familiar with the writings of Hegel, Marx, Nietzsche, Freud, Wittgenstein, and Derrida. Perhaps this is simply to say that though there are many ways in which we have thankfully left this conservative patriarch behind, there are other ways in which we have yet to catch up with him" (x). Incidentally, Eagleton's book was published the same year as the French edition of *Memoires for Paul de Man*, which contains the famous line about *Allegories of Reading* that Derrida alludes to with his comment about the future and promise that awaits de Man's readers ("Like all of Paul de Man's work, it still awaits us, in advance of us") (*Memoires* 149).

Bibliography

Adelman, Janet. *Blood Relations: Christian and Jew in The Merchant of Venice*. Chicago: University of Chicago Press, 2008. Print.
Auerbach, Erich. "Figura." *Scenes from the Drama of European Literature*. Minneapolis: University of Minnesota Press, 1984. Orig. 1959. 11-76. Print.
Colley, John Scott. "Launcelot, Jacob, and Esau: Old and New Law in *The Merchant of Venice*." *The Yearbook of English Studies*. 10 (1980): 181-189. Print.
de Man, Paul. *Allegories of Reading: Figural Language in Rousseau, Nietzsche, Rilke, and Proust*. New Haven: Yale University Press, 1979. Print.
Derrida, Jacques. "Like The Sound of the Sea Deep Within A Shell: Paul de Man's War." Trans. Peggy Kamuf. *Critical Inquiry* 14 (Spring 1988): 590-652. Print.
—. *Memoires for Paul de Man*. Rev. Ed. New York: Columbia University Press, 1989. Orig. 1986. Print.
Eagleton, Terry. *William Shakespeare*. Oxford: Blackwell, 1986. Print.
Freud, Sigmund. "The Theme of the Three Caskets." *Writings on Art and Literature*. Stanford: Stanford University Press, 1997. 109-121. Print.
Hoeniger, F. David. "Gower and Shakespeare in *Pericles*." *Shakespeare Quarterly* 33.4 (Winter 1982): 461-479. Print.
Jackson, MacD. P. *Defining Shakespeare:* Pericles *as Test Case*. Oxford: Oxford University Press, 2003. Print.
Kofman, Sarah. "Conversions: *The Merchant of Venice* Under the Sign of Saturn." Trans. Shaun Whiteside. *Literary Theory Today*. Eds. Peter Collier and Helga Geyer-Ryan. Cambridge: Polity Press, 1990. 142-166. Print.
Lewalski, Barbara. "Biblical Allusion and Allegory in *The Merchant of Venice*." *Shakespeare Quarterly* 13.3 (Summer 1962): 327-343. Print.
Lupton, Julia Reinhard. "Exegesis, Mimesis, and the Future of Humanism in *The Merchant of Venice*." *Religion & Literature*. 32.2 (Summer 2000): 123-139. Print.
Mullaney, Steven. *The Place of the Stage: License, Play, and Power in Renaissance England*. Chicago: University of Chicago Press, 1988. Print.
Murphy, Andrew. *Shakespeare in Print: A History and Chronology of Shakespeare Publishing*. Cambridge: Cambridge University Press, 2003. Print.

Orgel, Stephen. *The Authentic Shakespeare: And Other Problems of the Early Modern Stage*. New York: Routledge, 2002. Print.

Rochester, John Wilmot, Earl of. "On Mrs Willis." *The Works of John Wilmot, Earl of Rochester*. Ed. Harold Love. Oxford: Oxford University Press, 1999. 37. Print.

Shakespeare, William and George Wilkins. *Pericles*. Ed. Suzanne Gossett. The Arden Shakespeare Third Series. London: Thomson Learning, 2004. Print.

Shakespeare, William. *Cymbeline*. Ed. J.M. Nosworthy. The Arden Shakespeare Second Series. Walton-on-Thames: Thomas Nelson & Sons, 1997. Orig. 1955. Print.

—. *Hamlet*. Second Quarto. Eds. Ann Thompson and Neil Taylor. The Arden Shakespeare Third Series. London: Thomson Learning, 2006. Print.

—. *The Merchant of Venice*. Ed. John Drakakis. The Arden Shakespeare Third Series. London: Methuen Drama, 2010. Print.

—. *The Tempest*. Eds. Virginia Mason Vaughan and Alden T. Vaughan. The Arden Shakespeare Third Series. London: Thomson Learning, 1999. Print.

Sinfield, Alan. "How To Read *The Merchant of Venice* Without Being Heterosexist." *Shakespeare, Authority, Sexuality: Unfinished Business in Cultural Materialism*. New York: Routledge, 2006. 53-67. Print.

Taylor, Gary. *Reinventing Shakespeare: A Cultural History from the Restoration to the Present*. Oxford: Oxford University Press, 1989. Print.

Vickers, Brian. *Shakespeare, Co-Author: A Historical Study of Five Collaborative Plays*. Oxford: Oxford University Press, 2002. Print.

HATH NOT A JEW A NOSE?
OR, THE DANGER OF DEFORMITY IN COMEDY

JEFFREY R. WILSON

Identified and apprehended dialectically, as both individual and stereotype, "Shylock the Jew" is a complex blend of subject and object, of human particularity and cultural abstraction, of a *person* understood legally as an autonomous being who has rights and obligations and a *persona* understood etymologically as the lifeless wooden mask worn by an actor on stage. One stereotype, which happens to be a mask, has been routinely attached to Shylock: an obnoxiously large nose. This prosthetic comes not from the text of *The Merchant of Venice* (1596-97), nor from a Shakespearean theatrical tradition, but from "the artificiall Iewe of Maltas nose," as William Rowley's *A Search for Money* (1609) remembers the costume of Edward Alleyn's Barabas in Christopher Marlowe's play *The Jew of Malta* (12). Rowley even describes the "two casements" fastened on either side of the nose, "through which his eyes had a little ken of vs." In other words, a pair of eyeglasses holds the nose on the actor's face, just like that insufferable device meant to make you look like Groucho Marx, the Jewish-American comedian.

In *The Jew of Malta* (1589-90), Ithamore thrice salutes Barabas's beak, roaring "I worship your nose for this" when Barabas schools him to "smile when the Christians moane" (2.3.173-74). Marlowe makes the nose the mark of a Jew who is exceedingly villainous: merciless, malevolent, and hell-bent against Christianity. Spying Barabas's "villainy" (3.3.1), Ithamore laments how he has "the bravest, gravest, secret, subtle, bottle-nosed knave to [his] master" (3.3.9-10). The nose concludes this catalog of Barabas's immoralities because Marlowe loads it up with moral significance, aligning a perceived pattern in the Jewish body with a perceived pattern of villainy in the Jewish nation. Thus, when two Christian clergy come for Barabas, he "smelt 'em e're they came," and we might imagine Alleyn indicating his prosthetic, to raucous laughter, as Ithamore exclaims, "God-a-mercy, nose" (4.1.24-25).

If the play influencing Shakespeare's Shylock uses an artificial nose to signal a Jewish villainy, so do at least two plays influenced by Shylock. A character in George Chapman's *The Blinde Begger of Alexandria* (1598) disguises himself as "Leon the rich vsurer," presumably but not explicitly a Jew, as the others note "he hath a great nose." In *Jack Drum's Entertainment* (1601), John Marston's *dramatis personae* lists "Mamon the Vsurer, with a great nose," and news of the (again presumably) Jewish merchant's sunken ship causes Mamon to cry, "My nose will rot off with grief" (E3). Elizabethan dramatists like Marlowe, Chapman, and Marston associate the nose broadly with a Jewish antagonism to Christianity, and specifically with a stereotyped Jewish avarice, manifested in either mercantilism or usury.

Coming upon passages such as these, nineteenth-century scholars scampered to stamp the prosthetic on Shylock. In 1836, John Collier had "little doubt that the part of Shylock was originally played in a false nose" (38). An 1840 edition of Rowley's text agrees: "It was usual in the time of Shakespeare, to furnish Jews and usurers on the stage with artificial noses, and so Shylock was probably originally represented by Richard Burbage" (46n19). According to Moncure Conway's book *The Wandering Jew* (1881), "Shylock, as acted by Shakespeare's friend Burbage … consisted of exceedingly red hair and beard, a false nose preternaturally long and hooked, and a tawny petticoat" (125). This astonishingly precise costume comes from two dubious sources, first a funeral elegy for Burbage that was actually forged in the nineteenth century by Collier, and second the "deformed Father" in the actor Thomas Jordan's seventeenth-century verse adaptation of *Merchant*:

His beard was red, his face was made
Not much unlike a Witches.
His habit was a Jewish gown,
That would defend all weather;
His chin turn'd up, his nose hung down,
And both ends met together. (2-3)

In 1911 E. E. Stoll took Jordan's ballad as the best estimation of an Elizabethan Shylock, and in 1949 John Moore suggested the comparably cartoonish Italian clown Pantaloon (See Figure 1). Shylock's artificial nose survives in the more recent scholarship of, say, Jay Halio (10), Frank Felsentein (162), and Gary Taylor (11), but it survives in the absence of any direct evidence that Shakespeare's character actually wore the nose. More cautious criticism by Toby Lelyveld (8), James Smith (3), and John Cooper (117) has doubted and often denied Shylock the nose. As these

Figure 1: Maurice Sand, *Pantalon (1550)*, in vol. 2 of *Masques et Bouffons (Comedie Italienne)* (Paris: Michel Levy Freres, 1860), front matter.

studies indicate, the evidence for an artificial nose is not contemporary with Shakespeare, and Elizabethan notices of *Merchant* do not evidence the nose. Charles Edelman puts it nicely when he writes that Alexander Pope's famous comment about "the Jew / That Shakespeare drew" (292) "shows a yearning, shared by all students of the play, to reconstruct somehow the first Shylock, about whom there is no reliable contemporary information whatsoever" (99). In sum, a historicist might reason an artificial nose onto Shylock on the basis of early English theatrical and cultural conventions, but the strict textualist will refuse to credit this unsubstantiated suggestion. In 2010 this very debate was staged in *The New York Review of Books* with Stephen Greenblatt playing the historicist and James Shapiro the textualist. The issue of Shylock's nose is so tricky, however, that Shapiro himself (*Shakespeare and the Jews*, 240n96), and such able analysts as Joan Holmer (136n11) and Peter Berek (56), have thrown up their hands in uncertainty.

Did Shylock wear a false nose on the Elizabethan stage? Shakespeare never mentions it, though he has ample opportunity to do so, as when Antonio spits on Shylock's gabardine and beard. Why not also spit on the most obvious target, his huge nose? Is it because the Elizabethan actor playing Shylock wore no nose? Nothing in *Merchant* precludes the nose, but nothing calls for it either, which, in the wake of Marlowe's eager symbolism, creates a present absence in Shakespeare's portrait of the Jew. The bard's disregard for this pungent theatrical device does not certify its absence, but it is cause for consideration. If Shylock wore no nose, why did Shakespeare abandon this theatrical tradition? If he did use the prosthetic, why did Shakespeare avoid making any moral significance of the nose, as Marlowe, Chapman, Marston, and Rowley clearly did?

This chapter responds to these questions, not by scouring the historical record of Elizabethan performances, which yields no answer, but by extrapolating from Shakespeare's other thematic considerations and compositional decisions in *Merchant*. Such a critique cannot settle the historical question with absolute certainty, I know, but it does allow us to explore a series of possibilities and the likelihood and significance of each. From where I stand, this is the very best response to Shakespeare's drama, where so much – not just material details of Elizabethan performance, but more importantly key issues in the drama – is open to alternate readings of the text and renderings of it on stage. As I ask whether or not Shylock wears an artificial nose on the Elizabethan stage, therefore, I hope to use the indeterminacy of this historical question as an opportunity to discuss the composition and reception of Shakespeare's irony. By *irony* I mean the author's veiled attitude toward the characters and actions in his text, which is the compositional posture that creates such persistent debates over, for example, the origin of Shylock's anger, the terms of his bond, and the propriety of his forced conversion.[1] In the shape of a question mark, the

---

[1] I mean Socratic irony, not what Puttenham calls the "drye mock" (157), but the manner of articulation described by Bacon: "It was not without cause, that so many excellent Philosophers became *Sceptiques* and *Academiques,* and denyed any certaintie of Knowledge, or Comprehension, and held opinion that the knowledge of man extended onely to Appearances, and Probabilities. It is true, that in *Socrates* it was supposed to be but a fourme of *Irony, Scientiam dissimulando simulauit:* For hee vsed to disable his knowledge, to the end to inhanse his Knowledge" (51). See Knox.

artificial nose is the material, theatrical, and dramaturgical object that commemorates Shakespeare's irony in *The Merchant of Venice*.

The Figure of Stigma in Early English Drama: Abnormality, Villainy, Irony, Tragicomedy

Critics such as Lisa Freinkel and Julia Reinhard Lupton have recently updated the typological readings of the Christian treatment of Judaism in *Merchant* by considering the text in the terms of figural interpretation as it is mapped out by Erich Auerbach. Rather than rehearse the Christian attempt to cancel and supersede Judaism, Freinkel and Lupton remind us that our criticism of Shakespeare's text, like criticism of the Bible, is exegetical, especially when meaning is manifold or allegorical. I would like to continue this conversation by using Auerbach's analysis of the mimetic style in *Genesis* to articulate the coy compositional mode behind Shakespeare's description of Shylock's Jewishness, and the crazed interpretations consequently created by Shakespeare's Christian characters and his often-Christian audiences.

In the famous first chapter of *Mimesis*, "Odysseus' Scar," Auerbach juxtaposes the "realistic" style of Homer's poetry, particular facts here on earth strung together in an explicit series of causal connections and a "figural" style in *Genesis* that aims for truth rather than reality. To take nothing away from Auerbach, the mark of Cain might be a better point of contact with Odysseus's scar than the Akedah is, for it allows the marked body to serve as a touchstone, a shared feature that renders differences in mimetic styles apparent. On the one hand, Homer represents a natural reality by linking a bodily mark with its material cause, a hunting accident from Odysseus's boyhood. On the other hand, the *Genesis* writer fashions a supernatural world in which the mark of Cain is "mysterious, containing a second, concealed meaning," as Auerbach describes Hebraic figuralism (15).

Genesis announces and abandons the mark of Cain in one quick verse. Cain murders Abel, and God banishes Cain, but Cain fears retribution, so "the Lord set a marke vpon Káin, lest anie man finding him shulde kil him" (Gen. 4.15).[2] What is this mark? What does it look like? Who are these other men who would kill Cain? How will the mark stop them? Does the plan work? Unlike Odysseus's scar, which Auerbach calls "of the foreground" (13), leaving nothing in darkness, the mark of Cain is unclear, "fraught with background" (12), implying more than is said. As Auerbach

---

[2] All Biblical citations are to the Geneva Bible, i.e. *The Bible and Holy Scriptures*.

puts it, the Hebrew text is "tyrannical" (14), announcing but not
elucidating history, the kind of mysterious mimesis displayed for example
in the English Bohun Psalter that shows God marking Cain on an obscured
cheek, leaving its exact nature unclear (See Figure 2).

Figure 2: Detail of Cain and Abel, in the Bohun Psalter (1370-80), at the Bodleian
Library (Oxford, England), 40.

The withholding of information in the Hebrew text over-excites our
interpretive faculty, which is why the mark of Cain surfaces variously in
later cultures as a letter on his body, a trembling in his limbs, a set of
horns, a cross, a tattoo, black skin, beardlessness, or leprosy (Mellinkoff).
One particularly vigorous fourteenth-century English illumination displays
a thoroughly marked Cain: the Lord's outstretched hand hunches the spine
of the murderer, who also exhibits negro features and horns to announce
his collusion with the dark and the demonic (See Figure 3). If the Bohun
Psalter can stand for the coyness in the composition of the Hebrew figure,

this anonymous English psalter suggests the consequent abundance in the interpretation of it.

Figure 3: God Punishing Cain, in an Anonymous English Psalter (ca. 1397-1400), at St. John's College Library (Cambridge, England), 6.

While Samuel Taylor Coleridge famously said Edmund Kean's acting was "like reading Shakespeare by flashes of lightning" (38), another nineteenth-century critic, Douglas Jerrold, thought something else about Kean's Shylock in particular: he impresses an audience "like a chapter of *Genesis*" (11). I would like to suggest that the mystery and the history of the mimesis in *Genesis* can illuminate the operation of Shakespearean irony, both its composition and its reception. With respect to Shylock's Judaism, Shakespeare writes *Merchant* in a way reminiscent of *Genesis*, where a shocking scarcity of facts is cagily delivered in contradistinction to the moral absolutes at play in the text. Shakespeare's irony, always

difficult to describe, can be viewed as a version of the Hebraic figuralism
Auerbach adumbrates:

> Certain parts brought into high relief, others left obscure, abruptness,
> suggestive influence of the unexpressed, 'background' quality, multiplicity
> of meanings and the need for interpretation, universal-historical claims,
> development of the concept of the historically becoming, and
> preoccupation with the problematic. (23)

In *Genesis* and *Merchant* alike, an eerie absence of information in the text
evokes an alarming presence of interpretation in the critical tradition,
much of it trying to ascribe its exegetical claims to the text itself. The
other characters in *Merchant*, as well as the play's audiences, often
interpret Shylock's Judaism frantically, like the Christian treatment of
Cain, which subordinates the sparse historical facts of the text to the
relentlessly moralized meanings of Christian allegory.

For example, imagine you were the costume designer for the Lord
Chamberlain's Men in 1597, asked to gather materials for *Merchant*,
specifically for the costume of "*Shylock the Jew*" (1.3.1sd). Your text tells
you very little else: Shylock is "old" (2.5.2, 4.2.11), wears a "Jewish
gaberdine" (1.3.112), and has a "beard" (1.3.117). You don't even have
the *dramatis personae* first given in the 1637 quarto to tell you Shylock is
"a *rich* Jew." The text of *Merchant* tells you Shylock is Jewish, but not
what it means to be Jewish or to look Jewish. It's difficult to find Jews
around you in Elizabethan England, so you have no unmediated
experience with Judaism (Glassman). To stage Shylock, you must fill in
the gaps of Shakespeare's text with reference to other representations: oral
tradition, travel literature, previous plays, and the occasional printed
image. Your Jew will be at least thrice removed from truth, an imitation of
other imitations.

Since Shylock's gabardine is specifically "Jewish," you might put a
badge on it, perhaps the yellow *rota* worn in Germany, or maybe the more
English tradition of the two stone tablets bearing the Ten Commandments.
Shylock's costume should be elegant enough to indicate the avarice early
English plays attach to their Jews: you recall Barabas bragging of his
"clean shirt" (*Jew*, 4.4.70). Speaking of Barabas, "The Hat he weares,
Iudas left vnder the Elder when he hang'd himselfe" (4.4.74-75), but
should your Shylock wear one of the large pointed hats that identify Jews
in medieval art? If so, a Venetian Jew's hat might be red, yellow, or
orange, depending upon which travel literature you consult, or it might be
a yarmulke. In any event, you must also determine the color of the hair
underneath his hat. Shylock's beard might be the "little yellow beard, a

Cain-color'd beard" that Shakespeare mentions in *The Merry Wives of Windsor* (1.4.23); or it might be "the dissembling color," as Shakespeare calls the red hair of Judas in *As You Like It* (3.4.7). Scuttling to supply information Shakespeare leaves out, actors, directors, and critics have saddled Shylock with all these costumes and more. That is, Shakespeare's Shylock is the Cain of the Bohun Psalter (See Figure 2), but he has been made into the monster in the other psalter (See Figure 3). I would venture to say, however, that the anonymous sixteenth-century German print of *A Judge, a Jew, and a Woman* (See Figure 4) offers the best approximation of an Elizabethan Shylock drawn strictly from Shakespeare's text: aged, balding but with a long grey beard, and no hat, but richly dressed with identifying Jewish marks (a *rota* on the left shoulder and Hebrew gibberish on the gabardine), holding his bag of money, and – in this case – displaying a large nose (not however obnoxiously artificial).

Figure 4: HW, *A Judge, a Jew, and a Woman* (16th c.), 215 x 168 mm, in vol. 13 of *The Illustrated Bartsch* (New York: Abaris Books, 1978), 122.

The long, bridged, and hooked nose appears on two English Jews drawn in the late thirteenth century (See Figures 5 and 6), the last time the country housed any significant Jewish presence. The more famous of these caricatures includes the caption, *Aaron fil Diaboli,* "Aaron, Son of the Devil," which is meant to evoke the the murderous pack of Jews insisting to Jesus, "Abraham is our father" (*John* 8:39). Allegorizing the parentage of the Jews, Jesus responds, "Ye are of your father the deuill," who "hath bene a murtherer from the beginning" (*John* 8:44), lumping the Jews and the devil in with Cain, the world's first murderer. Some early Christians said that Satan, not Adam, had fathered "Cain whiche was of the wicked" (*I John*, 3:12). When Cain is made into an agent of evil, his mark gains additional significance. In *Genesis*, it is the Lord's blessing of protection for an exile, but the Christians who demonize Cain make this mark into the original instance of the mark of the Jews, a mark elsewhere iterated as circumcision, horns, a big nose, badges, hats, or distinctive clothes (nevermind the transparent contradiction of needing to distinguish in their dress Jews supposedly identified by their bodies).

Figure 5: Caricature of an English Jew, in an anonymous English liturgical manuscript (late 13th c.), at St. John's College (Cambridge, England), 50v.

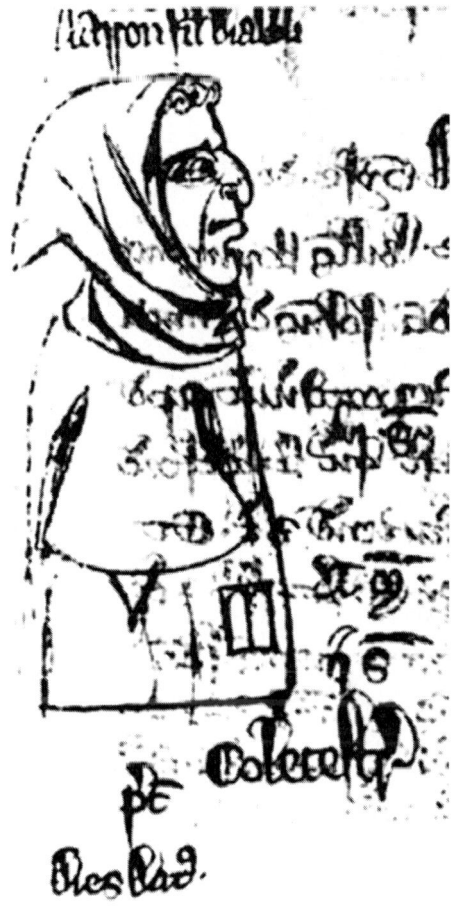

Figure 6: *Aaron fil Diaboli*, in the Forest Roll of Essex (1277), at the National Archives (London, England), "5 Edward I."

Rather than clarify how to costume a Jew, *Merchant* sends a series of insults toward Shylock that makes the Jew sound a lot like the devil. Antonio says Shylock has an "evil soul" (1.3.99), and the Jew is called "devil" on five occasions by four different characters. Most memorably, Launcelot Gobbo thinks "the Jew is the very devil incarnation" (2.2.27-28), and when Salanio sees Shylock, "the devil ... comes in the likeness of a Jew" (3.1.19-21). Here, Gobbo's "incarnation" parodically inverts the incarnation of God in Jesus, and Salanio also displays what social

anthropologists like Stuart Clark call magical or oppositional thinking
when he reasons a "likeness" between the Jew and the devil. Visually,
because spiritually, the Jew and the devil are a "match," as Salanio says
when he sees Shylock's friend, Tybalt: "Here comes another of the tribe: a
third cannot be matched, unless the devil himself turn Jew" (3.1.77-78).
Their bodies "match" each other, devil and Jew, and their bodies also
"match" their morals. Same morals, same bodies, and both are wicked, so
both should be ugly, because that is what evil is said to look like.[3]

    With no evidence to demonstrate he does, one reason to think Shylock
wore the false nose on the Elizabethan stage is that this device thoroughly
demonizes the Jew. This is because the other character to wear an artificial
nose on the sixteenth-century stage is the devil of the Tudor interludes. In
Thomas Lupton's *All for Money* (1578), Sin calls Satan a "bottell nosed
knaue," a phrase Nichol Newfangle also uses to describe Lucifer in Ulpian
Fulwell's *Like Wil to Like* (1587). If Shylock perhaps borrows Barabas's
"bottle-nose," Marlowe's Jew himself inherits this prop from one of the
previous generation's devils, a legacy that configures at least three layers
to the character of Shylock – man, Jew, and devil – each identity offering a
different valence of villainy.

    It is a complicated bit of costuming, the false nose, meant to represent
a natural physical feature of the Jew's body yet so obviously artificial
when affixed to the Gentile actor. The Jew's nose is a part of the
character's body, but not the actor's, just like the hump propped up on the
shoulder of Shakespeare's Richard III. The fact that Barabas and Richard
wear similar dramaturgical devices suggests that some issue prior to "race"
or "deformity" is at play. When a character is socially disqualified on the
basis of an innate difference from some cultural norm, the phenomenon
Erving Goffman identifies as "stigma" reveals its representational force.
Goffman lists three kinds of stigmata: physical, mental, and racial, the first
being Richard's, the last Barabas's. The collapse of these three discrete
categories in a single concept shows that stigma is not an attribute of the
human body but a social relationship that only arises after birth. In other
words, stigma is not nature but second-nature, which is what makes it such
a compelling rhetorical device for poets. Like culture, poetry presents

---

[3] Certainly this comparison of Shylock and Satan benefits from the memory of
Marlowe's Barabas sinking into a cauldron at the end of *The Jew of Malta*, just like
the devil diving into a hell-mouth at the end of earlier mystery and morality plays.
See Lupton on the "Pauline architecture of typology" in Marlowe's stagecraft
(*Citizen-Saints* 67). In *Merchant*, the Jew's "house is hell," over which he lords
like Satan, complete with a "merry devil," Gobbo, whose comic villainy frustrates
while foregrounding the tragic villainy of his master (2.3.2).

"another nature" (in Phillip Sidney's words [14]), not the world as it is but the world as it seems or ought to be, and the visibility of stigma is what makes it so available to the dramatist, the one poet possessed of the power of spectacle. Other characters can submit their words and deeds to an audience for interpretation, but stigma on stage consumes our attention, prejudicing us against he who has it. A stigmatic's actions are not to be judged good or bad: the interpretive task is to determine how his actions are bad, since he has been stigmatized. At the same time, the overt artifice of a nose or a hump draws attention to the theatrical event. It insists we acknowledge the act of representation. During the Elizabethan age, it is in the ironic drama of Shakespeare, where the artifice of both mental and cultural assumptions is habitually exposed, that the interrogation of stigma is most evident. Thus, our currently unanswerable question, *Did an Elizabethan Shylock wear the artificial Jew's nose?*, can stand for an unstable moment in the intellectual history of England, when the reading of stigma was under revision.

Seeing Barabas and Richard III together illuminates what I would call – combining the vocabularies of Auerbach and Goffman – the figure of stigma on the Elizabethan stage. The stigma, be it a crooked nose or a crooked back, incorporates and envisions a particular crime, such as avarice or murder. At the same time the stigma also embodies a cultural enmity to the beautiful and good state suggested in contrast, either Christendom or England. The stigmatic spectacle at the start of an early English play points into the soul of a villain, but also forward to his evil actions, and even up to a divinity that defeats and erases all manner of abnormality (physical, mental, spiritual, and moral) through an attractive and heroic earthly agent like Ferneze or Henry Tudor. In the interim, the stigmatized villain speaks directly to the audience, as in the opening addresses of both Barabas and Richard, trying to avert tragedy with farce, usually by way of some hilarious double-dealing. His invigorating wit endears the stigmatic to the audience, who goes along for the ride, until the playwright slaps us back to our senses with a tragic catastrophe in Act 5. In sum, Barabas and Richard evidence a dramatic strategy early English playwrights use to organize physical abnormality as dramatic spectacle, moral villainy as dramatic character, verbal irony as dramatic speech, and tragicomedy as dramatic plot.

In the comparison of Barabas's nose and Richard's hump, the stigmatic is, among other things, the protagonist of a revenge tragedy, returning woe unto a world that has dealt with him unfairly. In Marlowe's play, when the Maltese coffers are empty, and they owe the Turks ten years' tribute, the governor callously confiscates the wealth of the Jews. Barabas vows revenge, for which the stage is set in Act 5, but he dies in a plot of his own design. In Shakespeare's first tetralogy, the Lancastrians kill Richard's father, and he laments the innate disadvantages of his deformity. Richard vows revenge against his enemies and in fact the entire world, though he cannot kill enough to quiet his anger, which persists until he himself dies in battle during Act 5 of *Richard III*.

Physically and generically, Barabas and Richard are twins, in a manner of speaking, but what about the physical and generic form of their other brother, Shylock? If stigma ends in tragedy on the early English stage, is it possible to think of *The Merchant of Venice*, like *The Jew of Malta* and *Richard III*, as a tragedy? No, frankly, it is not, though it is important to recognize revenge tragedy as the genre against which *Merchant* works. Shylock wants the play to be a revenge tragedy, fuming he will have "no satisfaction" if he has "no revenge" against Antonio (3.1.94). The Christian merchant freely lends out money in Venice, lowering the rate of interest Shylock can charge on his loans, and Antonio does so in a particularly public and racially charged fashion. Shylock vows revenge and plans to exact it through the elaborate contract for a pound of Antonio's flesh if the Christian defaults on his loan from Shylock: "If it will feed nothing else, it will feed my revenge" (3.1.53-54). Here Shylock plays a Janus-faced revenger, like Barabas and Richard III, "a villain with a smiling cheek," as Antonio puts it (1.3.100). In the wake of *The Jew of Malta* and *Richard III*, though, the revenger ought to die in Act 5. The too theatrical public event at the play's climax ought to end in bloody catastrophe, littering the stage with bodies. In *Merchant*, however, Shakespeare locates his public gathering in Act 4, and he emphatically allows "no jot of blood" (4.1.306). *Merchant* is not the revenge tragedy sought by Shylock and written by Marlowe. It is not another play about some Jewish villainy. It is a play about Christian virtue. That virtue is mercy, which is what Shakespeare exercises in Act 4 with a dramatic antinomianism that dispels the laws of revenge tragedy in the same moment that Shylock begrudgingly suspends civic law by reneging his right to Antonio's flesh.

The mixed mode of tragicomedy brings the play's first printer to classify it as "*the most excellent history of the Merchant of Venice*," though the running title in the Quarto calls the play a "*comicall History*," and it is easy to see why both Francis Meres (282) and the First Folio group *Merchant* with Shakespeare's comedies. The marriages of Bassanio and Portia, Gratiano and Nerissa, and Lorenzo and Jessica are only the most obvious reason *Merchant* is a comedy, with a fifth act offering not catastrophe but – nearly a *deus ex machina* – the safe harbor of Antonio's ships. If Shakespeare clearly alters the generic distinction of Marlowe's revenge tragedy, then what does Shakespeare do with the stigma in Marlowe's play, the artificial nose, which is the seal of both villainy and tragedy according to the figure of stigma in early English drama? The question of Shylock's nose can be considered by reasoning inversely: the changes Shakespeare made to the genre of Marlowe's play suggest to me that Shakespeare would have directed the actor playing Shylock to avoid the artificial nose and its tragic implications.

Hath not a Jew a Nose? The Trouble with Stigma in *The Merchant of Venice*

If *Merchant* is clearly no tragedy, it is the enigmatic moral character of Shylock that opens the play up to two possible species, as it were, within the genre of comedy. As I specify the genre of *Merchant* in the following pages, I want to think about the consequent strategies available to Shakespeare for characterizing Shylock. I hope to show a new resonance for the old distinction between a character that is drawn from either art or nature, since this familiar conceit fits so nicely into a discussion of Shylock's nose as also either artificial or natural. Here Stevie Simkin has perceptively unpacked "the artificiall Iewe of Maltas nose": "The description is a transferred epithet – that is to say, a phrase where the adjective ('artificial') is transferred from the appropriate noun ('nose') to another noun ('Jew').… It is not only the false nose (worn presumably by Edward Alleyn when playing the role) that is artificial, but Barabas himself" (149). In this section, I weigh the implications of visually figuring Judaism in either the Jew's clothes or the Jew's nose, coordinating these options with the two kinds of characters I have named, natural and artificial. If Shylock wears an artificial nose, I argue, then his moral character is absolute, coded in his race: he could never not be Jewish. Thus *Merchant* is a moral comedy replacing a Jewish vice with a Christian virtue. If, however, Shylock wears no artificial nose, only Jewish clothes, then his character is variable, open to alteration: he can convert religions (which means moral regeneration) as he can change clothes. Now *Merchant* is a comedy of errors correcting the religious foolishness of the Jew with a Christian education.

Here I am referring to a *comedy of errors* and a *moral comedy*, two different kinds of comedy that come from two different traditions, the one classical and the other medieval. The first kind comes from Aristotle, who gives this surprisingly corporeal definition of comedy in the *Poetics*:

> Comedy is, as we have said, a representation of people who are rather
> inferior – not, however, with respect to every kind of vice, but the
> laughable is only a part of what is ugly. For the laughable is a sort of error
> and ugliness that is not painful and destructive, just as, evidently, a
> laughable mask is something ugly and distorted without pain. (1449a)

Laughing at what is "ugly" and "distorted": Is this our response to the
stage-Jew and his artificial nose? It might be "a laughable mask" that
makes him "ugly," but I have suggested that stage-stigma signals an
essentially villainous character that is "painful and destructive," like
Richard or Barabas. Whether physical or moral, "inferiority" in Aristotelian
comedy is not something absolute. Aristotle calls it "error." In ancient
Greece and Elizabethan England, there are no corrective measures for the
physical differences that are loaded with stigma; they signal something
more serious than "error."

The second kind of comedy comes from Dante, who explains the title
of his epic, *Commedia*:

> Comedy, then, is a certain genre of poetic narrative differing from all
> others. For it differs from tragedy in its matter, in that tragedy is tranquil
> and conducive to wonder at the beginning, but foul and conducive to
> horror at the end, or catastrophe…. Comedy, on the other hand, introduces
> a situation of adversity, but ends its matter in prosperity. (100)

Contrary to the laughably ugly *characters* in Aristotelian comedy, Dante
understands comedy as a simple trajectory in the *narrative*, from
"adversity" to "prosperity." If the genre of comedy is about finding felicity,
the comedy of errors does so in spite of the inferiority in its characters,
while moral comedy does so on account of the good fortune found at the
end of its plot.

It is the comedy of errors that Shakespeare initially establishes in
Merchant by using the Roman stock characters he had explored a few
years earlier in *The Comedy of Errors* (1592-94). Bassanio plays both the
adulescens amator and the *parasitus*, a "willful youth" (1.1.146) but with
a "disabled … estate" (1.1.123). From this perspective, he is little better
than the six other "sponge[s]" Portia enumerates during her introduction
(1.2.39-94). With a carefully crafted garrulity the *servus callidus* Gratiano
"play[s] the fool" (1.1.79), in contrast to the "clown" Launcelot Gobbo
(2.2.1sd), who actually is a fool, or *servus stultus*.[4] In Belmont, the "lady
richly left" (1.1.161) is the *virgo* Portia. "*Her waiting woman*" (1.2.1sd),

---

[4] In Italian, *gobbo* means "hunchbacked," and some scholars have sought to
deform Launcelot, but this allusion is tendentious.

Nerissa, plays the maid, or *ancilla*. Together they provide suitable sexual pairings for the lusty youth and his clever slave. Antonio, so dearly "lov[ing]" Bassiano (1.1.131, 132, and 154), is a *senex amator* of a sort, while the *senex iratus* is "old Shylock" (2.5.2), whose body Shakespeare characterizes as aged, not Jewish. As Shakespeare starts *Merchant* in the manner of Roman comedy, the character types from that tradition fill the stage with what Shylock calls "shallow fopp'ry" (2.5.35). Revenge tragedy destines such a society for destruction, but not Shakespeare's Venice, here in this comedy of errors.

If Shylock can be seen as a Roman stock character, the more English tradition of moral comedy offers another, equally evident, aspect. Shylock cannot be a revenger like Barabas – the genre of *Merchant* does not allow it – but Shakespeare's comedy can handle the aspect of Barabas that resembles the Tudor Vice. Like the Vice, Shylock enjoys "merry sport" (1.3.145), through which he produces his "merry bond" (1.3.173), although it is formulated with "a villain's mind" (1.3.179). In the comedy of errors the *senex iratus* is a morally inferior curmudgeon, but in a moral comedy Shylock is the "enemy," as Antonio puts it (1.3.135). With virtue and vice clearly cut, Portia can say, "I stand for sacrifice" (3.2.57), and Shylock can insist, "I stand for judgment" (4.1.103) or "I stand here for law" (4.1.142). Informing the audience exactly which ethical principle they designate, these two sound just like the allegorical abstractions of sixteenth-century moral comedy. If *Merchant* is a moral allegory, then Portia is the Christian virtue Mercy and Shylock the Jewish vice Law, and the two personifications battle for control of Everyman's soul, as depicted during Antonio's hearing, until Mercy finally conquers Law. As Law, Shylock carries the appropriate allegorical accouterment, the scales of justice (4.1.255). As Vice, Shylock also wields a knife (4.1.124), one certainly sharper than the Vice's dagger of lathe.

Like Benedick in *Much Ado About Nothing* (1598-99), the early English stage does not distinguish between "villain" and "Jew."[5] To see Shylock alternately as the *senex iratus* and as the Vice, however, is to see that Shakespeare's character can accommodate different versions of villainy, ranging from error to enmity. It is important to remember the semantic range of the word *villain*, from the Latin *villa*, "country house." Etymologically *villain* signals a low-born and base-minded social inferior, but in literary usage the word comes to signify a more sinister antagonist.

---

[5] Benedick does not distinguish "villain" from "Jew" thematically, nor does Shakespeare grammatically: "If I do not take pity of her, I am a villain; if I do not love her, I am a Jew" (2.3.262-63). On this proverbial phrase, see Shapiro, *Shakespeare and the Jews*, 8.

It is these various villainies possibly present in Shakespeare's characterization of Shylock that lend *Merchant* alternately to a classical comedy of errors or the medieval moral comedy.

The comedy of errors is about the confusion that ensues when characters forget to balance their personal desires with their social responsibilities, so the character types of Roman comedy each represent a mixture of virtue and vice. This kind of comedy creates a world in which the confused stand around, or more often scuttle about, awaiting reformation. The comedy of errors finds felicity because each character can be educated up out of his or her mistakes and brought back to social propriety. If *Merchant* is played as a comedy of errors, then Shylock's anger toward Antonio, boorishly performed, leads him down a steepening path of moral mistakes, which are compounded until finally corrected into the socially responsible morality of mercy inaugurated with his conversion to Christianity.

This comedy of errors cannot possibly handle an artificial nose, insofar as the figure of stigma establishes an innate and absolute villainy, as well as certain tragedy. For this reason, there are (to my knowledge) no physical deformities in the Elizabethan comedies of error that are modeled on Roman new comedy. Like the artificial nose, the Vice has no place in the comedy of errors. As an allegorical aspect of the greater human or social whole, the Vice is uneducable. Without other allegories to oppose it, the Vice would wear down and annihilate the naturalized characters of Roman comedy, who could not endure an incessant evil that constitutionally resists all attempts to reform it. Conflict in the comedy of errors comes from misperception, right and wrong, but the Vice creates a conflict in moral comedy between good and evil. If *Merchant* is played as a moral comedy, then Shylock's enmity toward Antonio, soberly performed, leads to a confrontation between a Christian good and a Jewish evil, until Shylock is bested by his moral superiors and vanquished from the stage.

In Shakespeare's play, is the villainous Jew morally mistaken, an inferior in need of education, or actually an enemy, a Vice at war with a virtue to which it can never acquiesce? Shakespeare allows both species of comedy into the middle acts of *Merchant*: in Act 2 Jessica's conversion shows a comedy of errors where villainy can be corrected, and in Act 3 Shylock's inconsolable rage shows moral comedy pitting virtue against an irreconcilable vice. First, Jessica's conversion reveals that the Jew in *Merchant* is not necessarily the enemy of the Christian. In this iteration, the Jew is ignorant but educable, not evil nor innocent, so still a villain, but open to reformation. No morality is necessarily written into the Jewish

nation, nor the Jewish body, as Jessica says, contrasting herself with her
father: "Though I am daughter to his blood, / I am not to his manners"
(2.3.18-19). For Jessica to "become a Christian" (2.3.31) is for religious
identity – which in *Merchant* means moral character – to be contingent on
conscious decision rather than attached absolutely to the conditions of
one's birth.[6] Thus when Jessica becomes "a gentle, and no Jew" (2.6.51),
Shakespeare envisions her conversion in her clothes: she disrobes her
Jewish fashions to appear "*above in boy's clothes*" (2.6.25sd). An artificial
nose on Shylock is possible, but it seems highly unlikely on Jessica, whose
religious identity exists not absolutely in her Jewish body but contingently
in the clothes she chooses to wear, Jewish or Christian. She is not
regulated by the figure of stigma, because her body is not marked off. As
Salerio says to Shylock when the Jew laments his lost daughter, "There is
more difference between thy flesh and hers than between jet and ivory"
(3.1.39-40). The line suggests another stigma to identify and discredit
Shylock, tawny skin, and in his Arden edition of *Merchant* John Drakakis
speculates that the roles of Shylock and Morocco were doubled (404). If,
like the Prince of Morocco, Shylock has "the complexion of a devil"
(1.2.130), Jessica shares the "fair flesh" of the Christian Antonio (1.3.130),
or the "fair" skin of the Christian Portia (1.1.162), with color moralized
here into a virtuous light skin and a vicious dark skin. Shakespeare
repeatedly figures religious conversion in the skin color of "fair Jessica"
(2.4.28, 39), who writes to her Christian fiancée with "a fair hand, / And

---

[6] Much of *Merchant* interrogates, as Portia puts it, "the word *choose*" (1.2.22-23),
especially the tension between the human desire to choose one's own destiny and
the angst of a situation where one has no choice. Early in *Merchant*, Shakespeare
poses the problem of religious choice, or conversion, when Antonio calls Shylock
a "gentle Jew" after they seal their bond: "The Hebrew will turn Christian: he
grows kind" (1.3.177-78). Here "kind" means "nice," but it also sounds its
etymology, *kin*, or family, even race, the people to whom you are naturally nice. In
Antonio's statement, Shakespeare suggests the possibility of "growing kind," or
becoming familiar with those who are foreign, asking whether kinship is
determined by blood or by manners, whether it is something one can "grow" into
through, say, religious conversion. Is *kindness* written into our birth, or is it
predicated on our action? These two perspectives produce two readings of the
statement that there is "much kindness in the Jew" (1.3.153). In one interpretation,
there is "much [hospitality] in the Jew," suggesting a cross-cultural kindness; but
in another interpretation, there is only, tautologically, "much [Jewishness] in the
Jew." This latter kind of *kindness* references a Jewish identity that can be nothing
other than Jewish (including hospitable, the former kind of *kindness*). This
tautological kind of "Jew" is synonymous with "villain," as in Gobbo's polyptoton:
"I am a Jew if I serve the Jew any longer" (2.2.112-13).

whiter than the paper it writ on / Is the fair hand that writ" (2.4.12-14). Jessica's conversion to Christianity even signals a moral education that might emanate to Shylock: "If e'er the Jew her father come to heaven, / It will be for his gentle daughter's sake" (2.4.33-34). As Lorenzo continues, however, he says the Jewish nation might have a necessarily tragic fate operating independent of any conscious moral choice: "And never dare misfortune cross her foot, / Unless she do it under this excuse, / That she is issue to a faithless Jew" (2.4.35-37). For this reason, Gobbo later playfully pontificates to Jessica, "I think you are damned" (3.5.5-6). There will be, Jessica mocks, "no mercy for me in heaven because I am a Jew's daughter" (3.5.32-33), to which she responds with a summary of her comedy of errors: "I shall be sav'd by my husband, he hath made me a Christian" (3.5.19-20).

In the idiom of Elizabethan comedy, the error of Jessica's Judaism in Act 2 is open to education, but the enmity of Shylock's Judaism in Act 3 is unalterable and must be attacked. Seeing Jewishness as a villainy alternately to be corrected or to be conquered drives us to the core question of what exactly Shakespeare's Jew is: how does Shakespeare want us to see this character, as a human being or as a cultural stereotype? Here we can separate the two identities Shakespeare collapses in his stage directions for "Shylock the Jew." I shall speak of one possibility called "Shylock" and one called "the Jew."[7] The first is a "he," the second an "it," so "Shylock" refers to an un-nosed character, while "the Jew" invokes the artificial device. "The Jew" is the Vice, so it is a dramatic convention, an artificial construction of evil, but when he is only morally inferior, not evil, "Shylock" is a human being, fully naturalized. In my reading, *Merchant* is about Shakespeare's attempt to make a character ("the Jew") into a human ("Shylock"), which I say thinking about Charles Lamb's juxtaposition of a Barabas that is stigmatized and a Shylock that is not:

> Shylock in the midst of his savage purpose is a man. His motives, feelings, resentments, have something human in them…. Barabas is a mere monster brought in with a large painted nose to please the rabble…. It is curious to see a superstition wearing out. The idea of a Jew (which our pious ancestors contemplated with such horror) has nothing in it now revolting. We have tamed the claws of the beast, and pared its nails, and now we take it to our arms, fondle it, write plays to flatter it: it is visited by

---

[7] Although I have not seen this formulation elaborated, it is suggested by Brooke: "He is not only Shylock, he is a Jew" (140); and Cohen: "Shylock is addressed as 'Shylock' only seventeen times in the play. On all other occasions he is called 'Jew' and is referred to as 'the Jew' " (54).

Princes, affects a taste, patronizes the arts, and is the only liberal and
gentlemanlike thing in Christendom. (31)

Amidst this notionally refined but really inhumane conceptualization of
"the idea of a Jew," Lamb articulates two possible ways to play "it." On
the one hand, "the Jew" in *Merchant* could have been a monstrous bogey
like Barabas, where "it" is an artificial construction, either the revenger or
the Vice. On the other hand, Shakespeare's "Shylock," though still a
villain, seems more human than Barabas, for "he" is a naturalized
character, not a monster.

Shakespeare shows these two strategies for characterizing "Shylock the
Jew" in the altered basis of the character's identity, which comes from
"its" religion in 1.3 but from "his" bare human being in 3.1. First, when
the Christians invite it to dinner, the Jew identifies itself through a
religious difference allowing no communion: "I will not eat with you,
drink with you, nor pray with you" (1.3.33-38). Later, however, Shylock
famously subordinates his Jewish identity to a universal human community
based not on religious difference but on biological similarity: "Hath not a
Jew eyes? hath not a Jew hands, organs, dimensions, senses, affections,
passions? fed with the same food, hurt with the same weapons, subject to
the same diseases, healed by the same means, warmed and cooled by the
same winter and summer, as a Christian is?" (3.1.61-64). It is significant
that Shakespeare's blazon passes over the nose, the one body part that
might determine whether we should see a naturalistic "Shylock" or an
artificial "Jew." Moments like this illustrate what I mean by Shakespeare's
irony. In his assertion of bare human being, Shylock could have said,
"Christians and Jews smell with the same noses," which would have
confirmed Shakespeare's rejection of the artificial nose; but Shakespeare
goes out of his way to avoid the most obvious physical feature of the Jew's
body, leaving open the possibility that Shylock dons the nose. This
dramaturgical indeterminacy actually fits the thematic irony of this scene
perfectly, for Shylock only appeals to a universal human community in the
service of his quest for revenge: "If a Jew wrong a Christian, what is his
humility? Revenge. If a Christian wrong a Jew, what should his sufferance
be by Christian example? Why, revenge" (3.1.68-71). In other words,
Shylock's most human and usually sympathetic moment is tethered to his
intensely artificial heritage as a Vice and a revenger who cannot act
otherwise.

The possibility that an Elizabethan Shylock wore the nose refocuses
the famously problematic question Portia asks upon arriving in Venice:
"Which is the merchant here? and which the Jew?" (4.1.174). Portia seems
to say neither Antonio nor Shylock appears in such a way that makes his

identity self-evident. Shylock wears no Jewish nose, it would seem, nor
even Jewish clothes. Insofar as Shakespeare usually minds the relationship
between spectacle and character closely, an identical appearance could
suggest a moral equivalence between Antonio and Shylock, each partly
responsible for letting their bond get so out of hand. Shakespeare might be
making this point, but completely indistinct appearances seem highly
unlikely to me, and Portia's line does not land if Shylock has even the
most moderate Jewish attire. I can easily imagine, however, Portia uttering
the line sarcastically, to roaring laughter, as she recovers from the shock of
seeing a hyperbolically Jewish Shylock, clothed head-to-toe in Jewish
regalia and wearing an obnoxiously bulbous nose: "Which is the merchant
here? and which the Jew?" In the void of evidence that the Elizabethan
Shylock wore an artificial nose, Portia's disarming question is a rare
reason to think he did.

Even though Portia starts by insulting "the Jew," she proceeds, like the
Duke, with an appeal to an individual. "Is your name Shylock," she asks,
and he answers, proudly, surprised to be addressed as a man rather than a
monster, "Shylock is my name" (4.1.176). When Portia insists, however,
"must *the Jew* be merciful" (4.2.182), she undercuts herself, since "the
Jew" that is abstractly constructed to signify Law is not capable of mercy.
"Shylock" is, but not "the Jew." Thus Portia pleads once more with
"Shylock" (4.1.227), but her appeals do not resonate with "the Jew," as the
character is called for the rest of the scene (4.1.231, 280, 292, 321, 346,
393).

The shifting appellations used by Shakespeare's Venetians express the
nebulous identity of their opponent, as well as the alternate possibilities for
the scene's comic resolution. When Antonio's bond is eventually forgiven,
and felicity finally found in Venice, it is punctuated with the demand that
"Shylock the Jew" convert to Christianity. Since Charles Macklin's
sympathetic performance of the character in 1741, and acutely since
World War II, it has been popular to view Shylock as a man wronged by
Antonio before the play begins, then wronged again by Portia during the
scene at court. I doubt many Elizabethans saw Shylock's conversion in
this way. They would not have asked if it was a good thing done fairly.
They would have assumed it was, then spent their interpretive energy
asking what kind of comedy they had seen come to completion, asking
how the comic promise of felicity had been fulfilled: had the villainy of
"the Jew" been conquered in a moral comedy, or had the villainy of
"Shylock" been corrected in a comedy of errors?

To summarize: on the one hand, *Merchant* can be a moral comedy,
featuring "the Jew" and its artificial nose. To stigmatize Shylock with this

dramaturgical device is to suggest that the character is equally artificial, an allegorical abstraction of a certain kind of immorality, like the Vices that annoy the Tudor interludes. With its character predetermined by its conceptual significance, thus absolute and impervious to change, this villain is an enemy whose actions can be altered no more than the stage-Jew can hide its humongous nose. From this perspective, *Merchant* is a morality play depicting the conquest of a Christian virtue, Mercy, over one of its most persistent challenges, Law. Thus the Jew and it legal absolutism are expelled from the play in Act 4, left to wander the earth like Cain, while the Christian characters find felicity in Act 5. Even Antonio gets his ships. On the other hand, *Merchant* could be seen as a comedy of errors featuring "Shylock," who wears no artificial nose. To abandon this dramaturgical device is to humanize the character according to the naturalized stock characters of Roman comedy. As *senex iratus*, Shylock is still a villain, but his villainy can be corrected with religious conversion. Rather than an enemy, this version of Shylock is an inferior whose errors can be amended, just as he can change into Christian clothes. While the character of the Vice is absolute, the *senex iratus* is open to education. It is this willingness to change his behavior, howsoever begrudgingly, that allows Shylock to remain in the state of Venice after his hearing. Barabas isn't so lucky.

We cannot know with any certainty which way an Elizabethan experienced *The Merchant of Venice*, for two reasons. First, Shakespeare's irony is often canceled in performance when a company must make dramaturgical decisions that privilege one interpretation over another, like whether or not Shylock should wear the artificial nose. In the dramatic illusion Shakespeare envisioned and we recreate for ourselves when we read his text, Shylock may or may not wear the artificial nose. In a theatrical performance, with all the finality of the material world, Shylock either is or is not stigmatized. Until we know whether or not the Elizabethan actor playing Shylock wore the artificial nose, we cannot know how Lord Chamberlain's Men encouraged their audience to interpret the character.

Second, in the Christian ethics an Elizabethan draws from the Bible, there are inconsistent instructions about how to respond to inferiority, as evident in the plight of the stigmatic. Throughout the Bible, stigma always signals inferiority, but the stigmatized are excluded from God's sacred society in some books of the Bible and included in others. In *Leviticus* the Lord tells Moses to deny priesthood to anyone with a "blemish … lest he pollute my Sanctuaries" (21.18-23). Here, with impure souls somehow expressed in their defective bodies, the stigmatized are encountered and exiled by God's lieutenant on earth, as occurs in the figure of stigma in early English drama. In the terms of my discussion on dramatic genre, *Leviticus* and its ethics of exclusion align with the concerns of moral comedy, where vice is vanquished by a superior virtue. It is when *Merchant* is seen from this perspective that "the Jew," a sinister evil stigmatized by its artificial nose, must be attacked and vanquished from the blessed community of Christians Shakespeare creates in Act 5.

In contrast, other books of the Bible welcome the stigmatic into God's fold, although this inclusion takes two different forms. First, the stigmatics are sometimes accepted, inferiority and all. When David wants to "shewe the mercy of God" to his friend Jonathan, he hosts a dinner for Jonathan's son, Mephibosheth, who was "lame of his feete" (*2 Sam.* 9.3). Jesus moralizes this gesture: "When thou makest a feast, call the poore, the maimed, the lame, and the blind" (*Luke* 14.13). These are the ethics of acceptance at play in *Merchant* when Bassanio invites Shylock to dinner. It is heartening to imagine a stigmatized Shylock sharing table fellowship with Venetian Christians in a moment of mutual recognition, but Shylock throws the invitation back in Bassanio's face. Racial tensions are so strained in Shakespeare's Venice that there can be no communion between Christian and Jew. In the play Shakespeare wrote, Shylock cannot be accepted for who he is. His inferiority must be either conquered or corrected.

Thus, if Shylock is to join the sacred society, this inclusion is predicated on the correction of his inferiorities, moral and possibly physical as well. Rather than exclusion or acceptance, some Biblical stigmatics experience what might be thought of as a "messianic orthopedics." From the promises of the prophets, to the miracles of Jesus, to the healings of his apostles, these stigmatics have their inferiorities magically amended by the awesome power of God. While discussing correction in the comedy of errors, I sought to associate it with a "Shylock" who shows no stigma, since the deformities, disabilities, and differences that are stigmatized in the pre-modern world have no corrective measures available to them. The notion that God can miraculously correct organic inferiorities, however, opens up a new possibility for *The Merchant of Venice*.

At Shylock's hearing, and at other times in *Merchant*, Portia speaks – more than mercy, equity, or justice – a rationality that borders on the divine *logos* of Christianity. Her dad set up the ridiculous business with the caskets to select Portia's husband, but when her suitors come to Belmont, she quickly sees how stupid it would be to leave love to chance. When she directs Bassanio to the lead casket, she does not capriciously suspend the laws of the land so much as she amends an outdated edict based on circumstance. She must massage her father's law into the actual affairs on the ground, just like Jesus in the Gospels. Thus she is a "demigod" (3.2.115) bringing "the joys of heaven here on earth" (3.5.76) and "drop[ping] manna in the way / Of starved people" (5.1.294-95). Shakespeare makes Portia the mediation of deity and humanity, romance and realism, Belmont and Venice. I think it would be too much to associate her transformation into Balthazar with the incarnation of God in the Christian gospels, but her trip to Venice does carry a certain sense of grace. It allows Shakespeare to cancel his bond to the dramatic laws of revenge tragedy in the same moment that Portia cancels Antonio's bond to the civic laws of Venice. In this reading, Portia's appearance in Venice figures the appearance of the messiah awaited by the Jews – she is one of Shylock's "godfathers" after all (4.1.398) – and the conversion of Shylock recalls the conversion of Paul. *Acts* commemorates Paul's conversion to Christianity with a memorable metaphor, the scales falling from his eyes (9.18), which might prompt us to consider a corporeal correlative for Shylock's conversion, like the artificial nose falling from his face.

In 1894, Henry Vibart described an amateur Shakespearean travesty held by some boys at a military academy in south London:

When they essayed to play a piece called 'Shylock Travestied,' Shylock had become possessed by lawful purchase, of a magnificent Jewish nose made of gutta-percha. This nose, a most artistic one, stuck on beautifully in a cold climate; but in the air-excluded room, with the temperature at about 100° Fahrenheit, the case was altered. In the midst of one of Shylock's most telling speeches, the nose became detached, and had to be held on with one hand, whilst the requisite declamation was conducted with the other. (260)

With Jewish-Christian friction heating up in Europe during the 1930s, an Oxford dramaturge described another small and otherwise unremarkable production of *The Merchant of Venice* where "Shylock started so energetically when told he must become a Christian that his Jewish nose came off and fell with a resounding flop on the stage" (Foss 36). For Shylock's nose to fall off in the middle of a performance is one thing, literally revealing the Christian authority behind this representation of a Jew, as well as the unstable artifice of one race stigmatizing the physical differences of another. For Shylock's nose to fall off upon his Christening is another thing, configuring the elimination of this stigma with Shylock's forced conversion. We might imagine an Elizabethan production of *Merchant* planting the artificial nose on Shylock, announcing absolute villainy and unavoidable tragedy according to the figure of stigma; but then Portia converts the Jew, or *corrects* in the idiom of the comedy of errors, demonstrating the miraculous power of Christianity to alter the laws demanded by stigma on the early English stage. The notion that every Jew has inside a Christian trying to break out is utterly repulsive, though tonally this reading of *Merchant* rings more pro-Christian than anti-Semetic, for which it is hard to fault Shakespeare. If an Elizabethan *Merchant* did use the nose, and play Shylock's conversion as a correction (rather than a conquest), this play would be the only comedy of errors I have seen that can handle stigma, doing so by recruiting some supernatural element that can correct the uncorrectable, Portia, what the Romans called a *deus ex machina*.

Bibliography

Alighieri, Dante. "The Letter to Can Grande." Trans. Robert Haller. *Literary Criticism of Dante Alighieri*. Lincoln: University of Nebraska Press, 1977. 95-111.

Aristotle. *Poetics*. Trans. Richard Janko. Indianapolis: Hackett, 1987.

Auerbach, Erich. *Mimesis: The Representation of Reality in Western Literature*. Trans. Willard R. Trask. Princeton: Princeton University Press, 1953.

Bacon, Francis. *The Proficience and Aduancement of Learning*. London: Henrie Tomes, 1605.

Berek, Peter. "'Looking Jewish' on the Early Modern Stage." *Religion and Drama in Early Modern England*. Eds. Jane Hwang Degenhardt and Elizabeth Williamson. Burlington: Ashgate Publishing, 2011. 55-70.

The Bible and Holy Scriptures. Trans. William Whittingham, Anthony Gilby, and Thomas Sampson. Geneva, 1560.

Brooke, Stopford A. "Merchant of Venice" *On Ten Plays of Shakespeare*. London: Constable, 1905.

Chapman, George. *The Blinde Begger of Alexandria*. London: J. Roberts for William Iones, 1598. N. pag.

Clark, Stuart. *Thinking with Demons: The Idea of Witchcraft in Early Modem Europe*. Oxford: Clarendon Press, 1997.

Cohen, D. M. "The Jew and Shylock." *Shakespeare Quarterly* 31.1 (Spring, 1980): 53-63.

Coleridge, Samuel Taylor. "Kean." *Table Talk*. Ed. Henry Morley. London: George Routledge and Sons, 1884.

Collier, John Payne. "A Funerall Elegy on the Death of the Famous Actor Richard Burbage: Who Died on Saturday in Lent, the 13th of March 1618." *The Gentleman's Magazine* (1825).

—. *New Particulars Regarding the Works of Shakespeare*. London: Thomas Rodd, 1836.

Conway, Moncure Daniel. "The Pound of Flesh." *The Wandering Jew*. London: Chatto and Windus, 1881.

Cooper, John R. "Shylock's Humanity." *Shakespeare Quarterly* 21.2 (1970): 117-24.

Drakakis, John, ed. *The Merchant of Venice*. London: The Arden Shakespeare, 2010.

Edelman, Charles. "Which is the Jew that Shakespeare Knew?: Shylock on the Elizabethan Stage." *Shakespeare Survey* 52 (2003): 99-106.

Felsenstein, Frank. "'Ev'ry child hates Shylock'." *Anti-Semitic Stereotypes: A Paradigm of Otherness in English Popular Culture, 1660-1830*. Baltimore: Johns Hopkins University Press, 1999.

Foss, George Rose. *What the Author Meant*. London: Oxford University Press, 1932.

Freinkel, Lisa. "*The Merchant of Venice*: 'Modern' Anti-Semitism and the Veil of Allegory." *Shakespeare and Modernity: Early Modern to Millennium*, ed Hugh Grady. London: Routledge, 2000. 122-41.

—. *Reading Shakespeare's Will: The Theology of Figure from Augustine to the Sonnets*. New York: Columbia University Press, 2002.

Fulwell, Ulpian. *Like Wil to Like*. London: Edward Allde, 1587.

Girard, Rene. "'To Entrap the Wisest': A Reading of *The Merchant of Venice*." *Literature and Society: Selected Papers from the English Institute*. Ed. Edward W. Said. Baltimore: The Johns Hopkins University Press, 1973. 100 19.

Glassman, Bernard. *Anti-Semitic Stereotypes Without Jews: Images of the Jews in England 1290-1700*. Detroit, MI: Wayne State University Press, 1975.

Halio, Jay L. "Introduction" *The Merchant of Venice*. Oxford: Oxford University Press, 1998.

Heywood, Thomas. "The Prologue to the Stage at the Cock-Pit." *The Jew of Malta*.

Holmer, Joan Ozark. "Jewish Daughters: The Question of Philo-Semitism in Elizabethan Drama." *The Merchant of Venice: New Critical Essays*. Ed. John W. Mahon and Ellen Macleod Mahon. New York: Routledge, 2002.

Jerrold, Douglas. Quoted in George Henry Lewes, "Edmund Kean." *On Actors and the Art of Acting*. London: Smith, Elder & Co., 1875.

Jordan, Thomas. "The Forfeiture, A Romance." *A Royal Arbor of Loyal Poesie*. London: R.W. for Elizabeth Andrews, 1663.

Knox, Dilwyn "Ironia Socratica." *Ironia: Medieval and Renaissance Ideas on Irony.* Leiden: Brill, 1989. 94-138.

Lamb, Charles. *Specimens of English Dramatic Poets, who Lived About the Time of Shakspeare.* London: Longman, Hurst, Rees, and Orme, 1808.

Lelyveld, Toby. *Shylock on the Stage.* Cleveland: Western Reserve University Press, 1960.

Lupton, Julia Reinhard. "Exegesis, Mimesis, and the Future of Humanism in 'The Merchant of Venice'." *Religion & Literature* 32 (2000): 123-39.

—. "Merchants of Venice, Circles of Citizenship." *Citizen-Saints: Shakespeare and Political Theology.* Chicago: The University of Chicago Press, 2005.

Lupton, Thomas. *All for Money.* London: Roger Warde and Richard Mundee, 1578.

Marlowe, Christopher. *The Jew of Malta.* Ed. Roma Gill. *The Complete Works of Christopher Marlowe.* Oxford: Clarendon Press, 1987.

Marston, John. *Iacke Drums Entertainment.* London: Thomas Creede for Richard Oliue, 1601.

Mellinkoff, Ruth. *The Mark of Cain.* Berkeley: University of California Press, 1981.

Melnikoff, Kirk." '[I]ygging vaines' and 'riming mother wits': Marlowe, Clowns and the Early Frameworks of Dramatic Authorship." *Early Modern Literary Studies* 16 (Oct., 2007): 1-37.

Meres, Francis. *Palladis Tamia* London: P. Short for Cuthbert Burbie, 1598.

Moore, John Robert. "Pantaloon as Shylock." *Boston Public Library Quarterly* 1 (1949): 33-42.

Pope, Alexander. Attributed in "The Merchant of Venice." *The Dramatic Censor* 1 (1770).

Puttenham, George. *The Arte of English Poesie.* London: Richard Field, 1989.

Rowley, William. *A Search for Money.* London: George Eld for Ioseph Hunt, 1609.

—. *A Search for Money.* Ed. the Percy Society. *Early English Poetry, Ballads, and Popular Literature of the Middle Ages*, Vol. 2. London: T. Richards, 1840.

Shapiro, James and Steven Greenblatt. "Shylock in Red?" *The New York Review of Books* (Oct. 14, 2010).

Shapiro, James. *Shakespeare and the Jews.* New York: Columbia University Press, 1997.

Sidney, Philip .*An Apologie for Poetrie*. Ed. Forrest G. Robinson. Indianapolis, IN: Bobbs-Merrill, 1977.

Simkin, Stevie. "'Unhallowed Deeds' :*The Jew of Malta*." *A Preface to Marlowe*. New York: Longman, 2000.

Smith, James H. "Shylock: 'Devil Incarnation' or 'Poor Man … Wronged'?" *Journal of English and Germanic Philology* 60 (1961): 1-21.

Stoll, Elmer Edgar. "Shylock." *Journal of English and Germanic Philology* 10 (1911): 236-79.

Taylor, Gary. "Shakespeare Plays on Renaissance Stages." *The Cambridge Companion to Shakespeare on Stage* Ed. Stanley Wells and Sarah Stanton. Cambridge: Cambridge University Press, 2002. 1-20.

Trachtenberg, Joshua. *The Devil and the Jews: The Medieval Conception of the Jew and its Relation to Modern Antisemitism*. Philadelphia: The Jewish Publication Society of America, 1961.

Vibart, Henry Meredith. *Addiscombe, Its Heroes and Men of Note*. Westminster: A. Constable and Co., 1894.

READING LAW AND ETHNICITY
IN THE MANGA SHAKESPEARE
MERCHANT OF VENICE

RUSSELL MCDONNELL

Although for much of the twentieth century comic books were regarded with considerable disdain by the guardians of general morality and good taste,[1] in recent years they have achieved enormous popularity and respect, even in literary culture. The first comic book versions of Shakespeare's plays were produced more than sixty years ago, but since the turn of the twenty-first century, there has been an explosion in the publication of Shakespeare comics, many of them works of considerable literary and artistic sophistication. The medium of comics is characterized both by its sequential nature and by its combination of words and pictures to achieve its effects; therefore, its panel transitions and its word-image relationships are the major keys to understanding how a particular comic functions, and how it is managing its subject matter in effective and innovative ways. In 2011 the Manga Shakespeare series published its edition of *The Merchant of Venice*, a particularly impressive Shakespearean comic book, textually adapted by Richard Appignanesi and illustrated by Faye Yong. The opening pages of the work provide a great example of the kinds of sequential devices and word-image relationships that are featured throughout this comic book version of the play. In this chapter I demonstrate how these formal complexities operate and then trace some of the central debates within criticism of *The Merchant of Venice*, showing how this adaptation takes distinct positions within these debates, and that it can therefore be seen as a sophisticated, critical interpretation of Shakespeare's work.

The comic opens (after an illustrated Dramatis Personae) with an image of a Venetian canal. What in film would be called an "establishing

---

[1] For the most famous and influential example of this sort of critique, see Wertham, Fredric. *The Seduction of the Innocent*. New York: Rinehart and Co., 1954.

shot" is here an establishing panel, identifying where we lay our scene. Here begins Antonio's speech, as he reflects, "I know not why I am so sad" (Yong 12). In this opening panel, text and image stand side-by-side in what comics theorist Scott McCloud calls a "parallel" word-image relationship, the two components of the comic coexisting, but seeming to function independently, with no clear relationship to one another (154). Although the situation is quickly clarified with the zoom-in on Antonio's face, the immediate effect is ambiguous and unsettling, colouring the whole Venetian scene with a sense of sadness and uncertainty (See Figure 1). "Your mind is tossing on the ocean," explains Salerio, "where your argosies with portly sail, like pageants of the sea, do overpeer the petty traffickers" (13). This bit of text initially seems like a simple metaphor, explaining the nature of Antonio's distress by likening it to a ship tossing on an ocean, but after the main clause we quickly learn that although the likening of Antonio's mind to a ship is of course metaphorical, the purpose of the comparison is not to merely describe his distressed state of mind, but to do so in a way that links this state to its cause. Thus what initially appears to be a simple, evocative comparison becomes something more elegantly forensic, characterizing Antonio's mind as a ship on the same sea where his actual ships are sailing (See Figure 2). Salario certainly offers a complimentary account of these ships, embedding a simile within his metaphor to liken them to "pageants of the sea." The reference is a theatrical one: "pageants" refers to the decorated, movable outdoor stages that were traditionally used in the performance of open-air mystery plays in late Medieval and early modern Europe. Thus even as Salerio praises the grandeur of Antonio's ships, he does so by likening them to theatrical devices, implying not only a worrying degree of physical flimsiness but also hinting at their dubious epistemological status. How real are these ships?

In this adaptation Salerio's imaginative account of Antonio's ships at sea is accompanied by an image of them, sailing proudly along, making the "petty traffickers" look petty in comparison. Yet on the next page, Salerio takes his description along far more distressing lines, and this description comes with a correspondingly different set of images: "Should I go to church and see the holy stone, and not think of dangerous rocks, which, touching my vessel's side, would scatter all her spices on the stream, enrobe the waters with my silks ... and now worth nothing?" (14). These lines accompany a series of three panels that depict one of the grand ships crashing violently into rocks and sinking, sending sailors and valuable cargo tumbling into the sea (See Figure 3). Here the comic confronts the reader with some significant questions about the exact nature of these images and the relationship they bear to the text. It is first worth noting the tiny figures of the crew members, hurled to their deaths in the sea, who appear nowhere in Salerio's speech. Turning again to McCloud's terminology, we might initially have been tempted to characterize this word-image relationship as "duo-specific," that is, one in which text and image convey essentially the same information. Yet these sailors may prevent us from that easy assignation; they are a small visual detail in the picture, easy to miss, and yet they inject a human dimension into the tragedy which, in Salario's mind, is entirely financial. We may read this detail as a subtle comment from Yong on a certain selfishness or coldness implied in the motives that Salario attributes to Antonio. Is he perhaps a man more concerned with money than with people? Additionally, when we regard this sequence of images are we seeing a set of imaginary events that exist only in Salario's mind (and which he imagines exist in Antonio's mind)? Or is Yong here shifting the scene of the action to Antonio's actual ships at sea which, as we later learn, really do sink?

The relationship between the previous image of Antonio's ships and this sequence of them sinking could be a relationship between an optimistic and a pessimistic imagining, or between a falsely optimistic imagining and the terrible truth, or between two true images separated in time. The question is complicated by the fact that the panel depicting the first image of the ships is bounded by a swirling, watery pattern. As legendary comics creator Will Eisner has observed, "The frame's shape (or absence of one) can become a part of the story itself" in various ways (46). The frame can be used "to convey something of the dimension of sound and emotional climate in which the action occurs, as well as contributing to the atmosphere of the page as a whole" (Eisner 46). As one of his examples, Eisner notes that a "cloudlike enclosure" for a panel often "defines the picture as being a thought or memory" (47). Thus this method of framing might lead us to suppose that the first image, at least, is an imaginary one. Alternatively, however, we might suppose that the watery border simply reinforces the nautical theme of the image. The second sequence is bordered on the left-hand side by Salario himself, which might indicate that the series of images emerges from him just as the accompanying speech balloons emerge from him – creations of his imagination, or possibly the thing itself. Additionally, we should note that Salerio's speech does not just refer to the images of ships that it either describes or conjures up; it also stands side-by-side, after all, with the images depicting the friends in the gondola, with Antonio, significantly, standing at the prow. As the ships toss on the treacherous and uncertain sea, so Antonio stands on the potentially treacherous waters of the Venetian

Figure 1. (C) SelfMadeHero, 2009. Illustrations by Faye Yong, Adapted by Richard Appignanesi

Figure 2. (C) SelfMadeHero, 2009. Illustrations by Faye Yong, Adapted by Richard Appignanesi

Figure 3. (C) SelfMadeHero, 2009. Illustrations by Faye Yong, Adapted by Richard Appignanesi

canals. Given that he is standing up in the boat he may be said to "overpeer" those around him, even as he is unaware of the financial and legal dangers into which his sinking ships will soon plunge him.

Reading the Law

This opening sequence, with its complex play of image sequencing and word-image combinations sets up a sense of instability in the text: first there is an ambiguous sense of where the characters are and what's going on; second, there are ambiguous images of sinking ships which may or may not exist only in Salerio's imagination and which might be implying something about Antonio's own moral attitude; and third, there is Antonio's obliviousness to his own precarious position in the commerce and (consequently) in the law of Venice. This third theme—the nature and operation of law in the play—has been of persistent interest to critics, yet most of this criticism has shown little interest in the subtlety and ambiguity that the Manga Shakespeare version identifies and explores. Indeed, most of the criticism that has taken an interest in the nature of law and its uncertainties in *The Merchant of Venice* has been curiously literal in its focus and much of it has been the work of retired lawyers and judges with an amateur's enthusiasm for the Bard.

Dunbar Plunket Barton, in his book *Links Between Shakespeare and the Law* devotes a chapter to the play, discussing whether or not the trial is "duly conducted according to the strict rules of legal procedure" (146) with reference to sixteenth-century English law. In the end, however, he negates the entire chapter by reflecting, "But why should a dramatist's law, where the scene is laid in France or Venice or Navarre, be supposed to be strictly conformable to the Laws of England?" (Barton 150). Why indeed? One might expand the point: why should a dramatist's law be strictly conformable to *any* real law? And why should we assume that Shakespeare cared at all about the specific nuances of legal procedure? But Barton's conclusion did not stop George Keeton or O. Hood Phillips from continuing the discussion. Keeton, for no obvious reason, speculates about what defences would be open to Antonio if the case "could be tried in a modern law court" (132). Phillips, like Barton, sets himself the task of testing "the soundness and fairness of the legal proceedings arising out of the forfiture" (92) and wonders exactly how it is that Portia is permitted to participate in the trial, concluding with stern judicial authority that as she is "the wife of Bassanio, the principal debtor for whom Antonio (the defendant) went surety; and is housing Shylock's daughter . . . Her position is thus most prejudicial" (92). It is a little hard to understand why anyone would want to approach the play with such legalistic literalism, which manages to be simultaneously pedantic and irrelevant.

But we mustn't kill *all* the lawyers, as we do get some more interesting work from practicing attorney Daniel J. Kornstein in his book *Kill All the*

Lawyers?: Shakespeare's Legal Appeal. Kornstein's reading of *The Merchant of Venice* focuses on the play's treatment of two different attitudes towards the formal rules and structures of the law. He cites Shylock's repeated appeal to his "bond" throughout the trial scene and argues that "Shylock here symbolizes literalness, and technicality in the law, divorced from common sense, prudence, and practical wisdom" (Kornstein 68). But Shylock's insistence on "literalness and technicality" (Kornstein 69) leaves him vulnerable to Portia's counterattack. She promises "Thou shalt have justice, more than thou desirest" (4.1.317), observes that "This bond doth give thee here no jot of blood" (4.1.306), and warns "if thou cut'st more / Or less than just pound . . . Thou diest and all thy goods are confiscate" (4.1.326-32). In Kornstein's view, this argument is patently absurd: "Portia's interpretation is like granting an easement on land without the right to leave footprints" (70). But the ludicrousness of Portia's reply is part of her strategy: her judgement "seems to be a quibble, a ludicrously literalist reading of the contract; an empty, hypertechnical [sic] legalistic interpretation that is illogical, useless, impossible, and absurd" and thus she demonstrates that "law, literally construed, can be nonsense" (Kornstein 71). I think Kornstein is on to something here, and there is some overlap between his position and that of Terry Eagleton.

Eagleton's position resembles Kornstein's in its recognition of the absurdity of Portia's demands upon Shylock: "No piece of writing can exhaustively enumerate all conceivable aspects of the situation to which it refers: one might just as well claim that Shylock's bond is deficient because it does not actually mention the use of a knife" (37). Unlike Kornstein, he theorizes this problem in poststructuralist terms, observing that "Any text [...] can be understood only by going beyond its letter, referring it to the material contexts in which it is operative and the generally accepted meanings which inform and surround it. Portia's reading of the bond, by contrast, is 'true to the text' but therefore lamentably false to its meaning" (Eagleton 37). Eagleton cites Shylock's insistence that if the court denies his bond, then "There is no force in the decrees of Venice" (4.1.102), to suggest that "It is almost as though Shylock is defying the court to deny him in order to expose its own hollowness. Either way he will win: by killing Antonio, or by unmasking Christian justice as a mockery" (38). Eagleton asserts that "What is at stake in the courtroom . . . is . . . the law of Venice itself: will it maintain its proper indifference to individuals, penalize one of its own wealthy adherents at the behest of an odious Jew?" (38). He answers himself that "of course . . . it will not; but in order to avoid doing so it must risk deconstructing itself, deploying exactly the kind of subjective paltering it exists to spurn" (Eagleton 38).

In *Shakespeare's Language* (2000) Frank Kermode sees the play as treating "the theme of Justice in the light of a supposed distinction between the Old and the New Law" (Kermode 71). In this view the Old Law "is represented by Shylock and lacks any tempering by Mercy, as opposed to the 'gentle' Gentile dispensation, which embraces the idea of forgiveness and redemption" (Kermode 71). According to this interpretation, Shylock's error is his complete commitment to the law, independent of any concern for mercy or grace: "refusing to accept payment of his loan, he has refused a bid for a secular redemption that would have echoed Christian doctrine" (Kermode 71). Kermode points to Antonio's line "Hie thee, gentle Jew" (1.3.173) in which the epithet "gentle" is doubly ironic, for being inaccurate both in the sense of being a complimentary remark about Shylock's kindness, nobility, and social rank and also in the punning sense of "Gentile" – with the clear implication that the lack of the latter quality inevitably indicates the lack of the former. Although Kermode does not make additional connections here, Antonio's pun should also put us in mind once again of Salerio's opening speech, in which he imagines how, if he were in Antonio's position, the stone walls of the church would make him think of his ships at sea, and of treacherous rocks touching "my gentle vessel's side" (1.1.32). Although the reader or spectator does not necessarily know it yet, Shylock will soon become the rock that threatens the "gentle" (or gentile) vessel – a point more heavily ironic given that in the context of the speech, the hypothetical rocks Salerio refers to are ones he was put in mind of by a Christian church, "the holy edifice of stone" (1.1.30). In the mind of an anxious Christian merchant, an ungentle Jew may corrupt a society to such an extent that even church stone evokes dangerous sea rocks, to sink a "gentle vessel."

In his 2004 book, *Shakespeare and the Origins of English*, Neil Rhodes also sees religion as a crucial point in the play's attitude towards law, observing that although "Christian equity" should theoretically guarantee an impartial legal process, Shylock's status as a Jew is evidently sufficient to disqualify him from receiving it (109). Rhodes's reading leans heavily on Alexander Silvayn's *The Orator*, a text published in 1596 which comprises one-hundred judicial "Declamations" and whose ninety-fifth entry is a likely source text for the play: "Of a Jew, who would for his debt have a pound of flesh of a Christian" (Silvayn 400). In this text, the Jew appeals to the impartial procedure of the law while his Christian opponent replies not with a legal argument but a stream of vitriol, insisting that the Jew has no right to "dispute of equitie" when he has "no faith at all" and that his demand is an "abhomination" (404). Rhodes reminds us of the etymological roots of "abhominable," which derives from *ab homine* "to mean 'away from man, inhuman, beastly'" (110). He argues that the trial scene in *The Merchant of Venice* follows much the same form as that in *The Orator*, concluding that "humanity understood as mercy or generosity has to be predicated on an acknowledgement of the humanity, in the more fundamental sense of the word, of the different parties concerned" (Rhodes 111). That is to say, although Christian law may have to treat everyone equally, does a Jew like Shylock even count as part of everyone?

The problem with Rhodes's line of argument is that his reading of the play depends not at all on the words of the play itself but entirely on the text of one of its possible sources. In placing the word "abhominable" in quotation marks he rather neatly detaches it from *The Orator*, and thenceforward applies it freely to *The Merchant of Venice*, as if it actually appeared there. Furthermore, in the trial scene, Shylock differs crucially from the Jew in Silvayn's *Orator* in that although he does receive a stream of dehumanizing abuse from Gratiano, this has nothing to do with why he loses his case. His failure results rather from Portia's "hypertechnical" reading of the law, which makes a mockery of his insistence on the precise terms of his "bond," but which does not abandon the necessary fiction that the trial is about Justice taking her majestically impartial course based on appeals to formal procedure, rather than being about the defeat of a villainous Jew.

So what does Manga Shakespeare do when it approaches these questions and problems, and how does it deploy the formal devices peculiar to the medium of comics in dealing with them? To answer this question requires a brief background in comics theory, a small but growing body of work, the most important example of which is *Understanding Comics*, the seminal text of comics artist and writer Scott McCloud. The most important aspect of McCloud's argument in *Understanding Comics* comes with his discussion of "closure," which he defines broadly as the "phenomenon of observing the parts but perceiving the whole" (63). The type of closure that most interests McCloud occurs in the space between panels that "comics aficionados have named 'the gutter'" (66). In McCloud's view, "the gutter" is perhaps the most crucial feature of the comics medium because it requires the reader to fill in what happens in between the panels of the comic book (66). In this view, the reader becomes, as he says, "a silent accomplice … an equal partner in crime" because "closure in comics fosters an intimacy…a […] contract between creator and audience" (68-9). As an example of this principle, McCloud offers two panels. The first depicts two men, one of them wielding an axe and shouting "Now you die!" and the other cowering before him shrieking "No! No!" The second panel depicts a city skyline, over which the agonized shout "EEYAA!!" hangs in the air in jagged letters (McCloud 68). McCloud points out that although we read in these images a gruesome act of murder, in fact no murder is directly represented. The reader of a comic book must exercise closure – must imaginatively fill in the gaps between panels, in response to textual and artistic cues.

McCloud classifies six different types of panel-to-panel transition: Moment-to-Moment, Action-to-Action, Subject-to-Subject, Scene-to-Scene, Aspect-to-Aspect, and Non-Sequitur (70-74). This last category raises the question, acknowledged by McCloud, of whether it is possible "for any sequence of panels to be totally unrelated to each other" (73). He responds in the negative, maintaining that "no matter now dissimilar one image may be to another" there remains "alchemy at work in the space between panels which can help us find meaning or resonance in even the most jarring of combinations" (73). The other most crucial aspect of the comics medium that McCloud defines is that of word-image relationships: whenever text and image appear together they must have a particular relationship to one another. McCloud defines seven types of word-image combination that can occur in comics: Word Specific, Picture Specific, Duo-Specific, Additive, Parallel, Montage, and Interdependent (153-155). This final type is perhaps the most interpretively interesting, as it occurs when "words and pictures go hand in hand to convey an idea that neither could convey alone" (McCloud 155). Although this chapter does not discuss examples of all of these categories of transition and relationship, I do discuss some of them. Doing so should give an idea of how the recognition and classification of the formal features of comics can be crucial to the interpretation of works in this medium.

Reading Ethnicity

One key aspect of the critical conversation surrounding this play is the question of anti-Semitism and that of racism more generally; the intensely visual nature of comics prioritizes the question even further as a representational question on which a comics artist must make a definite decision. This is one of the classic questions in discussions of anti-Semitism: what does a Jew look like? This facet of the criticism includes discussions of the play's early performance history. Although there is a common account that Shylock was originally played in a clownish red wig and false nose, John W. Mahon observes that this idea derives from a ballad by Thomas Jordan published in 1664 titled "The Forfeiture: A Romance"; as Mahon observes "this is hardly a contemporary account" (21). Indeed, closer investigation reveals that the poem does not even describe a stage performance of the play but is rather a fresh adaptation of the story itself, making the physical description of the Jewish antagonist even more irrelevant to our understanding of Shakespearean theatrical practice. Jordan describes a Venetian Jew:

> His beard was red, his face was made
> Not much unlike a Witches;
> His habit was a Jewish Gown,
> That would defend all weather;
> His chin turn'd up, his nose hung down,
> And both ends met together. (11-16)

In this version, the disguised woman at the trial who turns the case against the Jew is not Portia but the Jew's own daughter, who is described as having "a Christian soul / Lodg'd in a Jewish body" (23-24). The poem might be an interesting glimpse into early modern anti-Semitic attitudes, but it remains a decidedly slender reed on which to rest any certain claims. The fact that this particular performance convention is mentioned nowhere in Andrew Gurr's authoritative *The Shakespearean Stage 1574-1642* is telling. Certainly, openly anti-Semitic depictions were standard in Nazi Germany[2] and the play's performance history can potentially cause anxiety for modern directors of the play who are anxious to avoid appearing racist.

Harold Bloom, for instance, declares that "One would have to be blind, deaf, and dumb not to recognize that Shakespeare's grand, equivocal comedy *The Merchant of Venice* is nevertheless a profoundly anti-Semitic work," though he adds that "every time I have taught the play, many of my most sensitive and intelligent students become very unhappy when I begin with that observation" (171). It is not clear how a student can be sensitive and intelligent, and yet at the same time blind, deaf, and dumb; neither is it obvious why Bloom considers it good pedagogical practice to begin a classroom discussion of a play by telling his students what interpretive conclusions they ought to draw about it, but perhaps we should bracket these pedagogical concerns. In any case, the position that the play is anti-Semitic is a common one, and even those scholars who reject this view

---

[2] For a detailed discussion, see Bonnell, Andrew G. *Shylock in Germany: Antisemitism and the German Theatre from the Enlightenment to the Nazis*. New York: Tauris Academic Studies, 2008.

acknowledge the importance of how Shylock is depicted. Yet Daniel Kornstein insists that a key factor in the play's appeal is generalizable nature of its theme. He maintains that "Shylock is not only a Jew; he is a symbol for any group that feels itself oppressed. Substitute African-Americans, women, or any other such group, and we understand the strength of their impatient feelings for full equality. We are all outsiders now, and Shylock looks better to us" (81). The coercive use of "we" is a hazard in the business of literary interpretation and claims so phrased are inevitably vulnerable to refutation by any reader or audience member who simply replies that he or she feels no such thing. Nevertheless, Kornstein's conclusion does represent an interpretive view worth noting: that the specific ethnicities represented and discussed in *The Merchant of Venice* are incidental to its themes of legality and prejudice. The Manga Shakespeare version exhibits the same tendency in its de-specification of the play's treatment of ethnicity. Although Appignanesi's textual adaptation does not erase the references to Shylock's Jewishness, Yong's envisioning of it effectively does so by converting Venice from a historically and geographically literal place to a fantastically altered version of itself, populated by characters whose pointed, elfin ears identify them as not precisely human. Although it retains some of its recognizable features, including canals and gondolas, these features are recognizable only because of what we know about the real-world city of Venice, not from any particular details in the text of Shakespeare's play. Furthermore, Yong refigures ethnicity in the play in a way that removes it from the zone of historical and religious specificity in order to convert the play into one that makes a more general point about racism and otherness. In the art of comics (and, indeed, in the art of illustration in general) one major key to the depiction of character types is that of the cartoon.

In *Understanding Comics*, McCloud defines the cartoon as "amplification through simplification," explaining that "by stripping down an image to its essential 'meaning,' an artist can amplify that meaning in a way that realistic art can't" (30). He argues that we tend to regard a photograph or a detailed, realistic drawing of a face as the face of a person who is distinctively other than ourselves, but that a simple cartoon fact, consisting only of a few dots and lines, is easy for us to identify with (McCloud 36). Although the phenomenological thrust of this claim makes it impossible to prove definitively (we cannot reasonably purport to know the subjective experience of readers and audience members) it does draw our attention to questions of how figures are represented and the attitude that the artist invites us to hold towards them. The Christian characters in the Manga Shakespeare *Merchant of Venice* are white-skinned and fine-featured, distinguishable mainly by their clothing and by the length and shade of their hair. And in discussing this topic we must not just look to the Jewish characters; as R. W. Desai observes, "besides Shylock as the Other, there are other Others like the first two suitors who make a bid for the hand of Portia and have, in general, been eclipsed by Shylock" (304). These characters are physically marked as Other – yet not by any means that corresponds obviously to real-world ethnicities. The Jewish characters in the play are pale-skinned, with long, braided black hair, while the Prince of Aragon has large webbed ears and webbed feet, and the Prince of Morocco wears a keffiyeh (a traditional Arabic headdress) and, as we can see in the opening Dramatis Personae pages, which depict all the major characters in colour, he has green skin.

The Prince of Morocco is a particularly interesting character to investigate in this adaptation, because Shakespeare's text makes pointed reference to the blackness of his skin. When she first learns of his arrival as a suitor, Portia remarks to Nerissa, "if he have the condition / of a saint and the complexion of a devil, I had / rather he should shrive me than wive me" (1.2.123-25). Upon their first encounter Morocco, evidently sensing or anticipating her distaste, urges her, "Mislike me not for my complexion, / The shadow'd livery of the burnish'd sun, / To whom I am a neighbour and near bred" (2.1.1-3). It is worth noting here that although the more dominant and obvious meaning of "mislike" here is simply "dislike," an early modern text may well be drawing on the more archaic alternative meaning of "displease" or "offend." On the former reading, Morocco is urging Portia not to be dismayed or displeased at the colour of his skin; on the latter, he is urging her not to displease *him*. On this reading, Morocco's statement becomes not a plea for favour but an instruction, perhaps even a warning. In this regard, Morocco's remark should remind us of Shylock's famous speech on the humanity of the Jew, which contains the pointed rhetorical question, "if you wrong us, shall we not revenge?" (3.1.56). Morocco does not promise revenge, but his remark perhaps contains a hint of defiance that puts him in an analagous position to the Jew.

In the play, Portia twice makes disparaging remarks to Nerissa about Morocco's dark skin. The first is the one quoted in the previous paragraph, which she makes upon first hearing of him, and the second upon his departure: "A gentle riddance. Draw the curtains, go. / Let all of his complexion choose me so" (2.7.76-77). These remarks directly contradict the praise she gives Morocco to his face. After reminding him that "the lottery of my destiny / Bars me the right of voluntary choosing" (2.1.15-16), she assures him that if she were allowed to choose her own husband, "Yourself, renowned prince, then stood as fair / As any comer I have look'd on yet / For my affection" (2.1.20-22). Desai reads this passage as Shakespeare's own unusual love of blackness shining through in his writing, reconciling the apparent contradiction between the statements of praise and disdain by reasoning that this must be evidence that "the negative capability Keats attributed to Shakespeare does break down occasionally" (313). He supports this argument with what he seems to regard as a perfect *reductio ad absurdem*: he maintains that the only alternative to supposing that Shakespeare loves blackness and allows that love to spill out into his characters' dialogue is the unthinkable notion that Portia's contradictory statements are evidence that she is "a hypocrite and a dissembler" (313). This is an imperfect argument because given Portia's behaviour in the trial scene, it is hardly a strange notion to characterize her as a dissembler, and because even an insincere compliment to a visiting suitor might reasonably be said to fall under the heading of politeness, rather than of dishonest hypocrisy. In the Manga Shakespeare version, Appignanesi removes Portia's first complaint about Morocco's colouring but retains the second. Thus although he maintains her disdain for Morocco's race, the line about him having a "devil's face," which by early modern cultural standards directly implies blackness, is removed. The retained complaint refers only to "complexion," which in the visual context of this comic version refers to greenness. Appignfanesi also abridges Morocco's appeal (or warning) to Portia, retaining the opening line, but removing any reference to "the burnish'd sun" to which he attributes his blackness. The much-shortened speech simply reads, "Mislike me not for my complexion. I tell thee, Lady, this aspect of mine hath feared the valiant" (Yong 50).

The treatment of the Jewish characters in the play is somewhat different, as the text indicates their lack of any skin colour for the Christian characters to object to. Lorenzo, in fact, actually praises Portia for her fair skin. As he reads her letter, her remarks, "In faith, 'tis a fair hand; / And whiter than the paper it writ on /Is the fair hand that writ" (2.4.12-3). The fact that he lauds the whiteness of her skin (an entirely conventional piece of praise) indicates that for Jewish characters, at least, skin-colour is not a problem. Yet at one point, Salerio angrily informs Shylock that he and his daughter are different: "There is more difference between thy flesh and hers than between jet and ivory; more between your bloods than there is between red wine and Rhenish" (3.1.33-35). Despite the lack of a literal difference of melanin, he wants to attribute Shylock's wickedness to his Jewish body. In the Manga Shakespeare version of the play, Jessica's ethnically-specific appearance does not change at the end of the comic. She marries Lorenzo and becomes a welcome and included member of the Christian group of friends, but is still allowed to retain the black braids that are the distinctive mark of Jewishness in Yong's imagined world (Yong 205). Therefore the problem with Judaism, in both Shakespeare's textual version and Manga Shakespeare's comics version seems not to be racial but theological, a point that is also confirmed when Shylock is given the chance to avoid seizure of all his wealth by converting to Christianity (4.1.381).

The problem of visually marking Jewishness in the medium of comics has been famously confronted by Art Spiegelman in his great work *Maus*, a Holocaust memoir about his father's time in Auschwitz. In this comic book, Spiegelman performs the darkly Aesopian transformation of representing the members of the various nations involved in the Second World War as different animals. Thus Americans appear as dogs, Poles as pigs, Germans as cats, and Jews as mice. A feature of the text well worth noting (and critics have noted it) is that Jews are always mice, regardless of the particular country in which they happen to live. Yong's representation of the Jewish characters in *The Merchant of Venice* is similar to Spiegelman's insofar as she appears to reinforce the immutability or unassimilability of ethnic identity: the non-Christian characters in the play are, after all, marked with evident, physical differences. To be sure, the Manga Shakespeare version lacks the element of allegorical fable that *Maus* exhibits, and by making the difference not one of species but of relatively superficial skin-colour and hairstyle, somewhat softening the ethnic essentialism of the text which, as we shall see in a moment, is rather complex.

The recognition of some of these categories in the Yong's envisioning of the opening scene of the play has already provided us with valuable interpretive insights into how the Manga Shakespeare *Merchant of Venice* operates. We have seen Antonio precariously floating, both literally and figuratively, on uncertain waters, unaware of his tenuous position. Yet as the play moves along, he becomes more and more aware of the exact nature of the trouble he is in, explaining to Salerio:

> The duke cannot deny the course of law:
> For the commodity that strangers have
> With us in Venice, if it be denied,
> Will much impeach the justice of his state;
> Since that the trade and profit of the city
> Consisteth of all nations. (3.3.26-31)

On its face, the word "justice" may appear to refer to a transcendent principle of absolute moral order, yet the fact of its impeachability works against that reading, particularly when the source of that impeachment is "commodity" – a word with a primarily economic signification. Although it can carry a more general sense of a benefit or advantage, the dominant sense here seems to be that of an item for trade, produced for sale and use. This fairly concrete economic term has an even less auspicious sense of "A quantity of wares, parcel, 'lot'" which refers essentially to a volume of material goods. If "commodity" has the power to "impeach the justice of his state" then we see that justice is therefore contingent upon trade, and is not divine, absolute, or self-sufficient. We should note the polyptotonic echo of "deny" and "denied" in the passage; the former is attached to "law" and the latter to "commerce," and the correspondence reinforces the point that Venetian law is effectively identical with the Venetian economy. It is also worth pausing over the word "his" in the phrase "his state." Although the use of the genitive case implies mastery and control of the state, it is evidently in the power of "strangers." Not only is "justice" here undermined by being subject to external forces and relegated to the realm of political-economic contingency, but even within this sphere, the official political head of the city is not in charge either. It may be officially "his state," but not truly under his control.

The Manga Shakespeare edition features an abridged version of Antonio's explanatory speech. It is split between two balloons, the first containing "The Duke cannot deny the course of law" and the second containing "For the commodity that strangers have with us in Venice, if it be denied, will much impeach the trade and profit of the city" (Yong 126). The first balloon is positioned on the divide between two panels, the one a small panel illustrating a close-up view of Antonio's worried face and the second depicting the figure of the Duke, proffering a set of scales, looming over a shadowy version of the city of Venice. This transition is "subject-to-subject," showing two distinctly different images but remaining within the same idea: Antonio discussing the nature of Venetian justice. Yet it is worth noting that the transition is only this coherent because of the shared speech balloon: on the basis of images alone, it would be hard to discern a definite connection between the two. As comics critic and theorist Charles Hatfield has observed, understanding panel-to-panel transitions depends not only on images but on words:

> Verbal cues do help to bridge the gaps within a sequence, as seen in common transitional captions such as "Later" or "Meanwhile" (devices that have fallen from favor as readers become more versed in reading comics, just as title cards, fades, irises, and other such transitional devices fell from favor in cinema). In fact verbal continuity can impose structure on even the most radically disjointed series. (44)

McCloud's own example of closure between panel transitions illustrates this point effectively: without the scream hanging in the night sky, the transition between the two figures and the city skyline might seem truly obscure – readable as scene-to-scene or perhaps even as a non-sequitur, rather than as the Subject-to-Subject transition that he labels it.

This splitting of a speech balloon between two panels relies significantly for its effect upon the way that it jumps the gap between dialogue and narration. Lines of dialogue simply emerge from a character and are unambiguously an expression of a particular point of view; narration, in contrast, by its very nature, possesses (or aspires to) an omniscient or objective status. While there do of course exist unreliable and fallible narrators, what makes them notable and interesting is the assumption of objectivity and correctness inherent in the fact that they are narrators. There is nothing remarkable, after all, about an unreliable character. The switch from dialogue to narration on this page sends a clear signal that we are to read Antonio's speech not just as the worried expression of a character (although it is that as well) but also as a general comment on the theme and situation of the play, although the image of Antonio in the small panel at the top left corner of the page never quite lets us forget that this speech emerges from a single, and potentially partial, point of view. Because the same piece of text spans two panels it participates simultaneously in two different word-image relationships. The smaller of the two panels contains an instance of what McCloud terms a word-specific relationship, in which the text conveys most of the relevant information and the image plays a secondary role – in this case, indicating only which character is speaking. From here we transition to the larger panel, which contains a fascinating "interdependent" word-image relationship in which words and images go hand-in-hand to express an idea that neither could convey alone (McCloud 154). Although the Duke bears the scales in the image, the text makes clear that he is powerless to interfere with their operation, because although he towers over the city as its official ruler, its welfare depends upon the economic activity of "strangers," whose activities he dares not disrupt. Significantly, Appignanesi here slightly abridges the Shakespearean text, converting the object of the verb from "justice" to "trade and profit," thus foregrounding the Duke's economic concerns: in this grammatical revision, justice does not just serve commodity but is literally replaced by it. This refocusing of the textual passage creates an ambiguity in the illustration, in which we may wonder whether the scales really serve as a symbol of justice or rather as a tool of commercial trade. The abridgment also removes the ambiguous "his" in Shakespeare's text, but we might regard the possession or domination implied by the genitive case as somewhat substituted in the towering dominant figure of the Duke; on this reading, the irony is retained.

The Manga Shakespeare *Merchant of Venice* continues to make intriguingly ambiguous use of the image of scales throughout, and sometimes deliberately avoids the image in scenes where we would normally expect it. When Shylock declares in the trial scene, "I stand here for justice" (Shakespeare 4.1.146), he means that he demands and awaits the proper fulfilment of the law, but the phrase "stands for" also conveys the idea that he *represents* the law. At the climactic moment of the trial, when Antonio "must prepare [his] bosom for the knife" (4.1.257) Portia confirms with Shylock that he has his "balance" ready (4.1.270) and, as Theodore Ziolkowski points out, it is hard not to see "Shylock with his knife and balance" as "a striking image of Justicia" (174). The opportunity to represent Shylock as a parodic figure of Justice would seem tempting to a comics artist, yet Faye Yong avoids taking this opportunity. In fact, the image of scales never occurs in the Manga Shakespeare *Merchant of Venice* except as entirely metaphorical images: no literal scales ever appear in the book. At the moment of the trial in which Portia asks for the balances, Yong shows us an image of the scales alone in a panel with a black background, free from any of the immediate, literal context of the play's action.

The question of what sort of panel transition we have here is somewhat difficult. It is not quite a subject-to-subject transition, as it does not simply switch to a different subject within the scene, but to a subject quite outside the immediate reality of the courtroom. Yet neither is it a scene-to-scene transition, as we are not moving to a new location *per se*, but to an object just referred to in the dialogue. Although this question might spark some debate among comics theorists, I would argue that this transition best fits within the McCloud's category of action-to-action transitions, in which we switch not to a different spatial aspect of the current scene but to a different thematic aspect, regarding the scales not so much as a physical object in the courtroom but as a symbol of law whose function threatens to become gruesomely literal in a moment, as promised in the dialogue: "Are there balance here to weigh the flesh?" (149). Placed thus before the black background, the scales here become a visual realization of precisely what Eagleton describes: the law progressing according to its literal letter, independently of the "material contexts in which it is operative" (37). Here Justice is truly blind, that is to say, operating in darkness, according to the strict text of the bond, without concern for context – although this fact turns out to be Shylock's downfall rather than his triumph.

In conclusion, I should explain that the purpose of this volume is to showcase and demonstrate new approaches to *The Merchant of Venice* and that to my mind, such a collection should demonstrate not only the interpretations that can be produced by the application of current critical theories, but also those that can be produced by the operation of current artistic media. I hope to have demonstrated that this comic book adaptation of Shakespeare's play is a robust interpretive engagement in its own right and that I have showcased not just the benefits of applying McCloud's comics theory to a comic book, but also the fresh critical perspective that an excellent work of comic book art can bring to our understanding of Shakespeare. In other words, the critical approach that I wish to demonstrate here is that embodied in the medium of comics itself, which can take on a complex, sophisticated text like *The Merchant of Venice* and (if you will forgive the pun) truly do it justice.

Bibliography

Barton, Sir Dunbar Plunket. *Links Between Shakespeare and the Law.* London: Faber & Gwyer Limited, 1929. Print.

Bloom, Harold. *Shakespeare: The Invention of the Human.* New York: Riverhead Books, 1998. Print.

Desai, R. W. "'Mislike Me Not for My Complexion': Whose Mislike? Portia's? Shakespeare's? Or That of His Age?" *The Merchant of Venice: New Critical Essays.* Ed. John W. Mahon and Ellen MacLeod. New York: Routledge, 2002. 305-20. Print.

Eisner, Will. *Comics and Sequential Art.* Tamarac: Poorhouse Press, 1985. Print.

Gurr, Andrew. *The Shakespearean Stage, 1574-1642.* Cambridge: Cambridge University Press, 2003.

Hatfield, Charles. *Alternative Comics: An Emerging Literature.* Jackson: University Press of Mississippi, 2005. Print.

Jordan, Thomas. "The Forfeiture: A Romance." *A royal arbor of loyal poesie consisting of poems and songs.* London: R. Wood, 1664. 36-40. Print.

Keeton, George W. *Shakespeare's Legal and Political Background.* London: Sir Isaac Pitman & Sons Limited, 1967. Print.

Kermode, Frank. *Shakespeare's Language.* London: The Penguin Press, 2000. Print.

Kornstein, Daniel J. *Kill All the Lawyers?: Shakespeare's Legal Appeal.* Princeton: Princeton University Press, 1994. Print.

Mahon, John W. "The Fortunes of *The Merchant of Venice* from 1596 to 2001." *The Merchant of Venice: New Critical Essays*. Ed. John W. Mahon and Ellen Macleod Mahon. New York: Routledge, 2002. 1-94. Print.

Spiegelman, Art. *Maus: A Survivor's Tale*. New York: Pantheon Books, 1999. Print.

McCloud, Scott. *Understanding Comics: The Invisible Art*. New York: HarperCollins Publishers, 1993. Print.

Phillips, O. Hood. *Shakespeare and the Lawyers*. London: Methuen & Co Ltd, 1972. Print.

Rhodes, Neil. *Shakespeare and the Origins of English*. New York: Oxford University Press, 2004. Print.

Shakespeare, William. *The Merchant of Venice*. *The Norton Shakespeare*. Ed. Stephen Greenblatt,Walter Cohen, Jean E. Howard, Katharine Eisaman Maus. New York: W. W. Norton & Co., 1997. 1111-175. Print.

Silvayn, Alexander. *The orator handling a hundred seuerall discourses*. Trans. Anthony Munday. London: Adam Islip, 1596. Print.

Yong, Faye, illus. *The Merchant of Venice*. By William Shakespeare. Adapt. Richard Appignanesi. New York: Amulet Books, 2011. Print.

WITH THESE ESSAYS IN HAND:
RE-STAGINGS OF *THE MERCHANT OF VENICE*

SIDNEY HOMAN

I have known this play as an actor and director, teacher and scholar, and as a member of the audience for almost fifty years now.[1] But I invoke the past here only to bring it into the context of this present collection of essays. What have they to tell us about options the actor might take in fashioning his or her character? How might the essays contribute to the director's concept for the play?

Whatever else *The Merchant of Venice* is about—and I use that word "about" in the two senses of meaning and happening (as in, "Is your mother about the house?")—it is about how we, in our age, read or stage the play or the film, or, with a nod to Russell McDonnell's analysis of the Manga Shakespeare comic version, experience it as a reader in a medium combining word and image. Bassanio has his choice among three caskets, their three metals, and three inscriptions encouraging interpretation. We have an almost infinite number of caskets, the only warning being: be careful to avoid the situation where "one person's individual reason or meaning can be asserted as *the* reason or meaning" (Newlin 116).[2]

The essays in this collection, while not primarily performance criticism, let alone accounts from directors and actors, are, no less, *performances*—upon the text. And for this very reason I find them of great value because they allow me to imagine how their readings might inform a production, indeed, the next chance I get to do this play. While using the methods and language of scholarship, as calibrated to the principles of the scholar's

---

[1] Most recently I directed a production of *The Merchant of Venice* for a conference, "Convergences and Conversions: *The Merchant of Venice* into the Twentieth Century," sponsored by the Center for Women's Studies and Gender Research and the Center for Jewish Studies at the University of Florida, April, 2010. And the play is part of my yearly production *An Evening with William Shakespeare.*
[2] All citations to the work done by the scholars in this collection line up with their page number in this book.

own critical approach, be it historical or feminist, or psychoanalytic —or "whatever," as our students would say— each essay does precisely what responsible directors do. In that isolated period before rehearsals begin, or meetings with the design staff, even before the first read-through with the cast, they develop their concept, what they think the play is "about" — again, with that double meaning I use above.

While the contributors often cite productions of the *The Merchant of Venice*, I confine my remarks mostly to my own experience with the directors and actors with whom I have worked, for while the ultimate text for the essays in this volume is Shakespeare's play, my immediate text is really the essays themselves. I use what that great Shakespearean scholar Alfred Harbage, my own teacher, would call "the test boring method," taking eight specific moments in the play that have intrigued or puzzled or, most often, stimulated those charged with performing *The Merchant of Venice*. Given the tight construction so typical of Shakespeare, where every moment contributes to the play's larger pattern, however the latter is defined by the director or the scholar, these eight moments can serve, I believe, as microcosms for the macrocosm.

"In sooth, I know not why I am so sad" (1.1.1)

Shakespeare's plays start off like some well-tuned race car, going from 0 to 60 in a matter of seconds.[3] Antonio is feeling "sad," overly reflective, possibly morose, at least not his usual happy self. But why? He claims not to be worried about the safety of his ships, and we may chose to believe or not believe him when, in response to Salanio's alternative speculation that he is in love, he replies with an abrupt "Fie, fie" (1.1.47). The actor will want to have an immediate subtext for that single word "sad," for this condition that "wearies" Antonio but —again if we believe him— whose cause he does not know, although he does add that he is "to learn" (2-5).[4]

Examining the opening panel in the 2011 Manga Shakespeare comic version of the play, McDonnell points to the "parallel" relation between text and image, "the two components ... coexisting but seeming to function separately," with the effect being "ambiguous and unsettling" (162). The picture of a ship sinking gives form to Salerio's "argosies with

---

[3] The text for Shakespeare is *The Norton Shakespeare*, gen. ed. Stephen Greenblatt (W. W. Norton and Company: New York, 2008).
[4] Only line numbers are given after the first reference to the act and scene division that coincides with the act and scene division cited in the title for each section of this chapter.

portly sail" crashing on the rocks as a metaphor for Antonio's distress and, no less, depicts an actual event now with a "human dimension" when we see the tiny figures of sailors ("who appear nowhere in Salerio's speech") drowning in the sea. For McDonnell the panel may make a "subtle comment" by Salerio about a "certain selfishness or coldness" in Antonio: he cares for his ship, but not his men.

For McDonnell, in this way "the comic confronts the reader with some highly significant questions about the exact nature of these images and the relationship they bear to the text" (163). This possible aspect of Antonio's character, his indifference to the sailors, sustains a point McDonnell makes at the end of his essay: that new interpretations of the play can come from the "current artistic media" of the comic no less than the "critical theories" applied elsewhere in this collection (180).

Whatever option the actor takes, in collaborating with the director, will very much shape Antonio's character in the play, will explain what his real object is when two scenes later he enters into that foolish bargain with Shylock for a pound of flesh.

Is that bargain Antonio's desperate attempt to show Bassanio how profound his feelings are, driven by a homosexual love that the courtship of Portia threatens to render impossible? Paul Digman calls this option "intriguing from a modern standpoint" but one that "veer[s] sideways from medieval and early modern associations of close male friendship with nobility and ethics" (49). He does cite Michael Radford's film (2004) where Bassanio and Antonio lounge on a bed "somewhat suggestively together" and the 2010 Broadway production in which the homosexual attraction was more obvious (48, note). Dingman opts instead for Antonio's suffering a "lovesickness [as] described in several romances of the medieval era" (49), with Shakespeare's main plot turning on "this early agreement" (the bond for the pound of flesh) between close friends, underscoring the "clear trust" they have for each other (51).

For Horacio Sierra, Antonio is in love with Bassanio, yet fears he will lose him to Portia, and, while he cannot confess this love to the well-intentioned Salerio and Salanio, this is why he is "sad." For the actor, if this Antonio knows why he is "sad," then his "But how I caught it found it, or came by it" (3-4) is a smoke screen. Alternately, Antonio is not yet sure of his feelings for Bassanio, or is caught between acceptance and denial, and thus his "I am to learn" and "I have much ado to know myself" (5, 7) will give the actor an arc for the character, from uncertainty to growing certainty (the first signs of this perhaps coming in 1.3 when he enters into the contract with Shylock that goes against his normal prudent business practices), to his moving expression of his love for Bassanio at the trial when he thinks Shylock has won:

> Grieve not that I am fall'n to this for you
> ... Commend me to your honorable wife.
> Tell her the process of Antonio's end.
>   Say how I loved you. Speak me fair in death,
> And when the tale is told, bid her be judge
> Whether Bassanio had not once a love (4.1.261-72)

Bassanio in turn would "lose" and "sacrifice" his "life, [his] wife, and all the world" if it would "deliver" his friend from "this devil" Shylock (4.1.277-82). The challenge here for the actors playing Antonio and Bassanio is to keep their exchange from becoming bathetic, for the expression of love is as sincere and passionate as that between Portia and Bassanio.

From his initial uncertainty about his feelings Antonio comes to a "queer acceptance of his seemingly interminable bachelorhood," which Sierra finds "a positive contrast with Shylock's fears and embarrassment about his negligible claim to being Jessica's father" (94). In Act 5, Antonio's being willing to vouch for his friend's fidelity signals his new "investment" in a "reproductive futurity ... via a homosexual triangle wherein he unties Bassanio and Portia," and, as Sierra adds, "whom we assume will have children" (95). Taking this option for Antonio would thus recall characters in Shakespeare who, whether the attraction is sexual or only social, must give up a friend to someone of the other gender: Mercutio's losing Romeo in *Romeo and Juliet*, Benedict's losing Claudio to Hero in *Much Ado about Nothing*, Celia's losing Rosalind to Orlando in *As You Like It*. Despite his desperate measure to retain the bond between himself and his general, Iago at length loses Othello to Desdemona, if we have a positive reading of Othello's death speech.

Audrey Birkett, however, is more tentative in identifying Antonio's love as homosexual, saying his relationship with Bassanio is "unclear at the outset" (20), the sexuality "never identified" (20). As a result, for her "Homosexual and heterosexual are not fixed identities in the play" (21).

I find that these readings of Dingman, Sierra, and Birkett are, at length, not that far apart, since all involve the testing of a friendship, whatever its nature, and the principle of sacrificing oneself for another. Each reading allows a choice of emphasis and subtext for the actor playing Antonio in his conversation with Basanio at the end of the opening scene. Antonio's "eye of honour" emphasizes his concern that Bassanio's plan to clear himself of debts be an ethical one, although his use of his "person" and "extremest means" may, or may not, admit a more emotional subtext. Still, in a play where caskets, once opened, can lead to abstinence or love, Antonio's trinity of purse, person, and means "Lie all unlocked to [Bassanio's] occasion," or requirements (135-39).

Bassanio has the greater number lines here, but as an actor once told me, "Anyone can say lines. It's what to do onstage when you have no lines that's difficult." At first, Antonio lightly chides Bassanio for being so round-about in asking for a loan and then he must listen to him praise Portia at great length as "fair" and then "fairer than that word, / Of wondrous virtue" (162-63). While Bassanio holds the stage, Antonio can still "speak" in his visual reactions, in gestures that are as important as the dialogue. How does he look at Bassanio as he goes on for fourteen lines about the woman who will, at very least, share in his affections? Does he sigh? Does he try to speak, interrupting his friend extoling Portia's beauty, virtue, and wealth? At some point, does he turn away to hide his disappointment? The stage direction has the two exit *severally* or separately. Would the director want to keep Antonio onstage alone for a split section, to signal for the audience his anxiety or outright disappointment, no less than his resolve to aid his best friend?

A "merry sport" and a "merry bond" (1.3.141, 169)

Why and when does Shylock hit upon the specifics of the pound of flesh contract, or what he calls a "merry sport" or "merry bond"? These are two related questions for the actor, though the first more readily admits interpretations beyond the immediate issue of staging implied in that "when," or the timing of the scheme.

The "why" is the actor's object, Shylock's reason, conscious or not, for doing what he does. He himself, of course, tells us he has cause for hating Antonio: "he is a Christian" and "lends out money gratis" (37-39). However, as James Newlin points out, Shylock's grouping the two stated reasons as an "ancient grudge" (42) only "confuses more than equates Shylock's cultural and personal animus" (111). For that matter, to what degree can we trust a character's self-diagnosis, even if it be in an aside, let alone delivered to some kindred spirit, as in the case in that opening conversation between Iago and his stooge Roderigo?

Again, why does Shylock do what he does? Jeffrey Wilson observes that "nineteenth-century scholars [and many directors] scampered to stamp the prosthetic [nose] on Shylock," in imitation of Marlowe's Barabas in *The Jew of Malta* (132). Later, he cites the five times other characters call Shylock "devil." The stigma of the Jew's nose, like the Biblical mark of

Cain, would push the play in the direction of what Wilson calls "a moral comedy," where Shylock becomes the Vice figure, whose actions are not "to be judged good or bad" but only "how they are bad" since—making a circular argument—"he has [already] been stigmatized" (144).

Wilson reminds us, however, there is no authority in Shakespeare's text for giving Shylock such a nose, such a stigmata. He does wear that "Jewish gabardine" on which Antonio spits (108). Still, the fact that no nose is mentioned, despite later theatrical tradition, is a "cause for consideration" (134), that missing Jewish nose transferring the play from an allegory of evil, where motive is irrelevant, to what Wilson calls a comedy of errors, where Shylock falls within the sphere of recognizable human behavior that can be diagnosed. The man has his reasons.

In an elaborate argument, to be revisited in the episode between Lancelot Gobbo and his father, Sierra suggests Shylock's fear is that his wife Leah has cuckolded him, that Jessica is not his daughter, an uncertainty making him doubt his own masculinity, his potency. This lead to Shylock's "displacement" (Sierra 97) of such fears on others, especially Antonio. Instead of begetting children, by his own admission he "breed[s]" money (92). This is Shylock's version of "the work of generation" (78). Through charging interest, he takes out his cuckold's revenge on younger men, so that Antonio's flesh becomes "the crossroads of many of the play's anxieties as it relates to fears about usury, interracial socializing, homoerotic relationship, and uncertainty about paternal status" (Sierra 101). Sierra notes that Shylock's desire to cut off Antonio's flesh undergoes "an exponential increase … after Jessica has eloped" (103), as he substitutes "financial regeneration for biological reproduction" (10). If this is Shylock's motive, the actor's object, getting revenge on younger, virile men, men who have not been betrayed by a wife or a child, it would be what Harold Pinter has called the "weasel under the cocktail cabinet,"[5] a subtext for motivations beneath those alluded to by the text, such as in Solanio's joke about Shylock's sexual appetite: "Out upon it, old carrion, rebels it at these years?" (3.1.31). Sierra, citing David Hawks, points out that in Renaissance literature usurers were sometimes portrayed as homosexuals "primarily to connote sterility" (96).

The options for when Shylock hits upon the idea of a pound of flesh are several. Knowing that Antonio will be coming to him for a loan, has the idea been hatching before the scene begins? Are Shylock's early negotiations pre-scripted, and only secondary to his real object, revenging

---

[5] Harold Pinter, "A Conversation with Harold Pinter," by Mel Gussow. *New York Times Magazine* (5 December 1971): 42-43, 126-36.

himself on Antonio? He asks Bassanio several times to go over the amount and length of the loan, perhaps boring or irritating him with the repetitions, which are aggravated by taunting Bassanio with doubts about Antonio's ability to repay. From Shylock's perspective, "Antonio is a good man" (11) but only "sufficient" (14), his means in "supposition" (15), and he has "squandered abroad" his ventures. He pointedly reminds Bassanio about the dangers of ship sinking or being attacked by pirates (13-23). But, again, is this only a tactic, prescripted, to hide his real object?

Or is it Bassanio's own use of "bound" that suggests to Shylock the picture of Antonio bound on a torture rack, that drives him from thinking about revenge to devising the actual means? If Bassanio delivers his "Be assured you may" (24) with what Shylock takes as an unwarranted confidence, does this set him off? Is Bassanio a little too aggressive, even testy with his "Shall I know you answer," which follows the more solicitous "May you stead me? Will you pleasure me?" (6-7). Or is he finally set off by Bassanio's well-intentioned but, from Shylock's view, insincere and thereby insulting invitation to dinner? Does Shylock signal his scheme's emergence in saying that Antonio "was the last man in our mouths" (55), or is Antonio's rebuke of Shylock's interpretation of Jacob and the sheep the final straw? An obvious moment is the aside when Shylock speaks of "catch[ing] Antonio on the hip" (41). Does Shylock's recounting how Antonio has humiliated him on the Rialto build on his earlier aside? Does Antonio's insistence that the deal be made not as friends but as enemies push him over the edge?

From the perspective of Marxist criticism, Birkett would see Shylock as the outsider who with the pound of flesh contract "relies more on a feudal system of bartering" (36) and thus challenges the business practices of Antonio and the other merchants. Whatever Shylock's object here, whether he acts out of anger or principle, or both, he remains the "Other" who, in Birkett's terms, would "re-colonize the colonizer" (32). This Other assaults what the Marxist would brand as Venice's "seriously flawed system in which all the character make choices based solely on their own interests and without thought of what might realistically happen in the future" (35). In the Manga Shakespeare, Antonio is shown in a small panel insisting that the course of the law cannot be denied, but in the larger panel, where the Duke holds the scales of justice, the narrator's text reminds the reader that the welfare of Venice "really depends upon the economic activity of 'strangers,' whose activities [the Duke] dares not disrupt." In Venice, justice serves not the law, as Antonio would have it, but is a "tool of commercial trade." (179).

The actor may opt not for a specific moment, but rather use some or all of the above as part of his build. The decision about "when" is inseparable from this issue of "why."

Like Birkett, McDonnell sees Shylock as representing the Other, noting that in the comic version there is a "de-specification of the play's treatment of ethnicity" (176). Shylock is clearly Jewish, but in "converting Venice from a historically and geographically literal place to a fantastically altered version of itself," a world "populated by characters whose pointed, elfin ears identify them as not precisely human," the illustrator Faye Yong "removes" *The Merchant of Venice* from the "zone of historical and religious specificity," freeing the work to make "a more general point about racism and otherness" (McDonnell 173). The cartoon, as argued by Scott McCloud in *Understanding Comics* (cited by McDonnell), provides an "amplification through simplification" that in turn strips down an image to its "essential meaning," in a way that more realistic art cannot (173).

For Antonio the overt reason he enters into a contract that goes against his normal business practices is simpler. Dingman sees his bargaining with Shylock as a "test" undergone by a medieval knight (54), a way to confirm his love for his friend. For Antonio, this test of his friendship is inevitable; indeed he is glad to accept the challenge.

For Shylock, the "when" is like the decision the actor playing Beatrice must make: at what moment does she decide to ask Benedict to kill his best friend Claudio? Is her weeping at the start of the scene (4.1) fake, a tactic to lure him in? Or is she hinting not so subtly with "It is a man's office, but not yours"? Or does the decision come to her suddenly, impulsively when Benedict says, "Come, bid me do anything for thee" (*Much Ado about Nothing*, 4.1.255-86). These are just three of a half dozen options in what actors call the "kill Claudio" scene.

Asking "when," whatever the answer, complements the "why," whether asked by scholars or actors. In staging the scene, this second question underscores how the play evolves moment by moment, line by line, beat by beat. The critic's overview of the scene, asking "why," is complemented by the actor's need to know "when," for the latter puts the former in motion, or, as Newlin suggest, "Readers may look *in* to texts for deeper meaning, but the figural model also moves those meanings forward and backward" (113).

"I will try confusions with him" (2.2.30)

"Confusions" is often glossed as "experiments." Lancelot tells the audience he will experiment with his blind father, and depending on the degree of his anger with Old Gobbo, those experiments can range from taunting, to misdirecting him ("Turn up on your right hand at the next turning, but at the next turning of all on your left, marry at the very next turn," and so on) thereby causing the old man to stumble about the stage, to physical abuse (banging into him, knocking his cane from his hand, pushing Old Gobbo so he loses his balance and falls). Sierra notes that many directors, thinking this scene (2.2.1-98) "distracting" (104), go so far as to cut it. I find that in Shakespeare such seemingly minor scenes, whether they be comic interludes or conversations that only tell us what we already know, always repay examination. Consider Hamlet's brief meeting with the anonymous Captain (4.4.10-20), where we get to see a rare side of the moody prince, as he chats up Fortinbras's soldier, feels for this man who wouldn't "pay five ducats" for the worthless land which will soon be a battleground," then exchanges a fond, brotherly farewell with him.

The old man may deserve his son's cruel joke, for, like Shylock, and perhaps Portia's father, he has not been the best of parents, has himself been "dead" (62) to his son. Blind and infirm, Old Gobbo has come seeking Lancelot not so much out of love but for financial support (a sort of comic extension of Lear's retirement plans). His first reaction to the "news" that Lancelot is dead is not grief, but dismay at losing someone he hoped would be "the very staff" of his old age, "his prop," and this last self-centered request leads to an angry aside from Lancelot: "Do I look like a cudgel or a hovel-post, a staff or a prop?" Lancelot's repeats his question "Do you know me, father?" and it might just as well have been asked by Jessica, or Portia for that matter. According to the son, even if the father had eyes, he still might "fail of ... knowing" him.

Lancelot is already debating whether to leave a bad surrogate father, Shylock, even as he anticipates a better surrogate in Bassanio (who will enter on cue in line 98). This resentment against his father has been building up for years, but once Lancelot gets it out of his system, then he can forgive the old man, or at least tell him the truth: his son is not dead. If we entertain Sierra's speculation that, following "in the footstep of his Arthurian namesake, Lancelot has slept with Leah and, as a consequence, is perhaps Jessica's biological father" (92), then a fourth father-child combination is added to the three we already have: Lancelot/Old Gobbo, Portia/her father, Jessica/ Shylock.

Even when Lancelot reveals the truth, and then confirms Old Gobbo's doubt by invoking the name of his mother, there is still room for one more joke or confusion at the old man's expense. But this time father and son become a comic duo. When he feels Lancelot's beard, Old Gobbo confuses it with the tail of his cart horse, only to be corrected by his son: "It should seem then that Dobbin's tail grows backward."

This scene is far from irrelevant for it provides a mirror to the larger issues involved in Shylock's history with Jessica, her feelings for him, though, as Newlin reminds us, "The scene with Gobbo seems to prefigure a reunion between Shylock and Jessica. But that scene never arrives" (116).

"You See Me, Lord, Bassanio, Where I stand" (3.2.149)

Many actors want to make this speech (3.1.149-74) a celebration of Portia's character, either one of a modesty and self-effacement recalling Cordelia's in her reunion with her father, or that of a woman who defines a higher love, one where she willingly sacrifices all she has for Bassanio, finding her identity, her self-worth, in prizing him above herself, in a way that, under any other circumstances, might seem like the submission of some un-liberated woman. In similar fashion, Kate's speech of marital fidelity at the end of *The Taming of the Shrew* has been taken either as recognizing the proper denial of the self in a union, an act incumbent on Petruchio no less than herself, or as an anti-feminist harangue. I directed one actress who had worked with battered women and refused to take this latter option.

Surely it is significant that Portia's definition of herself and of love adopts the commercial language of the men in the play, of those Venetian merchants whose crass business world stands in contrast to Belmont's romantic, pastoral atmosphere, at least on the surface. In this speech she is all figures, banking terms, money. To be even more worthy of Bassanio she would be "trebled twenty times" herself, made "ten thousand times more rich." She only wishes to "stand high in [his] account." In fact, if she had her way she would "exceed account." Portia's offers a dowry to end all dowries--her estate, her servants, her house, her very self. Clearly an intelligent woman, still, as a potential wife she calls herself "an unlessoned girl, unschooled, unpracticed," the eager student of her husband-to-be, to be "directed" by him.

In this play of potentially fatal contracts, she stipulates only a single ring that Bassanio must promise never to give away. Here at the conclusion of Bassanio's "trial" and later at Shylock's, Wilson argues that "Shakespeare makes Portia "the mediation of deity and humanity, romance and realism, Belmont and Venice" (156). Using the merchants' own language but in the service of love as an expression of her notion of sacrifice, she signifies the movement from commercial Venice to bucolic

Belmont. Not unaware of the business world, indeed, bound, in effect, to a post-mortem contract with her father, she may even be aware of Bassanio's initial motive in pursuing her. But the fact is that here, in this speech, she meets Bassanio and all men on their own terms, purposely speaking a language they can understand. And she would give all to him, even the ring.

Is she simply a woman overjoyed that the man who picked the right casket is not a loser like his predecessors? Perhaps she's confident that, whatever Bassanio's initial motivation, there must be something worthy in him since he gravitated to the lead casket.

Others see a sarcastic Portia who only "plays" the un-liberated woman in giving herself and her fortune to Bassanio, a Portia not unlike Kate, whose sarcasm in her wedding banquet speech, an option taken by some actors, may hint that she will not be Petruchio's obedient little "wifey" for very long. Others will ask, why does Portia fall head over heels in love with Bassanio? Is Bassanio good enough for Portia? After all, he is bankrupt and, like Petruchio, initially courts the heiress for her money.

Whatever the case, her speech is so powerful that Bassanio's first response is, "Madam, you have bereft me of all words" (3.2.175).

Portia's speech can be taken as the expression of a mature woman whose concept of love represents the play's gold standard, but what happens if we see Portia as something less than perfect? How can the actor then reconcile the self-effacing character presently onstage with a more qualified portrait of her elsewhere the play?

In the course of examining Portia's relationship with Nerissa, Rebecca Olson raises such qualifications. Noting that this relationship has "yet to be seriously contested," (73), Olson describes it, instead, as one characterized by "social asymmetry" (77), "the language of hierarchy" (79). While Portia and Nerissa share confidences, enjoy bantering with each other, even as Nerissa is allowed to be "practical, astute, and perhaps gently mocking" in her conservations with her mistress (71), Olson argues that Portia still preserves the distinction between "friend" (as Antonio is to Bassanio, and she will be as his wife) and "maid," Nerissa's actual status. Portia's character is "more domineering, and ultimately less sympathetic, than she is frequently taken to be, and in this way she defies generic expectation for comedy" (Olson 82). Olson is "surprised by the affection Portia elicits from modern audiences" (82). She points to Portia's explicit racism in her comments about the Prince of Morocco, both to his face and in private to Nerissa, and adds to this "her tendency to prolong the discomfort—to the point of torture—of other characters" (82). Portia's slight of Morocco ("A gentle riddance ... Let all of his complexion choose me so" [2.7.78-9]) provides "a suggestive counterpoint to the aggressive racist taunts directed at Shylock" and "highlight[s] the pervasive xenophobia in the script" (75). Olson recalls the casting of an African-American actor as Nerissa in the 2010 Oregon Shakespeare production (directed by Bill Rauch), where "Nerissa winced, visibly strung" (13) at her mistress's stereotype of Morocco. While Portia in the Oregon Festival production lamented her "overwhelming 'weariness'," the black maid was busy going about household chores. What Olson liked about this production, found "particularly fresh," was that Nerissa herself was included "among [the] outsiders" (75). In placing her among those maids, waiting gentlewomen, female confidants, even the supposedly BFF's of the upper-class, women who often create "avenues for treachery against the heroine" (such as Margaret in *Much Ado*, Emlia in *Othello*), Olson finds in Nerissa a mirror whereby we see something of a more human, a less perfect Portia (68). For Wilson, when Portia calls Shylock a Jew, she also takes part in this racial stereotyping, and further "undercuts herself" when she claims the Jew must be "merciful" (4.2.182) since "'the Jew' that is abstractly constructed to signify Law is not capable of mercy" (153).

Birkett raises the question, "Does Portia support the patriarchal society or does she subvert it?" (24), and concludes that our perspective on her depends on whether the reader is a feminist or not, and whether the reader likes or dislikes Portia. In "barking orders" at Bassanio she may appear to be "every feminist's worst nightmare" (24), at once upholding the male concept of the female as a prize and yet, by her imperious attitude, distorting it. She "challenges the patriarchal expectations by challenging the men, but she ultimately obeys them" (25). Definitions of "feminine" (Portia as subservient, modest, the "unlessoned girl," giving her all to "her man" Bassanio) and "feminist" (taking on the role of the male, cross-dressing at the trial, being assertive, challenging both the Venetian establishment and Shylock as their equal, if not superior) are too fluid and relative, both in our current society whenever *Merchant* is staged and in the play itself, to allow us to make a simple judgment of Portia, let alone reduce the complexities of her character. As Birkett points out, "feminist theory rejects a universal notion of what it is to be feminine" (23).

Newlin even qualifies the "romance" of Bassanio's choosing the right casket by arguing that he solves the riddle not through "any particularly special insight" into Portia's character (117), but by equating the "grossness of fair ornament" with "the word": "in a word / The seeming truth, which cunning times put on / To entrap the wisest" (3.2.100-01). For Newlin, there is nothing ultimately wrong with Morocco's and Aragon's "uncovered meanings"; they are just not "Portia's father's meaning," which is only a "predetermined, arbitrary meaning dictated as if on high (or, in this case, from beyond the grave)" (119).

McDonnell notes that in the Manga version characters branded as Other are not marked "by any means that corresponds obviously to real-world ethnicities" (174). The Prince of Morocco has green skin but in the Dramatis Personae page all major characters are in color. The imaginative atmosphere of the comic world allows for a more expansive reading of his character. McDonnell suggests that while Morocco's line to Portia, "Mislike me not for my complexion" (2.1.1), can be taken as a plea that she not be displeased by his appearance, it can also be seen as his urging "her not [in turn] to displease *him*," as "an instruction, perhaps even a warning to her." Morocco's line may contain "a hint of defiance that puts him in an analogous position to the Jew" (174).

As we will see in the next section, Portia's management of the case against Shylock may seem fair, just, perhaps even merciful, especially if we allow the play, as Newlin suggests, "an inherent authority granted a Christian reading" (120). If *The Merchant of Venice* is what Wilson calls a moral allegory, then Portia stands for Christian mercy, but if it is a comedy of errors, as Wilson defines it, then Shylock's anger at Antonio, "boorishly performed, leads him down a steepening path of moral mistakes" that are then corrected at the trial where Portia's sense of the "social morality of mercy is inaugurated with his conversion to Christianity" (149).

A marvelous woman equally "right" when it comes to love and the debate between mercy and justice, or something of a social snob, not exempt from the racism of her male counterparts in Venice, delighting in inflicting harsh judgment, even pain, perhaps as a way getting back at her ill treatment from the hand of her dead father at would-be fathers like Shylock—either way, Portia comes out the winner. And yet modern audiences, in this post-Holocaust age, are still bothered by the terms of Shylock's correction or punishment and by Portia's hand in determining it.

As with the Lancelot Gobbo scene, Portia's address to Bassanio fits in, *needs* to fit in with a director's overall concept of the play. Or would we want to make her "You see me" speech a free-standing piece, something more common in Brecht's Epic Theatre, where the actor playing Portia would be allowed to step fully out of character and deliver the playwright's opinion on that higher love to which, in varying degrees, the characters in the less than golden world of Venice, and even of Belmont, fall short? Or would we confer on Portia the perfection of a Cordelia, though even Lear's daughter can be played as a bit snippy, less than diplomatic in her opening exchange with her father?

Reject or even qualify one of these interpretations, and the question remains: how much does Portia believe what she says? Believe—consciously or unconsciously? Is she that sarcastic character some actors prefer? Does the bit with her ring at the end of the speech show that she has, in a way, read the play, knows that Bassanio will fail in his promise, albeit with the best of intentions? Pressing the ring into his hand and then folding his fingers around it, does this signify just how important the exchange is to her, along with her doubts about Bassanio? If this is so, such gestures qualify everything she has just said. Even while proclaiming an impossible idea of love as sacrifice, is she now being realistic, giving Bassanio a test that she suspects he might fail? Like Beatrice or even Juliet, is she suspicion that her lover's vow of love might not last? That he will soon "eat [his] word"? (*Much Ado about Nothing*, 4.1.276).

All this while Nerissa plays audience to the two. How does she react, speaking in her silence at the spectacle? For Olson, Nerissa's intentions are "more self-serving than is generally assumed" (74). She encourage Gratiano's suit "to adjust, even slightly, the social differences between herself and her mistress." And, again, what happens if we cast, as in the Oregon Shakespeare production, an African-American actor as Nerissa?

"It was my turquoise" (3.1.100-01)

When asked, my advice to an actor playing Shylock is to avoid the extremes: don't make him an innocent martyr of the Christian businessmen or a melodramatic villain.[6] When that didn't satisfy him, I suggested, "Why not come back tomorrow, and bring me some specific aspect of Shylock's life that catches your attention? Don't search for anything profound. Don't try to read behind the dialogue. Just find something specific. Trust your instincts." He came back the next day asking, "Why would Shakespeare mention someone like his wife Leah who never appears in the play? And a turquoise ring that wouldn't have to be in the props list?" After a long conversation, he came up with a portrait of Shylock as a young man, deeply in love with Leah, that love so engrossing that it compensated for the Christians' daily insults. Leah made Shylock forget all of this, the proof of her love that turquoise ring, not so valuable in itself as for what it signified. For my actor, the ring reminds us that there is also a normal, loving, human, domestic side to Shylock, that,

---

[6] For a production at Constans Theatre, University of Florida, September, 1993; and I speak at greater length about this conversation with the actor in *Directing Shakespeare: A Scholar Onstage* (Ohio University Press: Athens, 2004): 49-51.

like the Christian majority, he has been loved, has been a husband, a father, that a woman once gave him a ring to show her devotion, in this play about marriage rings given away to strangers. And while Shylock must be held accountable for his actions, he is also driven mad by the businessmen of Venice: they have denied him space, what the actor called "a larger stage," for that domestic life where one cultivates the virtues of love, devotion, caring for one's children, those private bonds that, as posited by the ideal society, then extend to the world outside the family. No one who does business with Shylock cares about his private life, about his wife; no one expressed sympathy when Leah died.

Sierra offers a somewhat different reading of the prop in this scene never making the stage. The ring does remind Shylock of earlier and, for a time, happier days with Leah, exposing "a movingly sentimental side" (Sierra 88) to this man otherwise branded as a Jew. But if the turquoise calls up fond memories, it does so before Leah betrayed him with a lover who was Jessica's true father. Sierra cites, among other references to this possible betrayal, Lancelot's "You may partly hope that your father got you not, that you are not Jew 's daughter" (3.5.8-9). To be sure, this is only a speculation that Jessica is not Shylock's daughter, just as we cannot be certain of Iago's charge: "I do suspect the lusty Moor / Hath leapt into my seat" (2.1.282-83). Indeed, it is a speculation just a bit less radical than Sierra's raising the possibility that Lancelot might be Jessica's father. Sierra plays with the exchange between Jessica and Shylock where to her hope that "The sins of the mother should not be visited upon" her, Lancelot's replies that, when he fears she is damned by both parents, he "shun[s] Scylla, your father, [and falls] into Charbydis, your mother" (3.5.10-14). Lancelot's "fall into" could intimate "sexual indiscretions in respect to entering the female anatomy" (92).

But proof is not the final issue here. Rather, what may be in Shylock's mind, how does he see himself, and his past with Leah? If he has doubts about Jessica's paternity, his own diminished sexuality, then when Jessica sells the ring she "symbolically divorces her parents and underscore more anxieties about Shylock's parental claim to her" (Sierra 4), a claim that, in its way, parallels the will of Portia's father, or Lear's attempted claim on Cordelia, his "joy" whom he wishes will draw "a third" of the kingdom "more opulent" than her sisters (1.1.74-77). Or Polonius's claim on Ophelia.

So, does the missing wife and her gift provide an insight into Shylock's character, a window into the past revealing a decent, normal, sentimental, romantic soul, that has been mostly buried, or is he divided here between his recollection of happy and then sad days with Leah, with a subtext roiling with anger at her adultery?

This division, at once conscious and unconscious, is inseparable from Shylock's vacillation here between joy and grief. One moment he is thanking Tubal for the "good news" that Antonio's argosies have sunk, the next recoiling in pain when his friend "stickst a dagger" in him with the bad news of Jessica's "spending fourscore ducats at a sitting." The rage when he vows to "plague" and "torture" Antonio since now he cannot pay the bond on time alternates with his extravagant romantic cry that he would not have sold the turquoise for "a wilderness of monkeys."

Shylock barks out a harsh order to Tubal even though he calls him "good," but the actor charged with Tubal's relatively small role might play him here as taking some pleasure in seeing his imperious business associate squirm under these conflicting reports. After Shylock's first long outburst, where his anguish ranges from the price of a diamond Jessica stole to the cost of the search for the couple to his expanding his complaint to "The curse [that] never fell upon our nation til now," he switches to the bathetic rhetoric of "no ill luck stirring but what lights on my shoulders, no sighs but of my breathing, no tears but of my shedding" (71-81). Tubal challenges him with what at first seems cold comfort: "Yes, other men have ill luck too." But this hardly answers Shylock's obsession with his own misfortune. Eager to find a brother in suffering, he excitedly interrupts Tubal when he mentions Antonio: "What, what, what? Ill luck, ill luck?" Tubal's response, that "Antonio is certainly undone," is at best partial comfort, with a subtext like: sure, you lost your daughter and the ring, but the glass is only half empty, for what about Antonio? There is some room for Tubal here as executing the comic revenge of the second banana, even as Shylock, whatever we make of the significance of his reference to Leah and the ring, hogs the stage. In the case of Tubal, the old cliché is applicable: there are no small parts, only small actors.

"Which is the merchant, and which the Jew?" (4.1.169)

After her perfunctory answer to the Duke's question "Come you from old Bellario?" and her assurance that she is "informed thorough of the cause," Portia in her disguise as the lawyer Balthazar asks, "Which is the merchant here, and which the Jew?" After both Antonio and Shylock stand forth, she appears to answer her own question with "Is your name Shylock?"

A fellow director always reminds his actors that whenever you take the stage you always have to know *where* your character is coming from, both physically and psychologically, what you are doing or thinking just before you enter, and, of course, why you are entering on cue. As Portia enters she understands the importance of the role she will be playing, her entrance itself anticipated by Nerissa's telling the Duke that she is "hard by" and awaits the Duke's invitation ("answer"). Perhaps just offstage, in one of the court's ante rooms, Portia is double-checking her costume, her disguise, going over the very advice she gave Nerissa earlier on how to impersonate a man (3.5.60-78), one of these "fine, bragging youths" or "bragging Jacks." Any friend of Bassano's is friend of hers, or, as Dingman says, her love for Bassanio "translates into concern for those he loves" (56). Nor is her entrance obscure, for she is accompanied by "three or four" attendants. The Duke himself greets her warmly, in large part because of the esteem with which he holds her master Bellario who has praised her highly in the letter he reads to the audience just before Balthazar enters.

As the disguised Portia comes onstage, does she or does she not recognize the plaintive? Surely, given the importance of her role, both as the lawyer hired to free Antonio of his bond and as a woman literally playing a role to rescue the best friend of her newly minted husband, she would pick her words carefully. And so, one line late, after the Duke's non-committal "Antonio and old Shylock, both stand forth," why does she ask for an identification for which there is no need?

Doesn't she recognize the Jew? Wilson, as we have seen, argues there is no clear textual authority for giving Shylock a Jewish nose, though here he might be wearing the Jewish gabardine Antonio mentions when he first meets the moneylender (3-4). The Duke helps in the identification when he calls Shylock "old." Nevertheless, we are back to the original question, about Portia's question: "Which is the merchant here, and which the Jew?"

The possibilities are several. She is being truthful: she cannot tell which is which, gabardine or age notwithstanding. She suspects which one is the Jew but, a careful lawyer, wants to be sure before she goes any further.

I think here of the questions Viola, also disguised as a male, asks when she takes the stage and sees both the Duchess Olivia and her maid Maria: "The honorable lady of the house, which is she?" (12N, 1.5.149). Surely, Olivia is dressed in a style befitting an aristocrat, the lady of the house, while Maria wears a maid's costume, at best that of a waiting gentlewoman. Besides, the Duchess is wearing that long dark veil signifying her years-long devotion to the memory of a dead brother! What is her object in acting so naïve and thereby insulting Olivia?

Perhaps, as Wilson suggests, Portia, playing the crowd who are intrigued by a lawyer who is so young, is being sarcastic, and the director can emphasize this by having the other onstage characters laugh at a question which parodies itself in its obvious answer. Or, Portia may deliberately ask a question which challenges the easy stereotypes of those Venetian businessmen who see Shylock not as a person but as a Jew, offering him no identity except that of a moneylender. Beyond her immediate character as Portia, she may thus address a larger issue in the play —the way Cordelia does in the final scene of *Lear*, or Desdemona, by her personal example of fidelity and trust, does or should do for Othello, or Hermione as the model of fidelity in *The Winter's Tale*. Again, Wilson goes beyond Portia as he raises the question: how does Shakespeare want us to see Shylock, "as a human being or as a cultural stereotype"? (151). The argument he has applied to the issue of whether or not Shylock had a prosthetic nose on Shakespeare's stage also applies, I think, to Portia's question here. She will not identify the Jew by what she sees, the surface—Jewish nose or not. He has a name, is a person, has a soul. Wilson speaks of how "an eerie absence of [such] information evokes an alarming presence of interpretation, much of it ascribing interpretation to the object being interpreted" (139). Within the space of two lines the plaintiff is referred to as both the Jew and Shylock, and so this brief moment, a mere three lines in the play's longest scene, can stand for what Wilson calls "the shifting appellations used by Shakespeare's Venetians [that] express the nebulous identity of their opponent, as well as the alternative possibilities for the scene's comic resolution" (153).

The director and the actors, no less than the audience, whether it be the spectator in the house or the scholar in the study, can make too much or too little of Portia's question. Knowing how much Shakespeare packs into every line, every word, the warming of the former is perhaps best heeded.

"I dare be bound again" (5.1.250)

For the second time in the play Antonio is willing to be the guarantor, or what Portia calls "his surety" for Bassanio--the term this time is spiritual (his "soul") rather than fiscal or physical. He refers to the past— "I once did lend my body for this wealth" (247)—and unwittingly compliments Portia, the "him that had [and now has her] husband's ring" (248), as the lawyer who preserved Bassanio's new-found "wealth" that otherwise would have "quite miscarried." Once more, the actor's concern for Antonio's object parallels the interpretations of the essays of this collection. Why does Antonio come forward, repeating, albeit under very different circumstances, his pledge to serve as Bassanio's surety?

It is interesting that the actor playing Antonio must stand onstage for more than one hundred lines before speaking. What is he thinking as he listens to this messy business about the husbands' having broken their marriage vows by giving away the rings or, until they are returned, Portia's threat to have sex with Balthazar, and Nerissa with his clerk? Is he secretly hoping that Bassanio's marriage will fail and the two friends will be back to where they were before she came into the picture? Would this cure the sadness that he confesses in the play's first line? Does he want to let things run their course or come to Bassanio's aid, caught as he is between principle and friendship? If he is the generic bachelor friend, or even like the Sassy Gay Friend (from the Second City video on YouTube) that Olson mentions in her essay (65), does he still recognize that Portia can make Bassanio happy, that he won't be excluded by their marriage, that he has to learn how to share his best friend with a woman? To accept what is inevitable? What he feared but knew would happen at the start of the play? When asked by one director friend "what to do with Antonio just standing like a log there onstage without speaking for one hundred lines," I suggested she place him downstage left, away from the two couples, so that while most of the audience's attention would be directed to them, every so often they could check and see how Antonio was responding to what he overhears and observes, in his facial expressions, even with a few gestures, perhaps a short cross without calling anyone's attention to draw nearer to the quarrel.[7] With his first line, "I am th'unhappy subject of these quarrels" (237), he would then join the bickering couples center stage.

In place of the reading that there is still friction between Antonio and Portia, comparing Antonio to Shylock as characters "forced 'outside' to live unhappily alone at the end of the play" (57), Dingman, instead, finds that Antonio here contributes to a happy union, that in joining with Bassanio in a new joint pledge involving the ring we have "symbolically another marriage" (57). This second episode involving the ring "combines monetary and chivalric themes" and thereby represents "a shared bond of service and prosperity owed to each member of the successful trio at the end" (59). Antonio's reward for stepping up invokes what Wilson calls "nearly a *deus ex machine*—the safe harbor of [his] ships" (145), the play itself moving from a possible revenge tragedy to a comedy or, using Dante's terms, replacing "adversity" with "prosperity (146). As Sierra describes the situation: Antonio here "publically recognizes that he can no longer meddle in [Portia's] marriage," and thus his "recognition of Bassanio's independence is antithetical to Shylock's maniacal reaction to being unable to control Jessica" (95). Antonio's mercantile background

---

[7] *Ibid.*

makes him understand "the risk of hazarding," and he is now "complacent with whatever Fortune gives him" (11). Having received "public recognition" of his love for Bassanio, he "gains nothing," yet his friendship with Bassanio is now "solidified," a "survival" that would not have been possible without Portia (13).

By my count, Antonio's offer to Portia constitutes the seventh of ten sections or movements in this rich and complex scene, in a play where every other scene is essentially singular in its focus or theme. One thinks of the distinct scenes given to Portia's suitors, or the Act 4 trial which, despite being the longest in the play, is focused on one, albeit complex issue. Or the scene where Lancelot Gobbo reunites with his father. Or the opening, whose two halves, given to Antonio's sadness and then Bassanio's request for money, are a matching pair.

Here, in the only scene of Act 5, the movements are like those of a musical composition, with distinct but no less related variations evolving from a single, encompassing multi-faceted theme. The first six movement build to Antonio's offer (movement seven), and that offer, once made, paves the way for the final five movements which bring the play to a comic resolution:

1. the love duet of Lorenzo and Jessica, bitter-sweet since the classical lovers cited had unhappy endings (5.1.1-38);

2. the brief comic interruption by Lancelot, announcing Bassanio's imminent arrival (39-47);

3. the lovers once again alone, this time the references to classical lovers giving way to Lorenzo's invocation of the Elizabethan cosmos and then, with the entrance of the musicians, his parallel celebration of the aesthetics of music (48-87);

4. Portia's entrance with Nerissa and their discussion of the more earthy topic of "how many things by season seasoned are" (88-107);

5. Portia's spotting the lovers and the practical household business of arranging for the husbands' arrival, capped with a brief return to the issue from the fourth movement about the relative antithesis between day and night (108-125);

6. the longest movement, where the husbands are charged with violating their marriage vows (126-247), a change from the cosmic or the practical to a potentially serious matter (though not to the audience), to whose resolution the wives hold the key, or what Sierra calls a situation where "metaphors of faithfulness" are mixed with "accusations of infidelity" (88);

7. then what I have called above "Antonio offer's of surety" (248-252);

8. that offer leading to a double resolution, first between the lovers and then Portia's *deus ex machina*, the letter informing Antonio all his ships are safe, perhaps a reward by the playwright for his recognition that Bassanio cannot be his alone, the cure, in effect, for his sadness from the play's opening line (253-278);

9. off to bed for the two couples, with Antonio happy but still single even as he calls Portia "sweet lady" (279-298); and

10. Grazianao's gross coda, where the wedding ring gives way to a vaginal ring (299-306).

These movements or divisions in the final act, standard practice for directors as they break down a long scene into manageable and somewhat distinct units, may find a parallel in McDonnell's comments on McCloud's classification of six different types of panel-to-panel transition in comics (171). The relations between two panels may be "Moment-to-Moment," "Action-to-Action," "Subject-to-Subject," "Scene-to-Scene," "Aspect-to-Aspect " (where the reader "bypasses time … and sets a wandering eye on different aspects of place, idea or mood"), and "Non-Sequitur" (where there is "no logical relationship between panels whatsoever," although this does not necessarily stop the reader from making a personal connection). Though several of these pairs might be defined by more than one of McCloud's six categories, I would suggest that 1 and 2 fall under "Aspect-to-Aspect," 3-4 and 9-10 "Subject-to-Subject," and 5-6 and 7-8 "Moment-by-Moment" or even, to some degree, "Action-to-Action."

Whether as movements or transitions, seeing the act structured in this way, its evolution a series of variations on a theme, puts Antonio's line "I dare be bound again," however we may interpret both his object and his subtext here, within a perspective where are intertwined love (from the bawdy to the romantic), friendship (whether heterosexual, homoerotic, or homosexual), and play (from verbal to the theatrical, from acting both as a means of testing and an agent for resolution). The short movement seven, given entirely to Antonio's renewed pledge, halts the downward spiral from the classical and cosmic opening movements to the bald accusations of disloyalty and threats of adultery, at least from the perspective of the four men in this scene. Antonio's offer to stand as surety for his friend opens the way to revelations, a reaffirmation of two unions, news of good fortune, and resolution, literally the play's own resolution as it moves—

again to cite Wilson—from a potential tragedy of revenge to a comedy of errors, now corrected.

The Script as Criticism, Scholarship as Performance

Newlin observes that Antonio's challenge to Shylock's reading of the Biblical account of Jacob's trick in getting all of Laban's newborn lambs is just one of the play's "competing allegorical readings," (123) "a conflict of one another's reason" (112). When Antonio "qualifies Shylock's entire rhetorical strategy as an insertion" (113) and equates "an evil soul" with the devil who would corrupt the inside of the scripture by placing, rather than finding meaning there (114), the debate over interpretation has shifted from the text's "inside" to a "concern for the interpreter's inside" (114). If "the goal of interpretation [is] to transfer one's meaning to another" (5), then Antonio "wins" here primarily because the play, Shakespeare's audience, and the age's culture are biased toward the Christian, not the Jew. As with Portia later, Antonio has "an inherent authority granted to *Christian* reading" (120). In the play generally, and especially at the trial, "meaning and explanation" are almost always described in "possessive terms" (112).

In their recreation of the text, the richer, the more complex, even contradictory, the Shylock fashioned by actors and their directors, as well as critics and scholars, the more the play itself, beyond its specific events, becomes a criticism of allegory, or any interpretation operating from what might be assumed are absolute principles, the "right" way. The meaning of *The Merchant of Venice* involves what the physicist Niels Bohr would call "complementarity," where no single interpretation, or reading, however logical, however appealing, however much it confines itself to the text, is right or exclusive, or is even right only by its own terms.[8] No reading can exclude that of others, let alone be inclusive in itself. In devising a concept for the play, broad as that concept may be, the director must, by necessity, make choices, for her concept imposes limits on its own interpretation. Or as Wilson reminds us, Shakespeare's irony, the rich field of responses he elicits, in this case by not specifying a Jew's nose, is often "canceled in performance when a company must make a dramaturgical decision that privileges one interpretation over another" (154). Practical

---

[8] One of the first critics to make this connection between Bohr's notion of complementarity and Shakespeare is Norman Rabkin, *Shakespeare and the Problem of Meaning* (Chicago: University of Chicago Press, 1981): 34.

advice, though I might suggest substituting "qualified" in place of "canceled."

To show the play's relevance to current issues, Birkett analyzes the play in the context of four major critical theories, only to suggest that *Merchant* has "limits in providing full answers to social questions" (16). But this "lack of a clear, distinct, and definite set of questions and answers explains why the play is so popular," for it allows directors, audiences, and scholars "to fit the work to any and all visions" (39).

The indeterminacy of language itself renders any interpretation relative. Lancelot, while hardly among the play's more intellectual characters, understands this, as Newlin maintains, when the clown observes, "How every fool can play upon the word" (3.5.37). In his sarcasm he recognizes "that the ambivalent zones of language are the place for *play*" (115), or what Newlin calls "the aporetic quality of language itself" (109).

If there has been some historical enmity between scholars and those who work in the theatre, between the director charged with staging *The Merchant of Venice* and the scholar or critic working in the study, that divisive past has been worn away by one obvious fact. Those commenting on the play, as literature, as a repository for the ideas of the age, even as material for reconstructing the playwright's personality, complement and often enhance the work of those having to deal with actors, designers, all those connected with the production. Including the audience. Shakespeare takes a full measure of such cooperation and support.

CONTRIBUTORS

Horacio Sierra is an Assistant Professor of English at Bowie State University. Dr. Sierra's teaching and research interests revolve around Shakespeare, Renaissance literature, early modern women writers, and Hispanic literature. He earned his Ph.D. in English from the University of Florida. He earned his B.S. in Communication from the University of Miami.

Audrey Birkett is a lecturer in the English department at the University of Colorado-Colorado Springs. She lectures on Shakespeare and Literary Theory and Criticism. Much of Dr. Birkett's work examines the use of paratext, the development of the text, and issues of authorship and authority in early modern drama.

Rebecca Olson is Assistant Professor of English at Oregon State University. Dr. Olson's ongoing research focus is the intersection between early modern works and material culture, and especially the relationship between texts and textiles. Her work has been published in journals including *Modern Philology*, *Word & Image*, and *Medieval and Renaissance Drama in England*.

Paul Dingman focuses his studies on the cultural history of Western Europe in the medieval and early modern periods; imaginative literature is of particular interest to him as a window to the past. Dr. Dingman teaches Medieval studies at Alfred University.

James Newlin is a doctoral candidate in the English department at the University of Florida. In addition to Shakespeare, his research interests include literary theory, psychoanalysis, and film.

Jeffrey R. Wilson completed his Ph.D. in English at the University of California, Irvine. Dr. Wilson's work explores the representational system that generates characters as various as Richard III, Aaron the Moor, Shylock the Jew, Falstaff, Thersites, Caliban, and the bastards.

Sidney Homan is Professor of English at the University of Florida and a Member of the Academy of Distinguished Teaching Scholars. Author of some ten books on Shakespeare and the modern playwrights, Dr. Homan is also an actor and director in professional and university theatres. In his most recent book, *A Fish in the Moonlight: Growing Up in the Bone Marrow Unit,* he tells stories of his youth in South Philadelphia and his experience sharing them with young patients at his university's hospital.